JESUS: STRANGER FROM HEAVEN
AND SON OF GOD

SOCIETY OF BIBLICAL LITERATURE
SOURCES FOR BIBLICAL STUDY

edited by
Wayne A. Meeks

Number 11
JESUS: STRANGER FROM HEAVEN
AND SON OF GOD
Jesus Christ and the Christians in Johannine Perspective

by Marinus de Jonge
edited and translated by
John E. Steely

SCHOLARS PRESS
Missoula, Montana

JESUS: STRANGER FROM HEAVEN
AND SON OF GOD
Jesus Christ and the Christians in Johannine Perspective

by
Marinus de Jonge
edited and translated by
John E. Steely

Published by
SCHOLARS PRESS
for
The Society of Biblical Literature

Distributed by

SCHOLARS PRESS
Missoula, Montana 59806

JESUS: STRANGER FROM HEAVEN
AND SON OF GOD
Jesus Christ and the Christians in Johannine Perspective

by
Marinus de Jonge
edited and translated by
John E. Steely

Library of Congress Cataloging in Publication Data
Jonge, Marinus de, 1925-
  Jesus, stranger from heaven and Son of God.

  (Sources for Biblical study ; no. 11)
  Includes index.
  CONTENTS: The fourth Gospel.—Nicodemus
and Jesus.—Jesus as prophet and king in the fourth
Gospel. [etc.]
  1. Bible. N.T. John—Criticism, interpretation,
etc.—Addresses, essays, lectures. 2. Jesus
Christ—History of doctrines—Early church, CA. 30-
600—Addresses, essays, lectures. I. Title. II. Series.
BS2615.2.H63   232   77-9984
ISBN 0-89130-134-8

Printed in the United States of America

Printing Department
University of Montana
Missoula, Montana 59812

5455 UM Printing Services

TABLE OF CONTENTS

PREFACE

This volume contains eight studies written during the past seven years for different purposes. Most of them appeared in print as articles in various periodicals and Festschriften in English and in Dutch. For the present collection, Chapters II-VII were translated and/or edited in order to avoid unnecessary repetition and to promote unity and uniformity; Chapters I and VIII were added to introduce and to conclude the volume.

The chapters should be read for themselves, as separate contributions to one main theme: Jesus Christ and the Christians in Johannine perspective. This book is a collection of successive connected attempts to bring some clarity to a very difficult problem rather than an exhaustive treatment of the subject. Considering the complexity of Johannine theology and the great number of theories and hypotheses put forward in an immense number of publications (which nobody can read in their entirety!), each approach will of necessity be limited in scope and restricted in the number of methods applied.

Behind the present studies lies the assumption that the Fourth Gospel is a meaningful whole, highly complicated in structure, with many paradoxes and many tensions in thought and syntax, but yet asking to be taken seriously as a (more or less finished) literary product in which consistent lines of thought can be detected. The same applies to the Epistles, which were studied by the present author at some length before he turned (again) to the Fourth Gospel-- see M. de Jonge, *De Brieven van Johannes* (Nijkerk: Callenbach, 1968, ^{2}1973) and C. Haas, M. de Jonge, and J. L. Swellengrebel, *A Translator's Handbook on the Letters of John* (London: U.B.S., 1972). Literary sources were used and non-literary traditions left their traces in the Gospel and the Epistles; the possibility of development in thought and ways of expression cannot be excluded and a

long literary process with different stages of redaction
may lie behind the present Gospel. Yet the first task of
an exegete should be to interpret the documents as they
lie before him; even if in some cases the present text
cannot be explained without some knowledge of its history
one can never be content with simply describing that history and restrict oneself to the "original" meaning and
function of the constituent parts.

The present author is very skeptical about the possibility of delineating the literary sources in the Fourth
Gospel and does not share the optimism displayed by some
of his colleagues when they try to distinguish between
sources and redaction. In many cases we cannot possibly
know what the redactor had in front of him and, consequently, we shall have to take him seriously as author,
i.e., as composer in his own right. Consequently in these
studies much emphasis is laid on the composition and structure of the Fourth Gospel as a whole, and the separate narratives and discourses are treated as literary units within
the framework of the Gospel. Great caution is exercised
in drawing conclusions regarding earlier stages of redaction, sources, or, for that matter, the historical circumstances reflected in the Gospel and the Epistles.

Chapter I was written especially for this volume; it
incorporates some material used for a lecture in King's
College, Aberdeen, in February 1974.

Chapter II is the text of the greater part of the
Manson Memorial Lecture 1970, given in the Faculty of Theology of the University of Manchester. It was previously
published in a complete form in the *Bulletin of the John
Rylands Library* 53 (1971), pp. 337-59.

Chapter III gives the text of a lecture given in
King's College, London, in January 1972 and in the Faculty
of Theology of the Katholieke Universiteit Leuven in March
1973. It appeared in *Ephemerides Theologicae Lovanienses*
49 (1973), pp. 161-77.

Chapter IV was originally read as a paper at the
S.N.T.S. meeting at Claremont, on September 1, 1972. It
was published in *New Testament Studies* 19 (1972-1973), pp.
246-70.

Chapter V is of more recent origin; it was written in
November 1975 for a colume called *Miscellanea Neotesta-*
mentica, to be published by E. J. Brill, Leiden, for the
Conventus of New Testament Scholars in the Netherlands at
the occasion of its 25th anniversary in the autumn of 1976.
In an earlier form the text was used for guest lectures in
Cambridge and Oxford in May 1973, and in Aberdeen in Feb-
ruary 1974.

Chapter VI is a translated and expanded version of
two connected lectures given on December 10 and 17, 1975,
in the "Theologische Etherleergang" of the N.C.R.V. (Dutch
Christian Broadcasting Association). They were previously
published in Dutch under the title "Gods Zoon en Gods
Kinderen" in *Rondom het Woord* 18 (1976), pp. 57-73. This
chapter is published also in *Saved by Hope: Essays in Honor*
of Professor Richard C. Oudersluys, ed. James I. Cook
(Grand Rapids: William B. Eerdmans, 1977).

Chapter VII is the translation of a contribution in
Dutch "Ethiek in de Tussentijd" written for the volume *Ad*
Interim. Opstellen over eschatologie, apocalyptiek en
ethiek, aangeboden aan Prof. dr. R. Schippers (Kampen: J.
H. Kok, 1975).

Chapter VIII was, again, written especially for this
volume. Earlier thoughts of the author on the subject,
partly incorporated in this paper, may be found in "The
Use of the Word ΧΡΙΣΤΟΣ in the Johannine Epistles" in
Studies in John presented to Prof. Dr. J. N. Sevenster,
NovTSup 24 (Leiden, 1970) and in "Ontwikkelingen binnen
de johanneische theologie," *Vox Theologica* 43 (1973), pp.
205-26.

I am grateful to many colleagues whose invitations to
give lectures and whose response in discussion and written

comments inspired me to formulate and to reformulate my own thoughts. Thanks are also due to those who gave permission to reproduce now in this form in this volume the studies which appeared earlier. I regard it as a privilege that Wayne A. Meeks, to whose publications on John I owe very much, accepted this little volume for the "Sources for Biblical Study" series edited by him. Finally I should like to thank my friend John E. Steely, translator of my *Jesus: Inspiring and Disturbing Presence* (Nashville: Abingdon Press, 1974), who encouraged me to bring these studies together and took a very active part in their translation and editing, as well as in the preparation of the final manuscript.

M. de Jonge

Theologisch Instituut
Rapenburg 59
Leiden
The Netherlands

August 1, 1976

CHAPTER I

THE FOURTH GOSPEL: THE BOOK OF THE DISCIPLES

The Purpose of the Fourth Gospel (20:30-31)

In two texts the author(s) of the Fourth Gospel address(es) his (their) readers directly. In 20:31, belonging to the so-called "first ending" of the Gospel (20:30-31), we read: ταῦτα (referring to the σημεῖα recorded in the Gospel) δὲ γέγραπται, ἵνα πιστεύητε ὅτι ᾿Ιησοῦς ἐστιν ὁ χριστὸς ὁ υἱὸς τοῦ θεοῦ, καὶ ἵνα πιστεύοντες ζωὴν ἔχητε ἐν τῷ ὀνόματι αὐτοῦ. In 19:35, clearly connected with the "second ending" 21:24-25, the purpose of the μαρτυρία of the man who witnesses the flowing of the blood and water from Jesus' side is ἵνα καὶ ὑμεῖς πιστεύητε. This second text will occupy us in Chapter VIII where all passages which mention the Beloved Disciple will be discussed. Here we shall concentrate on 20:30-31, a very important statement which will recur repeatedly in the following chapters, especially in Chapters IV and V.

Verse 31 presents us with a number of problems. First, there is the problem whether we should read πιστεύητε with p[66vid] ℵ* B 0250 892 or πιστεύσητε in ℵ[c] A C D and a great number of other witnesses.[1] The same diversity of readings is found in 19:35 and modern editors came to different decisions. The third edition of the U.B.S. Greek New Testament prints πιστεύ[σ]ητε twice. Nestle-Aland[25] πιστεύητε twice.[2] It is clearly difficult to decide in favor of one or the other of these readings. Of greater importance, however, is the question whether the aorist, if original, should be interpreted as an *aoristus ingressivus*. In that case the purpose of the Fourth Gospel would be to bring outsiders to faith in Jesus Christ, the Son of God. If either πιστεύητε is original or the ingressive aspect of the aorist is not intended here, the Gospel is directed

1

towards people who already believe, but read it to
strengthen and deepen their faith.

The syntactical arguments are just as undecisive as
are the text-critical ones. H. Riesenfeld, therefore, has
rightly turned to a comparison with other ἵνα-sentences in
the Gospel and the First Epistle of John.[3] Particularly
in the first Epistle these sentences express the author's
intention to bring home to his Christian readers the true
meaning and the real implications of their faith in Jesus
Christ (1 John 1:3, 4; 3:11, 23; 5:13, cf. 2 John 5, 6).
Similar statements are found in the Farewell-discourses in
the Gospel, directed to the disciples (13:15, 19, 34; 14:
29; 15:11, 12, 17; 16:33; 17:13). From this Riesenfeld
rightly concludes that the ἵνα-sentences reflect catecheti-
cal instruction within the Johannine communities rather
than missionary practice. His conclusion ties up with
other arguments in favor of the theory that the Fourth
Gospel is primarily if not exclusively a book of the
(Johannine) church.

The next question to be mentioned here is that of the
content of the Christian faith: ὅτι Ἰησοῦς ἐστιν ὁ χριστο-
τός ὁ υἱὸς τοῦ θεοῦ. As the relation between the various
christological titles will be dealt with in Chapters II-VI
in much greater detail, only a few remarks will be made
here. First, it is clear that ὁ υἱὸς τοῦ θεοῦ might be
taken as a synonym of ὁ χριστός; when Nathanael in 1:49
greets Jesus as "the Son of God" and "the king of Israel"
these two titles are closely connected. We should bear in
mind, however, that Nathanael here has only just discovered
Jesus and still has to learn to see the full implications
of his confession[4]--in vss. 50-51 Jesus himself speaks
about "greater things" which Nathanael will see and he
connects them with the designation "Son of Man." In
another related passage, 11:27, Martha expresses her faith
in the words "I am convinced that you are the Messiah, the
Son of God, who is coming into the world." This confession
follows upon Jesus' self-revelation "I am the Resurrection

and the Life" (vs. 25) and, for the evangelist, Martha's confession obviously is the right reaction to Jesus' words, as the whole context vss. 25-27 clearly shows.[5]

In the following five chapters of this book, we shall find over and over again that the title ὁ χριστός is combined with and interpreted by ὁ υἱὸς τοῦ θεοῦ or similar designations.

In 11:27 we hear that faith in Jesus as defined in this passage means eternal life. The same is expressed in 20:31 where the sentence beginning with ἵνα πιστεύητε... is followed by καὶ ἵνα πιστεύοντες ζωὴν ἔχητε ἐν τῷ ὀνόματι αὐτοῦ. The Johannine conception of "life," of course, cannot be treated here. It may, however, not be superfluous to point out that in a number of important passages (3:16-21, 31-36; 5:17-30; 6:32-59; 17:2-3, as well as 11:25-27) "life" is given to those who believe in Jesus, as the Son who has received his authority from the Father and who is intimately related to Him; 5:21 occupies a central position here: "As the Father raises the dead and gives them life, so the Son gives life to men as he determines" (see also the two following verses!).[6]

So much for vs. 31; in Chapter IV, pursuing a number of points already mentioned in II and III, I hope to show at greater length how the christological argumentation in the Gospel points to the inner-church directedness of the Fourth Gospel.[7] In our present context, we have next to discuss the connection between vs. 31 and vs. 30, and the relation between 20:30-31 and the whole of chapter 20. To that purpose we now turn to the role of the μαθηταί in the narratives of chapter 20.

The Mission of the Disciples 20:17, 19-23, 24-29

For the purpose of our investigation, we shall comment briefly on four points:
a. The meaning of Jesus' word in vs. 17, at the end of the story of the encounter of Jesus and Mary Magdalene.

4

b.   The giving of the Spirit to the disciples by Jesus and their commissioning in vss. 21-23.
c.   The function of the story about Thomas in vss. 24-29.
d.   The connection between vss. 24-29 and 30-31.

   Ad a. Verse 17 presents a number of problems; for our purpose it is essential to note that Jesus' ascension in the sense of his return to the Father is near. Whether we translate "But go to my brothers and tell them that I am now ascending to my Father and your Father, my God and your God" (with the *NEB* text) or "I am going to ascend..." (with *NEB* margin) is not as important as it may seem. The ἀναβαίνω is to be connected with the preceding οὔπω... ἀναβέβηκα. Jesus indicates the very moment of transition. The "hour" has come and Mary Magdalene's understandable but too human attempt to take up and continue her former contacts with Jesus has to be abandoned. From now onwards, the risen Lord communicates with his disciples in another way; the Spirit is about to be sent.

   Chapter 20 records the fulfillment of Jesus' promises in chapters 13-17,[8] but there is one great difference in perspective, expressed by R. E. Brown in the following words: "...the evangelist had to make the effort to fit the resurrection into the process of Jesus' passing from this world to the Father. If John reinterprets the crucifixion so that it becomes part of Jesus' glorification he dramatizes the resurrection so that it is obviously part of the ascension. Jesus is lifted up on the cross; he is raised up from the dead; and goes up to the Father--all as part of one action and one hour" and "(John) is fitting a theology of resurrection/ascension that by definition has no dimensions of time and space into a narrative that is necessarily sequential...."[9]

   We should note that here for the first time the disciples are called "my brothers." God is called "your Father"; yet the distinction between Jesus and the disciples is maintained in the double expression "my Father and your Father."[10]

Ad b. In 14:28 (cf. vss. 3, 18), Jesus says: "I am going away, and coming back to you." The second half of this sentence indicates a very complex reality.[11] One aspect of it is described in chapter 20 where the return of Jesus to his disciples is connected with the gift of the Spirit. In 7:39, 16:7 (cf. 6:62) we read that the Spirit could only come after Jesus' departure to the Father. In 14:18 the sentence: "I will not leave you bereft; I am coming back to you" follows the first passage about sending of the Paraclete who will be with the disciples for ever (14:15-17). After the direct connection in 15:26f. between "the Spirit of truth will bear witness to me" and "you also are my witnesses, because you have been with me from the first" the combination of the gift of the Spirit and the commissioning of the disciples in our passage does not come unexpected.

Verse 21 is most important, because it derives the mission of the disciples from the mission of Jesus by the Father. We shall return to this later;[12] the essential thing to be noted is that the disciples will act as Jesus' representatives and thus as God's representatives, on earth, i.e., over against the hostile world (17:18).[13] One aspect of the mission of the disciples is mentioned in vs. 23: "If you forgive any man's sin, they stand forgiven; if you pronounce them unforgiven, unforgiven they remain." This saying presents us with many problems (particularly if compared with other versions of it); for our present discussion it is useful to understand it against the background of 14:17, 16:8-11--again sayings about the Paraclete which indicate clearly that the κρίσις inaugurated by Jesus in his coming into the world is continued by the Spirit.[14] The Spirit, of course, operates through the disciples.

Ad c. No one who reads vss. 19-23 will suspect that one of the disciples was missing on that occasion. Yet vss. 24-29 tell us that Thomas, one of the twelve, was absent when the Lord commissioned the disciples. The Fourth Gospel singles out Thomas, obviously because it

wants to dramatize the motif of incredulity, traditionally
connected with the narrative of Jesus' appearance to the
disciples.[15] For this Gospel, Thomas' unbelief[16] is a
lack of faith in the testimony of his fellow-disciples who
declare that they have seen the risen Lord. His strong
affirmation that he will not believe unless he can see
with his eyes and touch with his hands shows that he has
no real idea of what Jesus' resurrection means.[17] Yet as
far as seeing is concerned, he asks no more than was ac-
corded to his fellow-disciples, and in the end he does not
touch Jesus' side.

The essential difference between Thomas and his
colleagues is that he is virtually in the position of the
later Christians who have not seen the risen Jesus but are
dependent on the divinely commissioned eye-witnesses.
Verse 29 does not oppose people who believe without seeing
and people who cannot believe without first having seen.[18]
The beatitude in vs. 29b has the reader of the Gospel in
mind.[19] Thomas expresses his faith in the confession, "My
Lord and my God." In this way the Gospel ends with the
highest possible christological pronouncement. It has
clearly reached a climax with this statement which refers
back to the beginning of the Prologue (1:1-3; cf. 1 John
1:1-4 and 5:20).[20]

Ad d. Verses 24-29, interpreted in this way, lead
up to the concluding passage, vss. 30-31. The Spirit
operates through the disciples who are now able to recall
what Jesus did and said and to interpret this correctly--
in the light of God's intentions laid down in Scripture
and confident of perpetual guidance. Their testimony is
authoritative for the Johannine community. If difficulties and differences of opinion arise, as at the time the
Johannine Epistles were written, believers are called back
to the basic testimony of the first witnesses who are,
also, the first believers (1 John 1:1-4).

In Chapter V I shall return to vs. 30 and consider
it from the point of view of the "signs" mentioned there

which occupy such a prominent place in the Fourth Gospel.
There we shall argue that it is essential that Jesus' signs
were performed "in the presence of the disciples" (20:30
corresponds to 2:11). The disciples, however, were only
able to grasp the full meaning of what they had heard and
seen after Jesus' return to the Father. This is stated
clearly in the hermeneutically very important statements
in 2:22, 12:16, 13:26, and 20:9 and in the passages dealing
with the Spirit in 7:39 and the Farewell-discourses which
we have already had occasion to refer to and which we
shall now discuss in some more detail.

The Disciples and the Spirit in Chapters 13-17 and Related Passages

Characteristic for the Fourth Gospel are a great
number of interpretative comments. As B. Olsson has remarked,[21] "the content of these 'footnotes' varies widely:
translations of words, identification of individuals, data
of time, place and customs, summarizing comments, explanations of speeches and events and longer theological exposi-
tions as in 12:37ff."

The remarks on the disciples' understanding before
and after Jesus' departure to the Father are of particular
importance for our view on the hermeneutical perspective
of the Gospel. The first statement of this nature is 2:21f.
which comments on Jesus' concluding word in the Johannine
version of the story of the cleansing of the temple (vss.
13-20). Jesus did not speak about the temple in Jerusalem,
but about the destruction and resurrection of his body.
This was not understood by the Jews who figure as Jesus'
opponents, nor by his μαθηταί who were present at the occasion. The latter, however, remembered (ἐμνήσθησαν) what
Jesus had said "after he had been raised from the dead."
At that time "they believed Scripture[22] and the word Jesus
had spoken." This comment stands in contrast to that at
the end of the preceding story of the wedding in Cana,
where it is said that Jesus revealed his glory and that

his disciples believed in him."[23] Although the disciples
saw and heard and believed, they did not receive full understanding of the meaning of Jesus' words and deeds and
of Scripture until after Jesus' return to the Father.

The interpretative comment after the story of the
entry into Jerusalem links up with 12:16: "This his disciples did not understand at first, but when Jesus had been
glorified (ὅτε ἐδοξάσθη Ἰησοῦς), they remembered (ἐμνήσθησαν) that this was written concerning him, and that they
had done this to him."[24] Also 13:7 which gives Jesus'
comment on Peter's refusal to have his feet washed announces a period of better understanding: "You do not understand now what you are doing, but one day you will."[25]
This does not refer to the explanation given in vss. 12-
17, but to the time after Jesus' death and resurrection,
the turning-point in history solemnly announced in 13:1-3,
the overture of the part of the Gospel dealing with Jesus'
teaching concerning his departure and the situation of his
disciples after that moment.

In 20:9 the comment "they did not yet understand
the Scripture, that Jesus had to rise from the dead" follows the remark that the disciple whom Jesus loved "saw
(the grave and all that was in it) and believed." The
real meaning of the events and of Scripture texts pointing
to these events is only disclosed to the disciples after
Jesus' return to the Father (20:9 is still before (20:17,
19-23!)--with regard to the events the beloved disciple is
ahead of the others.[26]

Interesting is Jesus' statement in 14:7b, which
comes between a question which reveals Thomas' lack of
understanding and a similar one by Philip: "From now on
you do know him (i.e., the Father); you have seen him."
The adverbial expression ἀπ᾿ ἄρτι separates two distinct
periods in history.[27] "From now on" real knowledge is
possible.[28] Jesus who is going to the Father is the way
along which one is able to go to the Father. Still, in
16:25 the decisive hour is yet to come: "Till now I have

been using figures of speech (ἐν παροιμίαις λελάληκα ὑμῖν):
a time is coming when I shall no longer use figures, but
tell you of the Father in plain words (ἐν παρρησίᾳ)" (cf.
also vss. 26-28). But when the disciples answer: "Why,
this *is* plain speaking, this *is* no figure of speech" and
add the confession "...we believe that you have come from
God" (vss. 29f.), Jesus announces a time of dispersion
which is near at hand (ἔρχεται...καὶ ἐλήλυθεν), during
which they will all go εἰς τὰ ἴδια.[29] He encourages them
by assuring them of his victory over the world (vss. 31-
33).

Jesus' departure to the Father is accompanied by
the sending of the Spirit. An interpretative comment in
7:39 states so clearly: "He was speaking of the Spirit
which believers in him would receive later; for the Spirit
had not yet been given, because Jesus had not yet been
glorified." This is a comment on Jesus' solemn declaration in 7:37, 38 which continues to present many problems
to the commentators. For the sake of brevity, I shall refer to F. Porsch's very full discussion of 7:37-39 in his
Pneuma und Wort[30] which *inter alia* rightly points to the
shift in perspective between Jesus' statement and the comment which is added. Jesus' declaration most naturally
refers to the present: one should come to him, the unique
Wisdom-teacher, in order to receive his revelation. The
comment refers to the future, connects Jesus' revelation
with the Spirit and emphasizes that this Spirit is given
to εἰ πιστεύοντες εἰς αὐτόν. Porsch rightly points out
that this verse is an important connecting link between
the statements on πνεῦμα in the first twelve chapters of
the Gospel and those in chapters 13-17 and 18-20. He tries
to show that the activity of the Spirit during Jesus'
earthly life is closely connected with the "word" (1:33;
3:3-8 and 34; 6:62f.). It is the life-giving power of
Jesus' word operating in those who believe in Jesus as the
unique Son sent by God.[31]

7:39 however looks beyond the earthly life of
Jesus; according to Porsch this is also the case in 4:10,
13f., 20-25 where the continuity between the revelation of
Jesus the Messiah now and in the future is stressed, and
where the worship in Spirit and truth is said to be future
and present.[32] Important also is 6:62f. The life-giving
power of Jesus' words is clearly expressed in vs. 63 (cf.
vs. 68)--also the fact that a number of his hearers, even
many of those who may be called μαθηταί, do not accept
them. In this context Jesus says: "Does this shock you
(σκανδαλίζει)? What if you see the Son of Man ascending
to the place where he was before?" The question is not
answered; the sentence has no apodosis and commentators
give a variety of explanations.[33] It is obvious that
there is a continuity in belief and unbelief. Those addressed here do not recognize the life-giving Spirit
operating in the earthly Jesus and will not be convinced
by his ἀνάβασις--they will not see the death on the cross
in the perspective of Jesus' return to the Father. And
the Spirit who enlightens man in order to lead him to a
full understanding will only be given to those who now already believe. Chapter 6 appositely concludes with the
positive reaction of the twelve whose faith is confessed
by Simon Peter (vss. 66-71).

We now turn to the five so-called Paraclete-
passages in the Farewell-discourses (14:16-17, 25-26; 15:
26-27; 16:7-11, 12-15).[34] The first passage (14:16-17)
gives the general setting of the sayings on the Spirit-
Paraclete. The Spirit of Truth will be given by the
Father as "another Paraclete."[35] He is both "colleague"
and successor to Jesus. He will remain with the disciples
for ever, and be in them.[36] With great emphasis it is
said that the κόσμος remains outside the orbit within
which the Spirit operates.[37]

In the following four passages, two deal with the
activity of the Spirit in the community of the disciples--
14:25-26 and 16:12-15; they will have to be examined in

some more detail. The other two, 15:26-27 and 16:7-11,
emphasize the Spirit's activity through the disciples over
against the world and will be passed over here.[38]

In 14:25-26, there is a clear distinction between
two periods: the period of Jesus who has spoken the word(s)
of God (see vs. 24) in the time he remained with the disciples.[39] Next, the Paraclete, the holy Spirit which the
Father will send in Jesus' name (note the δέ in the beginning of vs. 26!) will teach the disciples everything[40] and
will call to mind (ὑπομνήσει, cf. 2:22, 12:16!) all that
Jesus had told them. The καί in this verse is best taken
as explicative. The disciples will be taught many things,
but in the end their knowledge will consist of a better
and deeper understanding of all Jesus had said during his
time on earth.

This is borne out by 16:12-15. Verse 12 emphasizes
that there is much that Jesus wants to say but that the
disciples cannot bear now. The future activity of the
Spirit is described as ὁδηγεῖν to all truth (vs. 13).[41]
The word "truth" clearly refers to the revelation brought
by Jesus (see the γάρ in vs. 13b). The Spirit does not
speak on his own authority,[42] but is dependent on what he
hears.[43] He will be able to announce and to explain the
events which are to come in the time after Jesus' departure.[44] Verses 14-15, the final statement on the Spirit-
Paraclete, emphasize that the Spirit acts as representative and interpreter of the Son, just as the Son acts as
the representative of the Father. 16:12-15 are followed
by 16:25, a statement already discussed above. There is
an obvious parallel between the ταῦτα λελάληκα ὑμῖν in 14:
25 and the ταῦτα ἐν παροιμίαις λελάληκα ὑμῖν in 16:25.
This implies that Jesus' speaking in the period after his
departure and the teaching/recalling activity of the
Spirit are really one and the same.

In this connection, it is interesting to see that
14:16-17 and 14:25-26 precede and follow on important passages speaking about the return of Jesus (and the Father)

to the disciples. It may be argued that the Paraclete-
passages explain how Jesus will return and in what way the
Father and the Son will dwell among the disciples. 1 John
3:24 says so explicitly: "And by this we know that he remains in us, by the Spirit which he has given us" (cf.
1 John 4:13). Lord and Spirit remain closely connected,
also in the period after "the hour."

The Spirit operates in and through the community of
disciples which live in a hostile world (15:18-16:4).
There is a close connection between the witness of the
Spirit and that of the disciples (15:26, 27). The Spirit
is the dynamic companion of the disciples who are sent out
into the world as representatives of the Son (17:6-26;
particularly 17:18, to be connected with 20:21).

The conclusion which can be drawn from the analysis
of the passages in this section combined with the results
reached in the discussion of chapter 20 is clear: The
Fourth Gospel presents itself as the result of the teaching and the recalling activity of the Spirit within the
community of disciples leading to a deeper and fuller insight into all that Jesus as the Son revealed during his
stay on earth.[45] The Spirit does not really add anything
new, but sheds new light on the acts and the words which
were performed and spoken in the presence of those who had
been with Jesus from the beginning (15:27!). He is the
moving force behind an effective teaching about Jesus to
disciples of following generations (17:20, 21; 20:29)[46]
and a continuing witness to the world.

For the following generations it is absolutely essential to remain in fellowship with the disciples-
eyewitnesses, through the Spirit who continually refers
back to the earthly Jesus. The Gospel is an essential
component of the Spirit's testimony.

The True Nature of Discipleship

The first time the word μαθηταί occurs in the
Fourth Gospel it serves to denote disciples of John the

Baptist. In chapter 1:35-51 we hear how two disciples of John "follow Jesus," "come" and "see" and "remain" with him (1:37-39). They and others become disciples of Jesus and speak about him in terms typical of Jewish messianic expectation.[47] The word "to follow" is found in 1:37, 38, 40, 43 and is also used in 8:12; 10:4, 5, 27; 12:26; 13: 36, 37; 21:19, 20, 22 to denote discipleship. It implies a complete trust in Jesus, perseverance and martyrdom. Also the word "to remain" plays an important role in the Gospel and the Epistles. In 8:31 Jews who have believed in Jesus are exhorted: "If you remain in my word you are truly my disciples." There is no difference between "to remain in my word" and "to remain in my love" (15:9, 10) or "to remain in me" (elsewhere in 15:1-17). In the Farewell-discourses as well as the First Epistle it is made clear that we may speak of "mutual indwelling" of Father, Son, divine "activities" on the one hand and the believing community on the other. As far as the believers are concerned, there is a constant alternation between indicative and imperative.[48]

And as to the "come and see" of vs. 39: the encounters between the new disciples and Jesus are only the beginning. "You will see greater things than these," Jesus says to Nathanael who has just confessed his faith in him (1:50). This statement is followed up by 1:51; the greater things the disciples will see will give them deeper insight into Jesus' unique relationship to the Father.[49]

The pericope 1:35-51 is little more than a prelude to what follows in chapters 2-12. To "the greater things" belong the σημεῖα as revelation of Jesus' δόξα; the disciples who are present when Jesus changes water into wine in Cana in Galilee come to believe in him. The Cana-event, indicated as the "beginning of the signs," obviously also marks the real beginnings of discipleship for the small band who follows Jesus around and who are simply introduced as "his disciples" 2:2, 11, 12. The Gospel does not find it necessary to tell its readers who they were. They

are mentioned repeatedly as followers of Jesus, who believe in him and accompany him on his journeys.[50]

Yet there is also a wider circle of disciples: 4:1
tells us that Jesus made and baptized more disciples than
John the Baptist; 7:3 mentions a group of disciples (present and/or future) in Judea. When in 18:19-21 the high
priest asks Jesus about his disciples, Jesus points to his
teaching in public and suggests that the high priest should
ask all who heard him. In 6:60-71 a small group (here un-
expectedly called "the Twelve" [cf. 20:24]) is expressly
distinguished from a wider group of μαθηταί. The smaller
group remains faithful to Jesus while the others do not
follow him any longer. True disciples listen, see, believe, overcome offence, remain with Jesus and follow him.
In 13:35, Jesus exhorts his disciples to show their discipleship in mutual love; in 15:8 they are asked "to bear
much fruit and so prove to be my disciples." In chapter 9
we notice that, in the end, to be a disciple of Jesus is
considered by the Jews to be incompatible with being a
disciple of Moses and leads to expulsion from the synagogue (9:27, 28 and vss. 22, 34).[51]

Returning to chapter 2 for a moment, we find a contrast between 2:11 and 2:23-25. Why do the many people
in Jerusalem "who believed in his name, seeing the signs
which he did" obviously not qualify as disciples, whereas
the disciples who follow Jesus are able to see the revelation of his δόξα and believe in him? This question will
occupy us in Chapters II-V below. "Sympathizers" are
found everywhere in the Gospel (right to the burial of
Jesus, at which Joseph of Arimathea, the "hidden disciple"
[19:38], and Nicodemus play an important role); they lack
the insight into the real secret of Jesus' relationship to
the Father and fail to draw the ultimate consequences;
they do not break away from the synagogue.

The disciples form a separate group, centered
around Jesus and in one way or another remaining with him.
The essential point in Jesus' admonition to "the Jews who

believed in him" in 8:31f. is: "If you remain in my word, you are truly my disciples, and you will know the truth and the truth will set you free." Only by remaining with Jesus and following him (8:12; 10:4, 5, 27; 12:26, etc.) will they be and remain "in the light" and receive life. Only so will they also be able to continue after Jesus' departure to the Father and move from the period of the Son to that of the Spirit in which full insight is granted.

As T. L. Schram observed rightly,[52] the disciples are comparatively passive during the narrative; their role "is preparatory for the future the narrator is already involved in rather than contributory to the developing action....The disciples' function in the argument is to provide a model of accepting Jesus' words and to be the link between the Jesus of the narrative and the reader after the narrative is finished (17:20; 20:23, 27; 21:15-17)."

Before the giving of the Spirit in 20:19-23, the disciples show a lack of understanding at many occasions. The Gospel interprets this "structurally" as we have seen; at the same time, it is clear that the disciples, both in their acceptance and their misunderstanding of Jesus' word, are portrayed as models for future generations of believers. Misunderstanding on the part of the disciples and questions which show their lack of insight call for further instruction by Jesus, the true διδάσκαλος, or lead to new action by him.

This is, e.g., the case in the discussion between Jesus and his disciples after the encounter with the Samaritan woman (4:27-38), in which Jesus reveals the secret of his mission (and their own mission) to them (and not to the Samaritans!).[53] Next there is 9:1-5 where the disciples show their lack of understanding in the opening question: "Rabbi, who sinned, this man or his parents?" and Jesus directs their attention to what is going to be done in the name of God. In 11:7-16, the introduction to the story of the raising of Lazarus, the disciples do not understand what has happened and what Jesus intends to do, because they do not realize that Jesus has power over death. They are, finally, prepared to go with Jesus and to share his death (vs. 16), but they need the coming sign in order to believe more fully and to look beyond death (vss. 15, 42).[54] In the Passion-story, Peter is, traditionally, portrayed as denying his Lord (18:15-18, 25-27, cf. 13:38).[55]

Lack of insight is also displayed by the disciples in chapters 13-17. In 13:16-17 the foot-washing is the starting-point for further teaching concerning the relationship between the believer and Jesus (vss. 7-11) and for a lesson in true discipleship (vss. 12-17).[56] In 14: 4-12 the questions of Thomas and Philip lead up to new teaching of Jesus concerning the fundamental unity of intention and action between the Son and the Father. Similarly, discussions among Jesus' disciples on the meaning of his word, "A little while and you see me no more; again a little while and you will see me," in 16:16-18 lead to new teaching of Jesus concerning the times of mourning and the times of joy which are to come. In all the cases mentioned, the lack of understanding on the part of the disciples enables Jesus the teacher (and the evangelist!) to elucidate what is really meant, and all these cases are told from the perspective of complete understanding in the time of the Spirit.[57] And because there is not only discontinuity but also continuity between the period before and that after Jesus' "hour"[58] there are also instances where the disciples prove to have true faith and are able to formulate the right confession. So Peter says on behalf of the faithful "Twelve": "You have the words of eternal life, and we have believed, and have come to know, that you are the Holy One of God" (6:68f.).[59] And Martha replies to Jesus' teaching on the resurrection and the life with the confession: "I am convinced that you are the Messiah, the Son of God who was to come into the world" (11:27). They both speak as it were proleptically, they anticipate the faith of the Church expressed in 20:31.

There is continuity; the time for true worship is coming
and is now (4:21-24). It should be noted that in 6:69 and
11:27 perfects are used, together with a (here) emphatic
ὑμεῖς and ἐγώ. The same perfects are found in 17:7 and
1 John 4:14-16 which describe the situation of the believing community.[60]

The Christians belonging to the Johannine communities live in spiritual communion with Jesus' disciples,
whom they may regard as examples both before and after
Jesus' departure to the Father. What Jesus in 13-17 promises and commands with regard to the situation of the disciples in the time after his return to God is directed to
the whole church, not just to those present at the occasion. Yet there is also a distinction between the disciples who were eye-witnesses and those who are not. The
disciples of the latter category are dependent on the witness of the former (see 17:20, 21;[61] 20:29) and particularly in times of stress and uncertainty it is absolutely
necessary to go back "to the beginning" (15:27; 1 John 1:
1-4, etc.[62]).

Divine Initiative

In the preceding section of this chapter, discipleship was primarily described from the point of view of the
disciples themselves; yet it has become abundantly clear
that to become a disciple means reacting positively to the
One who is sent by God and understanding the real secret
of his being. In this concluding section we shall have to
pay some attention to the question, why and how some people were able to react positively while so many others remained skeptical, became hostile or did not get beyond
sympathy and inadequate understanding. We find that, in
the last resort, a divine initiative lies behind and mani-
fests itself in the human positive reaction. Paradoxically, faith is a human impossibility, made possible by God.

We will come back to this question in Chapter VI,
"The Son of God and the Children of God," and will there

also pay some attention to the relationship between divine
initiative and human reaction in the very first passage
speaking about a positive response, 1:12-13 (with the
terms γεννηθῆναι ἐκ θεοῦ and τέκνα θεοῦ γινέσθαι on the
one hand and λαμβάνειν αὐτόν and πιστεύειν εἰς τὸ ὄνομα
αὐτοῦ on the other).[63]

     In the present context I mention briefly the terms
"to draw" and "to give" found in chapter 6. "To draw,"
ἕλκειν, is used in 6:44 of the Father who sent Jesus and
now "draws" people who are then able to come to Jesus.
Jesus adds "I will raise (them) up on the last day." This
links up with 12:32 where Jesus announces that he will
draw all men to himself, when he is lifted up from the
earth.[64] In 6:65 the verb διδόναι is used in the sense of
"to grant," "to allow"--"...no one can come to me unless
it has been granted to him by the Father."[65] The same
verb also occurs with the meaning "to give to," with the
Father as subject, the believers as object, and the Son,
Jesus, as the one to whom the believers are entrusted.
Here we may point to 6:37, 39; 10:29 and especially to
17:2, 6-10, 24 and 18:9. The Son gives eternal life to
those whom the Father entrusts to him and whom he takes
out of the world. They accept his words and recognize him
as the unique representative of the Father. No one is
lost (3:16, 6:39, 10:28, 18:9) except Judas (17:12).

     Because of the complete unity of intention and ac-
tion between Father and Son,[66] the faith of the disciples
is often directly connected with an initiative on the part
of Jesus. The verbs used are "to choose," "to love," and
"to know."

     The verb "to choose" (ἐκλέγεσθαι) is used in con-
nection with "the Twelve" in 6:66-71. After Peter's confession on behalf of the small group of faithful followers
Jesus says, "Did I not choose you, the Twelve?" (vs. 70),
and immediately adds that among the chosen twelve there is
Judas who is going to betray him (vs. 71, cf. vs. 64).[67]
In the case of Judas, it is clear that Jesus keeps the
initiative even where the devil is at work (13:27).[68]

The verb ἐκλέγεσθαι is also used in 15:16 and 19.
The latter verse makes clear that Jesus' election means
separation from the world; in the former, Jesus states
categorically: "You did not choose me; I chose you."
This emphasis on Jesus' initiative follows on the image of
the vine and the branches (15:1-6) and its subsequent interpretation. It is clear that the Son is the giver of
life and that he shows what real love is (see esp. 15:13!).
Whereas μένειν and ἀγαπᾶν indicate reciprocal relations,
inspired by Jesus' initiative, and μένειν is used with
regard to the disciples in the indicative and the imperative, ἐκλέγομαι expressly emphasizes this initiative.

Jesus' love for those who belong to him is also
mentioned in other parts of the Farewell-discourses. These
begin with 13:1, "...He had always loved his own who were
in the world and now he was to show the full extent of his
love,"[69] and they end with 17:26, "I made thy name known
to them and will make it known, so that the love thou
hadst for me may be in them, and I may be in them" (cf.
vss. 23, 24). In 14:21-24 it is stressed that he who
loves Jesus and shows this in keeping his commandments
will be loved by the Father and the Son.

"To know," γινώσκειν, is found in the discourse on
the Good Shepherd (see 10:14-18, esp. vss. 14f.): "I am
the Good Shepherd; I know the Father--and I lay down my
life for sheep." Again there is reciprocity in the relation between the Son and those who belong to him (as there
is reciprocity between Son and Father), but again it is
the Son who takes the initiative and sets the example as a
singularly good Shepherd (10:15b corresponds clearly to
15:13). In 10:27-29, where this passage is taken up and
explained in the light of the unity of intention and action between Son and Father, Jesus is said "to know" his
sheep and the sheep are described as "listening to him"
and "following him."

In his important article, "The Man from Heaven in
Johannine Sectarianism,"[70] W. A. Meeks points to the

difference between "the Man from Heaven" whose descent and ascent are mentioned in the Fourth Gospel (not described!) and those who "hear" his words and react positively. They are never called *pneumatikoi* who, like the Son, have come down from heaven. They are "not of this world" (15:19, 17:14ff.), but this status is a confessed one, not an ontological one. Meeks refers here to 15:19 and 17:6, 14, and continues: "Thus we have in the Johannine literature a thoroughly dualistic picture: a small group of believers isolated over against 'the world' that belong intrinsically to 'the things below,' i.e., to darkness and the devil. Yet that picture is never rationalized by a comprehensive myth, as in gnosticism, or by a theory of predestination, as later in the western catholic tradition."

A passage like 3:19-21 shows that we can, indeed, go no further. Jesus' coming on earth brings κρίσις, separation between good and evil. Generally the response to the light which has come in the world is negative-- people avoid the light, because they do not want their ἔργα to be exposed. There are, however, people who "do what is true" and they come to the light. At that very moment it is made clear that *God* is behind their deeds and operates through them. The divine initiative becomes apparent in the actual positive response.[71]

NOTES

CHAPTER I

[1]See the note on this verse in *The Greek New Testament* (London-New York: U.B.S., [3]1975).

[2]See B. M. Metzger, *A Textual Commentary on the Greek New Testament* (London-New York: U.B.S., 1971) on 20:31 and the note on 20:31 in R. Schnackenburg, *Das Johannesevangelium* III, Herders Theologischer Kommentar zum Neuen Testament (Freiburg-Basel-Wien: Herder, 1975), p. 403, where other examples are mentioned.

[3]H. Riesenfeld, "Zu den johanneischen ἵνα-Sätzen," *Studia Theologica* 19 (1965), pp. 213-20.

[4]See Chapter III, below, pp. 58-59.

[5]See also Chapter VII, below, p. 175.

[6]See Chapter VI, pp. 148-49, and Chapter VII, p. 175.

[7]See, particularly, section IV, "Some remarks on the purpose of the Fourth Gospel," pp. 97-102.

[8]This is rightly emphasized by F. Porsch, *Pneuma und Wort. Ein exegetischer Beitrag zur Pneumatologie des Johannesevangelium*, Frankfurter Theologische Studien 16 (Frankfurt: Knecht, 1974).

[9]R. E. Brown, *The Gospel according to John (xiii-xxi)*, The Anchor Bible 29A (Garden City, NY: Doubleday, 1970), pp. 1013-14 (see also below, Chapter VII, p. 187, n. 21). A similar view is found in Porsch, *Pneuma und Wort*, pp. 370-74. Compare also W. A. Meeks's observation on 20:17: "We can only observe that, since the fourth evangelist's dramatic compression of exaltation and crucifixion motifs into one has left the traditional Easter appearances in a kind of limbo, this strange statement imparts to that limbo a sacred liminality" ("The Man from Heaven in Johannine Sectarianism," *JBL* 91 [1972], pp. 44-72).

[10]For ἀδελφός, see 21:23 and the Johannine Epistles passim. Cf. also 14:21, 23, and 16:27. On the distinction and connection between Jesus as the Son and the disciples as the children of God, see Chapter VI.

[11]See also Chapter VII below, pp. 172-75.

[12]See Chapter VI below, pp. 152-53.

[13]The whole section, 17:13-23, is important here; cf. 15:18-21; 13:16 (the word ἀπόστολος is used here as a general term), 20.

[14]See the very full discussion of 20:23 by Brown, *The Gospel according to John (xiii-xxi)*, pp. 1039-45. Sacramental elements and arguments pertaining to the exercise of authority within the Church should not enter into the exegetical discussion of this passage. The disciples represent the believers as such.

[15]See, e.g., C. H. Dodd, *Historical Tradition in the Fourth Gospel* (Cambridge: Cambridge University Press, 1963), pp. 145-46.

[16]See vs. 27: "Be unbelieving no longer, but believe" (*NEB*). μὴ γίνου should be understood as "do not persist in" (see Brown, *The Gospel according to John (xiii-xxi)*, p. 1026).

[17]In 11:16 and 14:5 also Thomas shows that he finds it impossible to look beyond death.

[18]This exegesis is also found in C. K. Barrett, *The Gospel according to St. John* (London: Macmillan, 1955), J. N. Sanders-B. A. Mastin, *The Gospel according to St. John* (London: Black, 1968), and Schnackenburg, *Das Johannesevangelium* III, ad loc.; Brown, *The Gospel according to John (xiii-xxi)*, pp. 1045-46, thinks that Thomas was criticized on two counts: "for refusing to accept the word of the other disciples, and for being taken up with establishing the marvelous and miraculous aspect of Jesus' appearance." He is right in stressing that in vss. 26-28 Thomas is led to true faith; cf. the royal official in 4:46-54.

[19]Verse 29a, like 1:50 and 16:31, may be read as an ironic statement or as a question.

[20]On the possibility of an antidocetic application of the Thomas story, see below, Chapter VIII, pp. 207, 210.

[21]B. Olsson, *Structure and Meaning in the Fourth Gospel. A text-linguistic analysis of John 2:1-11 and 4: 1-42* (Lund: Gleerup, 1974), p. 262. His whole fourth chapter on "The Interpretative Character of the Text and the Paraclete" is important for our present purpose.

[22]This refers to the adapted quotation from Ps 69: 10 in vs. 17. The ἐμνήσθησαν in this verse, which is ambiguous, should probably be connected with that of vs. 22.

[23]Already in the Cana-story, however, we find the statement οὔπω ἥκει ἡ ὥρα μου; see below, Chapter V, p. 124.

[24]On this passage, see further Chapter III, pp. 59-60.

[25]Cf. also the lack of understanding in 13:28.

[26]See further below, Chapter VIII, pp. 211-13.

[27]So Matt 23:39; 26:29, 64, and John 1:51. In John 13:19 it seems to mean no more than "now, at this moment" (cf. 14:29). Schnackenburg, *Das Johannesevangelium* III, p. 76, assumes this meaning here too; he connects vs. 7b with vs. 9 and 12:45. There is, however, also 14:20. See also J. Riedl, *Das Heilswerk Jesu nach Johannes* (Freiburg-Basel-Wien: Herder, 1973), p. 275.

[28]This is the meaning of this second half of this verse, regardless of the reading we prefer in the first half. On the text-critical difficulties there, see Metzger, *A Textual Commentary*, ad loc. *The Greek New Testament* prefers the reading εἰ ἐγνώκατέ με καὶ τὸν πατέρα μου γνώσεσθε (chosen by many commentators, inter alia Schnackenburg, whose interpretation centers around the paradox γνώσεσθε (vs. 7a)-γινώσκετε (vs. 7b). Nestle-Aland[25] and K. Aland, in a note to Metzger's comment, choose εἰ ἐγνώκειτέ με, καὶ τὸν πατέρα μου ἂν ἤδειτε. Metzger supposes secondary influence from vss. 8-9 (cf. also 8:19); Aland is of the opinion that a negative statement concerning the apostles is more likely to be original than a positive one (see also 14:28).

[29]Schnackenburg, *Das Johannesevangelium* III, ad loc., rightly emphasizes the negative overtones in this expression, and points to 8:44; 15:19.

[30]See note 8 above. Porsch discusses this passage on pp. 53-81.

[31]See, e.g., his summary on pp. 210-12.

[32]See Porsch, *Pneuma und Wort*, pp. 137-60. Olsson, *Structure and Meaning in the Fourth Gospel*, p. 196, connects the ἔρχεται with the time the prediction was made and the ἔστιν with the time it was realized. "We would have...a kind of co-projection of the time *before* Jesus' 'hour' and the time *after* Jesus' 'hour.'" I consider this interpretation unlikely; see also Chapter VII, pp. 175-77.

[33]See, e.g., Porsch, *Pneuma und Wort*, pp. 205-8. The interpretation given in the text is also shared by him.

[34]Of the many studies on these passages, see particularly G. Johnston, *The Spirit-Paraclete in the Gospel of John* (Cambridge: Cambridge University Press, 1970); Porsch, *Pneuma und Wort*, part II, pp. 215-303; U. B. Müller, "Die Parakletenvorstellung im Johannesevangelium,"

ZThK 71 (1974), pp. 31-77; and the commentaries of Brown
(esp. Appendix V, "The Paraclete") and Schnackenburg (esp.
Exkurs 16, "Der Paraklet und die Paraklet-Sprüche").
Short, but important for our purpose, is Olsson's "The
Paraclete as the Interpreter" in his *Structure and Meaning
in the Fourth Gospel*, pp. 266-72.

[35]The meaning and background of the terms παράκλητος and τὸ πνεῦμα τῆς ἀληθείας need not be discussed here.

[36]μεθ' ὑμῶν, παρ' ὑμῖν (cf. 14:25), ἐν ὑμῖν--see
Porsch, *Pneuma und Wort*, pp. 244-47, who, wrongly, refers
the μένει in vs. 17 to a continuity in the activity of the
Spirit before and after Jesus' departure. This seems to
be excluded by the δώσει in vs. 16.

[37]So also vss. 19, 23. There is a clear opposition
to 20:22; λαβεῖν means "to receive" as well as "to accept."
The consequences are worked out in 15:18-16:4 and 17:6-26.
On the οὐ δύναται in Johannine dualism, see my comments on
1 John 3:4-10 in *De Brieven van Johannes* (Nijkerk: Callenbach, 1968, [2]1973), pp. 139-59.

[38]15:26, 27 is an important part of 15:18-16:4.
Verse 26 and vs. 27 point to two sides of the same coin
(cf. also 1 John 4:13-14). In 16:7-11, the relationship
between the "exposure" (ἐλέγξις) of the world by the Spirit
and the testimony of the disciples is only implicit (but
the fifth Paraclete-statement follows directly). What is
essential is that the Spirit, acting as witness *à décharge*
for the disciples, is the witness *à charge* for the world,
sharing the final character of God's verdict on the world's
negative attitude towards Jesus' coming into the world--see
J. Blank, *Krisis. Untersuchungen zur johanneischen Christologie* (Freiburg: Lambertus, 1964), pp. 332-39, and cf.
Schnackenburg, *Das Johannesevangelium* III, p. 162.

[39]So also 16:7 and 16:12.

[40]Compare Jesus' teaching, e.g., in 7:14, 16, 17,
28; 8:20; 18:19-20, and see also 1 John 2:20, 27.

[41]The "contradiction" between vs. 12 and 15:15b is
intentional; vs. 13 shows that the πολλά to be disclosed
later is not quantitatively but qualitatively more. The
"teaching" and "recalling" of 14:26 are taken up in the
expression ὁδηγεῖν εἰς τὴν ἀλήθειαν πᾶσαν. The variant ἐν
τῇ ἀληθείᾳ πασῇ is chosen in *The Greek New Testament*, but
Metzger's note (*A Textual Commentary*, p. 247) shows that
the editors do not think that there was a difference in
meaning. They regard εἰς + acc. as introduced by copyists
who regarded it as more idiomatic after the verb ὁδηγήσει
than ἐν + dat. The "Spirit of Truth" leads the disciples
to a fuller apprehension of the truth already given to
them. Cf. 8:31, 32, 40, 44, 45 (and, of course, Ps 25:5).

[42]On ἀφ' ἑαυτοῦ, see Chapter VI, below, p. 143.

[43]ὅσα ἀκούει (or: ἀκούσει, preferred by *The Greek New Testament*) refers to a continuous activity in the future. It stands parallel to ἐκ τοῦ ἐμοῦ λήμψεται in vs. 14 and ἐκ τοῦ ἐμοῦ λαμβάνει in 16:15. The Spirit not only takes up and recalls what the Son said during his stay on earth. He also listens to what the Son, after his exaltation, has to say. We may compare here the two aspects of the relation between Son and Father. See, e.g., 5:30, "I can do nothing on my own authority; as I hear, I judge..." (cf. 5:19; 8:47) with 8:26, "...I declare to the world what I have heard from him" (cf. 8:40)--see below, Chapter V, p. 133.

[44]τὰ ἐρχόμενα probably refers to all the disciples will be able to say and to do in the time after Jesus' departure (cf. 14:12-14, 15, 21-24). Ἀναγγέλλειν is also used in 4:25 where the Samaritan woman expects of the Messiah that ἀναγγελεῖ ἡμῖν ἅπαντα. The verb means "to proclaim, to reveal something to someone." In Deutero-Isaiah this is a prerogative of the true God (see 41:23 and other passages mentioned by Porsch, *Pneuma und Wort*, pp. 297-99). The Son also is shown to be reliable because his predictions concerning the future become true (13:19; 14:29; 16:4). Ἀναγγέλλειν not only refers to the actual announcing but also to the revealing of the true meaning of the (coming) events (see, e.g., Isa 45:19 and Acts 20:27). See also Brown, *The Gospel according to John (xiii-xxi)*, p. 708.

[45]See the following quotation from Porsch, *Pneuma und Wort*, p. 300: "Es scheint dass Johannes hier (16,13-15) den ganzen Offenbarungsprozess in seiner inneren Struktur aufzeigen und zusammenfassen will: seinen letzten Ursprung im Vater, seine Vermittlung durch den Sohn an die Menschen, der die Wahrheit in die Welt gegenwärtig macht und schliesslich das immer tiefere Hineinführen in das Verständnis (in das Innere) dieses Wahrheit, die letztlich in diesem Geheimnis der Zuordnung von Vater-Sohn und Geist besteht."

[46]See also above, p. 17.

[47]See Chapter III, pp. 58-59 and the reference there to Schnackenburg, *The Gospel according to St John* I, Herder's Theological Commentary on the New Testament (New York: Herder and Herder; London: Burns & Oates, 1968), Excursus III, "The Titles of Jesus in John 1," pp. 507-14).

[48]See Chapter VII, below, pp. 172-75 and 177-80, and my commentary, *De Brieven van Johannes*, pp. 79-81.

[49]See also below, Chapter III, p. 59.

[50]See 2:17, 22; 3:22; 4:2, 8, 27, 31, 33; 6:3, 8,
12, 16, 22, 24; 9:2; 11:7, 8, 12, 54; 12:4, 16; 13:5, 22,
23; 16:17, 29; 18:1, 2; 20:18, 19, 20, 25, 26, 30; 21:1,
2, 4, 8, 12, 14. In addition, a number of individual disciples are mentioned. See also Exkurs 17, "Jünger, Gemeinde, Kirche im Johannesevangelium," in Schnackenburg,
Das Johannesevangelium III, pp. 231-45.

[51]See further Chapter III, below, pp. 61-63.

[52]T. L. Schram, *The Use of IOUDAIOS in the Fourth
Gospel. An Application of Some Linguistic Insights to a
New Testament Problem* (Dissertation, Utrecht, 1974), p.
138.

[53]In Chapters III (pp. 63-66) and IV (pp. 102-5)
the peculiar situation of the Samaritan believers is discussed. The relation between Jesus and the villagers in
4:39-42 is hardly different from that between Jesus and
the two disciples of John the Baptist in 1:38-39, and
their reaction to Jesus' words is a true Christian confession (cf. 1 John 4:14). The Gospel clearly wants to emphasize that Samaritans (as well as Greeks, 12:20-21, 32)
belong to the children of God (11:52). Yet they are nowhere called "disciples" and they do not figure in any
subsequent story or discourse in the Gospel. The disciples
remain a select group who receive further instruction on
Jesus' relationship to the Father (4:31-34) and hear that
they have a task as regards these Samaritans (4:35-38).
Compare also 4:22. See, particularly, Olsson, *Structure
and Meaning in the Fourth Gospel*, pp. 218-40 and 241-48,
Excursus III, "Mission in John." The passage vss. 31-38
presents many problems, but there is no doubt that in vs.
38 the harvest is entrusted to the disciples.

[54]On the faith of the disciples and Martha, see
Chapter V, below, pp. 124-26.

[55]See particularly μὴ καὶ σὺ ἐκ τῶν μαθητῶν εἶ τοῦ
ἀνθρώπου τούτου (18:17, cf. vs. 25). The word μαθητής is
not used in the parallel stories in the Synoptics.

[56]There is a certain tension between 13:7 and 13:
12-17, but no discrepancy. On the theory that vss. 12-17
belong to a later redaction of the Fourth Gospel (now also
defended by Schnackenburg, *Das Johannesevangelium* III, pp.
6-15), see below, Chapter VII, pp. 177-78.

[57]On this see also H. Leroy, *Rätsel und Missverständnis: Ein Beitrag zur Formgeschichte des Johannes-
evangeliums*, BBB 30 (Bonn: Peter Hanstein, 1968), esp. pp.
171-83.

[58]See above, p. 12.

[59]For a possible connection between 6:66-71 and 6:
16-21, see below, Chapter V, pp. 129-30.

[60]So also F. Mussner, *Die johanneische Sehweise*,
Quaestiones Disputatae 28 (Freiburg-Basel-Wien: Herder,
1965), pp. 30-32. The indicative of the perfect tense is
also found in 16:27, 20:29, and 1 John 5:10.

[61]These two verses may well be an insertion; see
Schnackenburg, *Das Johannesevangelium* III, pp. 214-16.
Schnackenburg rightly emphasizes that these verses, though
perhaps literarily secondary, do not constitute a foreign
theological element.

[62]See further Chapter VIII, below, and also my article, "Who are 'We'?", chapter X in *Jesus: Inspiring and
Disturbing Presence*, trans. by J. E. Steely (Nashville-
New York: Abingdon Press, 1974), from which I quote: "The
pluralis apostolicus passes over into the *pluralis ecclesiasticus*, and the *pluralis ecclesiasticus* is inconceivable
without the *pluralis apostolicus*" (p. 154).

[63]See particularly pp. 151-53.

[64]Commentaries usually point to Jer 38:3 (LXX) and
other parallels in the Septuagint. P. Borgen, *Bread from
Heaven. An Exegetical Study of the Concept of Manna in the
Gospel of John and the Writings of Philo*, NovTSup 10
(Leiden: Brill, 1965), pp. 160-61, points to the rabbinic
use of משׁך as "to take possession of" (by drawing or seiz-
ing an object). According to him, 12:32 is understandable
against the background of the rabbinic rules of agency.

[65]Cf. 1:12; 3:27; 5:26, (36); (17:4); 19:11.

[66]See, again, Chapter VI, below, passim.

[67]Cf. also 13:2 and 17:12. On foreknowledge and
announcement beforehand, see 13:19, 14:29, 16:4 (and 12!
cf. n. 44, above).

[68]In the whole Johannine Passion-story, Jesus is
not a victim, but "lays down his life of his free will"
(10:17, 18). See 13:26; 18:1-11; the omission of Simon
of Cyrene (19:17, βαστάζων ἑαυτῷ τὸν σταυρόν); 19:30.

[69]"The full extent of" is the *NEB* translation of
εἰς τέλος, which may also have a temporal meaning.

[70]See note 9. The quotation below is from p. 68.

[71]See also below, Chapter VI, pp. 153-54.

CHAPTER II

NICODEMUS AND JESUS: SOME OBSERVATIONS ON
MISUNDERSTANDING AND UNDERSTANDING IN THE
FOURTH GOSPEL

Nicodemus appears only three times in the Fourth
Gospel, and nowhere else in the New Testament. The first
time is in chapter 3, where we are told how he visits Jesus
at night, addresses him with what amounts to a confession
of faith and is corrected by Jesus in the ensuing dialogue
which changes into a monologue (3:1-21; cf. vss. 31-36).
There is no further mention of Nicodemus till he reappears
on the scene at the end of chapter 7 where we find him in
discussion with his fellow Pharisees, who react in a rather
personal and disagreeable manner when he asks for a fair
hearing for Jesus according to the Law (7:50-52). His last
appearance is in 19:38-42 where he joins Joseph of Arimathea in burying Jesus and brings a considerable quantity
of myrrh and aloes. The second and third occurrences are
connected with the first one by means of redactional remarks in 7:50, "the man who had once visited Jesus,"[1] and
19:39, "the man who had first visited Jesus by night."
This shows that at least those responsible for the final
edition of the Fourth Gospel wanted to indicate a connection between these three episodes.

The very scantiness of our information concerning
Nicodemus might tempt us to supply unknown facts from fan-
cy and to give a picture of a secret disciple, sympathetic,
but weak or (alternatively) tenacious and cunning--or of a
sympathizing outsider who did not, after all, acquire the
true faith and contented himself with paying the last
honor to a man whom he revered and whom he considered to
have been condemned to death unjustly. No doubt preachers
all through the ages have indulged in such fancies which
have no real basis in the Gospel itself, because this was
not written to satisfy our curiosity but to prompt and to
confirm faith (see 20:30).

29

Nicodemus is not pictured as an individual person, but as a representative of a larger group. He belongs to the Pharisees, he is a ruler of the Jews (3:1)[2] and as such he pleads Jesus' cause with his colleagues when they turn against him: "Is there a single one of our rulers who has believed in him, or of the Pharisees?" (7:48). Is Nicodemus the one exception among the rulers and the Pharisees? We are not told so; his argumentation remains within the limits of Pharisaic discussion of legal matters. But it is clear that Jesus' preaching has caused a split among the Jewish leaders, just as it had caused a σχίσμα among the ordinary people a little earlier (7:44).[3] In 19:39 Nicodemus's rank and affiliation are not mentioned, but it may not be farfetched to suppose that the Fourth Gospel implies that he was a μαθητὴς [τοῦ] 'Ιησοῦ κεκρυμμένος διὰ τὸν φόβον τῶν 'Ιουδαίων just like Joseph of Arimathea whose companion he has become.

Now there are more instances in the Fourth Gospel of secret discipleship and of schisms among the Jewish leaders. In 12:42 we hear that even among the ἄρχοντες many believed in Jesus (ἐπίστευσαν εἰς αὐτόν--the same expression is used in 7:48), but would not confess this openly because of the Pharisees, for fear of being banned from the synagogue. Verse 43 adds: "They valued their reputation with man rather than the honor which comes from God (τὴν δόξαν τοῦ θεοῦ)." This is said in a passage at the end of the first twelve chapters of the Fourth Gospel which intends to give a survey in retrospect of Jesus' activity in public.[4] The result is valued as negative. "In spite of the many signs which Jesus had performed in their presence they would not believe in him" (12:37). This in contrast to the disciples who saw the signs, came to believe and passed the message on to later generations in order that those might believe and hold their faith (20:30-31). Notwithstanding this general refusal to accept Jesus, which had already been announced by Isaiah "who saw his glory and spoke about him" (12:38-41), there were many even among the leading classes who believed. The fact, however, that they did not acknowledge Jesus openly proves that their faith was not genuine; 12:43 refers back to 5:44 where Jesus asks his opponents: "How can you believe if you want to receive honor from another and care nothing for the honor that comes from him who alone is God?"

A difference of opinion among the Pharisees is also recorded in 9:16 where some of them declare categorically: "This man is not παρὰ θεοῦ, because he does not keep the Sabbath," but others (probably also belonging to the Pharisees) object: "How could a sinful man perform such signs?" The opinion of the first group prevails and the blind young man who remains loyal to Jesus and, in fact, comes to faith in him, is expelled from the synagogue (9:34). His parents, in the meantime, have given an evading answer "because they were afraid of the Jews," for "the Jews (i.e., the Jewish leaders[5]) had already agreed that anyone who confessed Jesus as Messiah should be banned from the synagogue" (9:22; cf. 7:13, 16:2; 20:19).

Besides the sympathizers in leading circles we find also believers among the ordinary people in Jerusalem. The first passage which mentions them, 2:23-25, is rather important to our purpose because it immediately precedes the first Nicodemus-passage in 3:1ff. It clearly is intended as a general remark about the situation prevailing in Jerusalem after Jesus' first public appearance there. We hear of many who believed in him (εἰς τὸ ὄνομα αὐτοῦ) because they saw the signs he did (vs. 23). Jesus' reaction is negative. "He would not trust himself to them, because he knew all men well. He needed no information from other people about a man, for he himself knew what was in a man" (vss. 24-25).

This passage is difficult to reconcile with 2:11 and 4:54, which speak about the first and second sign performed by Jesus and seem to disregard the remarks about many signs in 2:23-25, 3:2 and 4:45. Nor does it agree with 2:18f., where the Jewish request for a sign which

would justify Jesus' action is refused--a problem to which
we shall return in Chapter V. The wording of the passage
does, however, correspond to that of 3:1-2. The word
ἄνθρωπος occurs twice in 2:25 and is used again in the beginning of 3:1, ἦν δὲ ἄνθρωπος,[6] and this "man" tells Jesus
that he and others (οἴδαμεν plural) are convinced that no
one would be able to perform the signs which Jesus performs
unless God were with him (3:2).

Similar remarks about sympathy for, and even belief
in, Jesus because of his signs are made in 4:45; 6:2; 7:31;
10:42; 11:45, 47-48; 12:11. No negative comments either
from Jesus or from the evangelist are added, but it is
clear that all these instances occur between the negative
opening statement in 2:23-25 and the equally negative final judgment in 12:37 and 12:42-43, already mentioned. In
this connection also 8:30-32 should be noted, where Jesus
tells the Jews who have come to believe in him (because of
his words) that they can only be his disciples if they
dwell in his word (cf. 5:38, and, of course, 15:1-10). It
is perhaps not insignificant that these verses are found
right in the middle of a long debate between Jesus and the
Jews which leads to an entirely negative response from the
Jews, culminating in an attempt to stone Jesus (8:59).

The result of this investigation of the evangelist's
description and appraisal of the believing sympathizers
among the ordinary people and the leading classes seems to
be clear. These believers stand on the wrong side of the
dividing line between the true believers who live in communion with him whom God sent to the world and the unbelieving world. Notwithstanding Nicodemus's opening affirmation "We know that you are a teacher sent by God" (3:1),
he is not among those for whom Jesus prays in 17:6-9: "I
have made thy name known to the men whom thou didst give
me out of the world...they know that all thy gifts have
come to me from thee; they have had faith to believe that
thou didst send me. I pray for them; I am not praying for
the world but for those whom thou hast given me, because
they belong to thee..." (NEB).

Is this negative conclusion justified, and is it
borne out by the three passages which mention Nicodemus?[7]

Let us look at 19:38-42 somewhat more closely. As
has often been noticed, this pericope, to which there are
synoptic parallels, shows some duplication with the previous one, vss. 31-37, in which there are very few connections with the synoptic narratives. Both the Jews and
Joseph of Arimathea ask Pilate for permission to remove
the body of Jesus (vss. 31, 38). It is not expressly
stated that Pilate granted the request of the Jews; it is
said that Pilate gave the permission to Joseph and that
Joseph, together with Nicodemus, in fact removed the body
and buried Jesus.[8] In the case of the Jews we are only
told that the soldiers (evidently called in by the Jews)
did not break Jesus' bones: one of the soldiers, however,
stabbed his side with a lance, and at once there was a
flow of blood and water (vss. 33-34). To this description
of what happened is added a declaration concerning the
trustworthiness of the one who saw this and gave his witness concerning it in vs. 35, a verse to be connected with
21:24 (and 20:30-31), which refers to "the disciple whom
Jesus loved" in a similar way. This first pericope ends
with a reference to the fulfillment of Scripture (vss. 36-
37) and is conveniently connected with vss. 38-42 through
the redactional phrase μετὰ δὲ ταῦτα at the beginning of
vs. 38.

This second pericope, which concerns us most,
clearly wants to emphasize that Jesus' burial was carried
out at great expense (vs. 39), according to Jewish custom
(vs. 40). Appropriately an entirely new grave was used
(vs. 41) and Jewish sabbath-laws were observed (vs. 42).
This passage also makes clear, in contrast to suggestions
to the contrary found in Mark 15:47, 16:1 and Luke 23:55f.,
24:1, that this burial was meant to be definitive.[9]

R. E. Brown, in his very full and illuminating comment on these verses, says about Joseph of Arimathea:
"Clandestine disciples were judged harshly and with con-
tempt in 12:42, but evidently Joseph's coming forward to

ask for Jesus' body has won the Johannine writer's es-
teem."[10] This may be so but this does not mean that the
evangelist's opinion concerning Joseph's and Nicodemus's
faith has changed. In a recent article,[11] B. Hemelsoet
has tried to argue that Joseph and Nicodemus who ἔλαβον...
τὸ σῶμα τοῦ ᾽Ιησοῦ are regarded as true believers. They
have accepted the Word (see the ἔλαβον αὐτόν in 1:12) while
accepting the body of Jesus as that of the new paschal
lamb. Hemelsoet sets great store by the fact that λαμβάνειν (with the meanings of "take" and "accept") is used
only in connection with Joseph and Nicodemus, not with the
Jews and the soldiers. He does not, however, pay attention to the contrast between the eyewitness mentioned in
vs. 35 and the two Jewish sympathizers mentioned later.
It is quite clear that the eyewitnesses play a very important role in Johannine theology, because the later living
Christians are dependent on their testimony (see 20:21-23,
29, 30-31; 21:24-25; 1 John 1:1-4,[12] and 17:20-21; cf. 17:
6-9 already quoted). And it is equally clear that in the
present Gospel Joseph and Nicodemus are pictured as having
come to a dead end; they regard the burial as definitive.
Jesus' work which, under a certain aspect, may be regarded
as accomplished (19:28, 30) is continued by his disciples,
especially by the disciple "whom Jesus loved" (19:25-27,
35; 20:2-10 and the passages just mentioned). A new era
in God's dealings with mankind through Jesus, the Messiah
and the Son of God, has begun; Joseph and Nicodemus have
not been able to look further than the tomb in the garden
near the place where Jesus was crucified.

Turning now to 7:50-52, we should first of all remark that this passage belongs to a series of "discussions"
between Jesus and the Jews in Jerusalem (7:16-24, 28-30,
33-36), introduced by debates among the crowds themselves
(7:11-13, 14-15, 25-27, 31-32). They are followed by a
solemn proclamation by Jesus (7:37-38), after which Jesus
no longer interferes in the controversies among the Jews
concerning him.[13] It is clear that this chapter has been

composed as a series of comments upon prevailing[14] Jewish
conceptions about the Messiah and refutations of Jewish
objections against Jesus (see vss. 27, 31, 42 and cf. 12:
34). We may compare here the section 1:35-51 where a
number of "messianic titles" are connected with Jesus in
order to show that Jewish expectations have found their
fulfillment in Jesus of Nazareth.[15]

On closer investigation it becomes clear that we
cannot really speak of discussions between Jesus and the
Jews (whether with the unbelievers or with the believers
among them).[16] We hear of controversies among the Jews;
no direct questions are put to Jesus and no direct answers
are given. Jesus only takes up a certain theme suggested
by the preceding Jewish discussion and develops it in his
own way; see vs. 16, "The teaching that I give is not my
own; it is the teaching of him who sent me," and vs. 28b,
"Yet I have not come of my own accord; I was sent by the
one who truly is." In vss. 33-36 Jesus announces his going away to the One who sent him, introducing a subject
which will later in the Gospel be treated repeatedly and
at greater length,[17] and this announcement is misunderstood (in a typically Johannine way) by the Jews who think
that he is to depart for the "dispersion among the Greeks."
After Jesus' proclamation in vss. 37-38 the debates are
continued between the two parties among the Jews themselves, first among the crowds in vss. 40-44 and later
among the rulers of the people, who react negatively with
the sole exception of Nicodemus, who advocates precision
in legal procedure in dealing with Jesus. This outcome
is not astonishing. Chapter 7 begins with the statement
that Jesus wished to avoid Judea because the Jews were
looking for a chance to kill him (vs. 1), and all through
the chapter remarks concerning the enmity of the Jews towards Jesus are found (vss. 13, 19, 25, 30, 44; cf. 8:37,
40, 59). Servants were, in fact, sent by the high priests
and Pharisees with the explicit instruction to arrest
Jesus (vs. 32).[18]

This analysis of chapter 7 is directly relevant to the question concerning the attitude of the Fourth Gospel towards Nicodemus. He takes part in an inner-Jewish discussion and does not take up one of the themes which were developed by Jesus in his own way in the course of this chapter--nor does any of the sympathizers mentioned before. Moreover, Nicodemus's remark does not deal with Jesus' teaching and acts as such; he only emphasizes the legal requirement that the accused should be granted a proper hearing (cf. Deut 1:16, 13:14, 17:4, 19:18).[19] In doing so he unmasks the hypocrisy of his fellow-Pharisees who scoff at "this rabble which cares nothing for the Law" (vs. 49) and evidently have no regard for the Law themselves if that is more convenient to them. I do not think that the Gospel wants to suggest that Nicodemus in fact has come to believe in Jesus and is, as such, an exception to the general rule laid down by his fellow-Pharisees in vs. 48. After all it refers the reader to chapter 3 and there is no indication of a development in Nicodemus's attitude since this rather unsatisfactory discussion with Jesus. Nicodemus is, and obviously remains, εἷς...ἐξ αὐτῶν (vs. 50).

A few words will have to be added about vs. 52. It reflects the controversy between Galilee and Judea which is so prominent in the Fourth Gospel.[20] Scornfully the Pharisees ask Nicodemus "Are you a Galilean too?" and they advise him to search the Scriptures in order to see ὅτι ἐκ τῆς Γαλιλαίας προφήτης (or: ὁ προφήτης, pap 66 and 75) οὐκ ἐγείρεται. There is some uncertainty as to whether the article before προφήτης is original or not. Modern schollars[21] prefer ὁ προφήτης as *lectio difficilior*. The prophet, already mentioned in 1:21, 25; 6:14 and 7:40, to be identified as the Prophet like Moses promised in Deuteronomy 18:15, 18, will not come from Galilee, at least according to these Jerusalem-centered ᾽Ιουδαῖοι.[22] If we read προφήτης, implying that no single prophet ever came from Galilee, we must suppose that the evangelist wants to

give another instance of a lack of regard for the Scriptures among the Pharisees. According to 2 Kgs 14:25 Jonah
ben Amittai came from Gath-hepher, a town in Galilee (Josh
19:13).[23] The former solution seems to be preferable.

The first passage which mentions Nicodemus, in chapter 3, presents us with many difficulties. It has a clear
beginning in 3:1, but no obvious ending. We do not hear
Nicodemus's final words nor are we told when he departed;
the dialogue is continued as a monologue. Are we really
allowed to call the first part of this chapter a dialogue,
or do we have to conclude that Jesus and Nicodemus speak
on entirely different wavelengths, if not about completely
different subjects? Some years ago S. Mendner, unable to
find any meaning in the dialogue as it stands, cut it down
to vss. 2, 3a, 7b, 9, 10, 12b and 13a and put it after 7:
45-52a.[24] Apart from the fact that this "solution" requires the theory of a thorough rewriting of the original
Fourth Gospel some time during the second century (a theory advocated by Mendner), it is clear that it does not
contribute towards the explanation of the text as we have
it before us. Does this text really make no sense?

I do not think that it is useful or even possible
to indicate where the dialogue with Nicodemus ends and
Jesus' monologue begins. The Nicodemus episode is the
starting-point for a typical Johannine discourse of Jesus,[25]
to which not only the verses up to and including vs. 21,
but also vss. 31-36, belong (though it is not easy to define exactly the relationship between the latter verses
and vss. 11-21).[26] If we agree to this we should see
clearly that Nicodemus does not come to Jesus with a question, but with a declaration, a declaration which is, in
fact, a confession of faith--the faith of the many who believed in his name (mentioned in 2:23), deepened by Nicodemus's insight into the predictions found in Scripture:
after all Jesus calls him ὁ διδάσκαλος τοῦ Ἰσραήλ (vs.
10).[27] His confession of faith concerns Jesus' mission on
earth, indicated by the words ἀπὸ θεοῦ ἐλήλυθας, διδάσκαλος,

σημεῖα ποιεῖν and ὁ θεὸς μετ' αὐτοῦ. This theme is taken up again in vss. 11-13 and elaborated upon in the rest of the discourse. Over against Nicodemus's οἴδαμεν stands Jesus' οἴδαμεν. The ἀπὸ θεοῦ ἐλήλυθας has to be interpreted as ὁ ἐκ τοῦ οὐρανοῦ καταβάς (vs. 13), ὁ ἄνωθεν ἐρχόμενος (vs. 31). Though it is said elsewhere that Jesus teaches[28] and may be called a διδάσκαλος[29] sent by God, the rest of the present discourse prefers the titles "the Son of Man," "the Son" and "the only Son"--see especially vs. 17...ἀπέστειλεν ὁ θεὸς τὸν υἱόν...; vs. 33...ὃν γὰρ ἀπέστειλεν ὁ θεὸς τὰ ῥήματα τοῦ θεοῦ λαλεῖ.

Now, if chapter 3 intends to give a deepening and correction of Nicodemus's christology in vs. 2, vss. 3-10 are no more than an intermezzo, though a very appropriate and necessary one. They show the essential difference between the οἴδαμεν of Jesus, and of the Christian Church living in communion with him, and the οἴδαμεν of Nicodemus and the other Jews, unbelieving *and believing* (strangely enough). The οἴδαμεν of Christ and the Christians[30] is that of ὁ ἄνωθεν ἐρχόμενος (vs. 31), i.e., ὁ ἐκ τοῦ οὐρανοῦ ἐρχόμενος who bears witness to ὃ ἑώρακεν καὶ ἤκουσεν (vs. 32). The result is negative: καὶ τὴν μαρτυρίαν αὐτοῦ οὐδεὶς λαμβάνει (vss. 32, 11), and this applies also to the sympathizers and believers represented by Nicodemus, who do not really understand (vs. 10).

The οὐ λαμβάνετε in vs. 11, and the οὐδεὶς λαμβάνει in vs. 32 refer back to the prologue (vss. 5, 10, 11). There, by way of contrast, are mentioned those who accepted the Logos, were allowed to become τέκνα θεοῦ, and of whom it is said that they ἐκ θεοῦ ἐγεννήθησαν. This theme is further developed in vss. 3-10 of the present chapter. Γεννηθῆναι ἄνωθεν (i.e., from above, misunderstood[31] by Nicodemus as δεύτερον, "again," vs. 4) or γεννηθῆναι ἐκ τοῦ πνεύματος (vss. 6, 8) or even ἐξ ὕδατος καὶ πνεύματος (vs. 5) is the necessary prerequisite for a true understanding of Jesus' mission and for the true faith. In order to recognize and to accept fully "the one who comes from

above," one has to be "born from above" oneself. The
second conditions the first, just as, in the prologue, the
first conditions the second. God's working in and through
Jesus is directly related to his dealing with the believers.
This is brought out very clearly in 6:37, 39, 44, 65, especially in the last verse: "...no one can come to me unless it has been granted to him by the Father."[32]

If we relegate the "birth from above" theme to a
secondary place within the whole discourse in chapter 3
and put the christological discussion in the center,[33]
Nicodemus's declaration in vs. 2 receives its full weight
and need not be regarded as a *captatio benevolentiae* cut
short by Jesus' remarks about "birth from above,"[34] often
supposed to answer Nicodemus's as yet unasked question
about the possibilities of "entering the kingdom of God."[35]
The evangelist wants to make clear in what respects the
faith of the group represented by Nicodemus fell short of
the true Christian faith and why their understanding was
in fact misunderstanding, putting them outside the community of the true believers of Jesus Christ.

It is necessary to dwell on this a little further
and to ask how the Fourth Gospel describes Nicodemus's
Jewish faith. If we confine ourselves to Johannine parallels we find that in 9:16 (a text mentioned already) the
Pharisees deny that ἔστιν οὗτος παρὰ θεοῦ ὁ ἄνθρωπος (=
Jesus), ὅτι τὸ σάββατον οὐ τηρεῖ whereas other Pharisees
object that a sinful man could not possibly perform such
signs (τοιαῦτα σημεῖα ποιεῖν) as Jesus performs. Here we
find a clear parallel to 3:2, in a context which is to be
understood against the background of a discussion of the
problem whether Jesus is a true prophet or a false one
(Deut 18:18-22 and 13:1-6).[36] We should also compare 9:
27-34, the final debate between the blind young man and
the Pharisees, ending with the former's expulsion from the
synagogue. The Pharisees call themselves "disciples of
Moses," for "we know (οἴδαμεν!) that God spoke to Moses,
but as for this man, we do not know where he comes from"

(vss. 28-29). The reply is to the point: It is strange
that you do not know where he comes from--i.e., that you
wish to deny that he comes from God--yet he has opened my
eyes (vs. 30). These parallels show that the terminology
used in 3:2 is elsewhere connected with a prophet, especially a prophet like Moses, and Moses himself.[37] As to
the expression ὁ θεὸς μετ' αὐτοῦ we may point to Jesus'
own use of parallel terms in 8:29, ὁ πέμψας με μετ' ἐμοῦ
ἐστιν, and 16:32, ὁ πατὴρ μετ' ἐμοῦ ἐστιν and (outside
John) to various OT texts which speak of God's being with
the patriarchs, Joshua, Judges, prophets[38] and Moses. Especially Exod 3:12 is illuminating here, where "I shall be
with you" occurs together with "I send you" or parallel
expressions (vss. 10, 12, 13, 14, 15), repeated five times.

Also at other places in the Fourth Gospel is Jesus
called διδάσκαλος, though this title does not occur very
often and is not in other ways prominent.[39] A useful
parallel is found in 7:16f., where Jesus, in the first
discussion with the Jews, speaks of his διδαχή and emphasizes that it is not his own, but that of "him who sent
him." Besides the expression τοῦ πέμψαντός με also ἐκ τοῦ
θεοῦ is used as qualification of this διδαχή; this as opposed to a teaching ἀπ' ἐμαυτοῦ.[40] This same expression
is used again in the second discussion (7:28-29) where
Jesus states emphatically: ἀπ' ἐμαυτοῦ οὐκ ἐλήλυθα, because
the One who truly is sent me...I come from him (παρ' αὐτοῦ
εἰμι) and he sent me" (ἀπέστειλεν). Chapter 8:42 is also
interesting, where Jesus says: ἐγὼ γὰρ ἐκ τοῦ θεοῦ ἐξῆλθον
καὶ ἥκω, οὐδὲ γὰρ ἀπ' ἐμαυτοῦ ἐλήλυθα, ἀλλ' ἐκεῖνός με
ἀπέστειλεν.

These parallels show that the terminology used by
Nicodemus is not wrong in itself: Jesus has come from God,
he is a teacher, he could not do the signs he performs unless God were with him. All these expressions, or at least
very similar ones, occur in the words of the Johannine Jesus himself, but then they are used within the framework
indicated in 3:11-21 and 31-36. In Johannine christology

a number of elements are very important, or even essential: the contrast between heaven and earth, spirit and
flesh, consequently the coming from the Father as coming
down and the returning to the Father as ascending; and the
unique relationship between Father and Son, implying that
the works of the Son are those of the Father and that the
words of the Father are the words of the Son.

In our chapter all emphasis is laid on ὃ ἑωράκαμεν
μαρτυροῦμεν (vs. 11), and this consists in a speaking
about τὰ ἐπουράνια (vs. 12). This presupposes the descending to earth of the Son of Man (vs. 13), for only ὁ ἄνωθεν
ἐρχόμενος (vs. 31), who is sent by God himself (vs. 34),
is able to speak God's words (vs. 34) and to act in God's
name (vs. 35). The essential thing is to believe in the
Son sent by the Father (vss. 16-18, 36) and to obey him
(vs. 36). Using a two-level scheme is, for the Fourth
Gospel at any rate, not simply a mythological way of
thinking. It serves to accentuate the unique connection
made between God's heaven and man's earth in and through
the sending of Jesus Christ, the only Son. In order to
indicate the nature of Jesus' work and teaching several
terms may be used, also those connected with prophecy,
with kingship, with Moses as the one great mediator between God and Israel in the past, with Jewish conceptions
of agency,[41] but if one fails to use them within the right
framework one fails to understand the essence of Jesus'
appearance and of God's dealings with the world--even if
one belongs to the Jews "who believed in him."

Jesus is ὁ ἄνωθεν ἐρχόμενος, he is ἀπὸ θεοῦ (3:2,
13:3) and παρὰ [τοῦ] θεοῦ (9:16, 33; 16:27; cf. 8:40; 1:6),
he is also ἐκ τοῦ οὐρανοῦ (3:13, 31; 6:31-58 passim) and
above all he is ἐκ τοῦ θεοῦ (8:42; cf. 16:28). Therefore
his teaching is ἐκ τοῦ θεοῦ (7:17) and it can only be understood by those who are ἐκ τοῦ θεοῦ (8:47, adding: διὰ
τοῦτο ὑμεῖς οὐκ ἀκούετε, ὅτι ἐκ τοῦ θεοῦ οὐκ ἐστέ, directed against Jesus' Jewish opponents).[42] Only the children
of God, of whom it may be said that they were born from

42

God (ἐκ θεοῦ ἐγεννήθησαν, 1:12, 13; 1 John 3:1, 2, 10; 5:
2), are able to understand and to follow the unique Son of
God.[43] And this is made clear in 3:3-9, a passage in
which Nicodemus is portrayed as having nothing to say. He
plays the typically Johannine part of the interlocutor who
understands Jesus wrongly (vs. 4) and asks: "How is this
possible?" (vs. 9). In fact, he reacts as an outsider; he
does not belong to the children of God.

Every passage in the Fourth Gospel, or group of
closely connected passages like those dealing with Nicodemus, can only be analyzed fully if the whole Gospel is
taken into account. Every feature of Johannine theology
forms an inseparable part of that theology. Therefore
every study of an aspect of the Fourth Gospel necessarily
remains a torso; still, at the same time, the student of
that aspect is confronted with the very center of Johannine theology, the christology outlined above.

CHAPTER II

[1]There are many textual variants at this point.
There is no need to suppose that ℵ*, which omits this
phrase altogether, represents the original text; in 19:39
all manuscripts have a similar cross-reference (with some
variation).

[2]οἱ ἄρχοντες is a somewhat vague term denoting "the
authorities" (see W. Bauer, s.v., 2a). In John perhaps
the members of the Sanhedrin are meant. Note that in 7:48
and 12:42 the ἄρχοντες are distinguished from the Pharisees, that in 12:42 secret believers are reported to have
been among them, who feared the Pharisees, and that in 7:
26 the crowd supposes that οἱ ἄρχοντες have recognized
that Jesus is the Messiah. J. L. Martyn's hypothesis,
that οἱ ἄρχοντες is used always in the Fourth Gospel for
those members of the Sanhedrin who believed secretly, cannot be substantiated--see J. L. Martyn, *History and Theol-*
ogy in the Fourth Gospel (New York-Evanston: Harper & Row,
1968), pp. 74-76.

[3]A schism among the Jews is also mentioned in 9:16
(see below) and 10:19.

[4]See C. H. Dodd, *The Interpretation of the Fourth
Gospel* (Cambridge: Cambridge University Press, 1953), pp.
379-83.

[5]On the many shades of meaning in the Johannine expression οἱ 'Ιουδαῖοι, see, e.g., R. Schnackenburg, *The
Gospel according to St John* I, Herder's Theological Commentary on the New Testament (New York: Herder and Herder;
London: Burns & Oates, 1968), p. 287, and E. Grässer, "Die
antijüdische Polemik im Johannesevangelium," in *NTS* 11
(1964-65), pp. 74-90. See also Chapter VI, note 33.

[6]Though in 3:1 ἄνθρωπος may be used in the meaning
of τις (BDF 301.2), it may give an extra "human" emphasis;
cf. 1:6; 3:4, 27. The connection between 2:25 and 3:1 is
a very close one; see the use of the simple δέ in 3:1 and
the reference to Jesus by means of the pronoun αὐτόν in
3:2.

[7]I disagree here with Schnackenburg, who in his introduction to the exegesis of chapter 3 (*The Gospel according to St John* I, p. 364) remarks: "The figure of Nicodemus does not remain entirely in obscurity. He is mentioned
twice again in the Gospel (7:50f.; 19:39), and in such a
way that his ultimate conversion to Christianity may be
deduced."

[8]We should notice the variants ἦλθον and ἦραν at the end of vs. 38 in some important textual witnesses. Do they represent the more difficult, and therefore original, reading? In that case Joseph is pictured as being helped by others. Or is the plural due to harmonization with vs. 40 (or vss. 31-32)?

[9]Matthew does not mention the women's intention to anoint the body, but he does not compensate for this with a story of an anointing by Joseph of Arimathea.

[10]*The Gospel according to John (xiii-xxi)* (Garden City, NY: Doubleday, 1970), p. 939. He goes on, however, with the words: "Or else, more simply, John mentions the detail only to explain why Pilate granted the request: the Roman prefect would scarcely have granted favors to an acknowledged follower of a man executed as a revolutionary."

[11]See B. Hemelsoet, "L'Ensevelissement selon Saint Jean," *Studies in John* presented to Professor Dr. J. N. Sevenster, NovTSup 24 (Leiden: Brill, 1970), pp. 47-65.

[12]See Chapter I, pp. 12, 17.

[13]In 8:12 another "Offenbarungswort" of Jesus introduces a new series of discussions.

[14]I.e., prevailing in the time of the Fourth Gospel.

[15]See Schnackenburg, *The Gospel according to St John* I, pp. 507-14, Excursus III, "The Titles of Jesus in John 1."

[16]See my "Onbegrip in Jeruzalem, Jezus en de Joden in Johannes 7," *Rondom het Woord* 15 (1973), pp. 61-80, and Chapter IV, below, pp. 82, 100.

[17]See 8:21-24; 13:33-36; 14:19; 16:16-19.

[18]R. Bultmann, *The Gospel of John* (Philadelphia: Westminster, 1971), arranges this chapter and the following one rather drastically. One of his principal difficulties is the inexplicable lapse of time between the sending of the servants by the Pharisees (vs. 32) and their report (vss. 45-46, after vs. 37). As D. M. Smith, *The Composition and Order of the Fourth Gospel* (New Haven and London: Yale University Press, 1965), pp. 152-55, has remarked, the question how and why the present arrangement replaced the supposed "original" one is not answered.

[19]For rabbinic and other parallels, see J. Blank, *Krisis. Untersuchungen zur johanneischen Christologie und Eschatologie* (Freiburg: Lambertus, 1964), pp. 49-52.

[20]See W. A. Meeks, *The Prophet-King. Moses Tradi-tions and the Johannine Christology* (Leiden: Brill, 1967), pp. 35-41, 313-18. His theory that the emphasis on Jesus' heavenly origin in the Fourth Gospel is the "spiritualization of an already existing tradition of Galilean origin of a saviour figure" (p. 41) seems to me not evident; 7: 37-52 adduced by Meeks in support of his thesis shows the Judea-Galilee controversy, but only to illustrate the absolute lack of understanding of *all* people involved. The χριστός, ὁ προφήτης does not come from Judea or Galilee, but from heaven. On "the prophet" in connection with Jesus, see Chapter III.

[21]See, e.g., Meeks, *The Prophet-King*, p. 24; Martyn, *History and Theology in the Fourth Gospel*, p. 105; Brown in his commentary ad loc.

[22]Martyn's conclusion, "The Mosaic Prophet is to come, of course, not from Galilee, but from the wilderness" (*History and Theology in the Fourth Gospel* (p. 105, n. 165), seems to me to disregard the context.

[23]See also Str-B II, p. 519.

[24]S. Mendner, "Nikodemus," *JBL* 77 (1958), pp. 293-323. I. de la Potterie's instructive article, "Naître de l'eau et naitre de l'Esprit," *Sciences Ecclésiastiques* 14 (1962), pp. 417-43, did not come into my hands until the present text had been sent to the printers. On pp. 425-35 the author gives a very detailed and interesting literary analysis of John 2:25-3:21 which agrees with the analysis given above. De la Potterie shows that there is "une correspondance antithétique entre l'introduction et le troisième discours; tous les deux ont pour thème principale *la foi*: la foi encore très imparfaite des Juifs dans 2,23-3,2, la foi chrétienne véritable et ses fruits de salut dans 3, 11-21" (p. 431). Consequently vss. 3-10 have to be considered as a "section intermédiaire": "La nouvelle naissance, dans les vv. 3-8, est donc présentée comme ce qui est absolument indispensable pour accéder à la vie de foi véritable et pour obtenir la vie éternelle" (p. 433).

[25]So also Bultmann in his commentary, p. 132: "The chapter begins with a realistically described *scene*, which, however, is never brought to a conclusion; for the dialogue between Jesus and Nicodemus, which begins in this scene, issues in a discourse by Jesus which is not related to any particular situation at all, and in which, from v. 13 onwards, the Revealer is spoken of in the third person. As far as the content of the composition is concerned, the primary element is the *discourse*."

[26]For a survey of the problems concerning the relationship between vss. 1-21 and vss. 31-36, see Smith, *The Composition and Order of the Fourth Gospel*, pp. 125-27.

46

^{27}One should note the plural οἴδαμεν with following
ὅτι in vs. 2, also used by the (believing) Samaritans in
4:42, the (unbelieving) Jewish leaders in 9:24, 29, the
blind young man in 9:31, the disciples in 16:30, and the
editors of the Gospel in 21:24. In all these cases a
group or an individual in the name of a group makes a
definite statement in a matter of faith. One should compare the singular οἶδα + ὅτι in 4:25; 11:22, 24, used by
believers in a similar way. It is impossible to delineate
the group indicated by the "we" in John 3 more precisely;
it stands over against another "we" in vs. 11a (see also
the plural "you" in vss. 7, 11b).

^{28}6:59; 7:14, 28, 35; 8:20; 18:20.

^{29}1:38; 11:28; 13:13, 14; 20:16.

^{30}Much has been written on the οἴδαμεν of vs. 11;
see, e.g., the surveys of previous opinion in the commentaries of Bultmann and Schnackenburg. This "we" could be
the *pluralis ecclesiasticus* which occurs frequently in the
Johannine writings, but it is difficult to understand how
Jesus could be included. Schnackenburg points to 3:32,
which makes clear that Jesus' testimony is the basic one,
and to 9:4, which he interprets as referring to the work
of Jesus and of the disciples connected with him.

^{31}On this case of misunderstanding and all other
instances in the Fourth Gospel, see H. Leroy, *Rätsel und
Missverständnis: Ein Beitrag zur Formgeschichte des Johan-
nesevangeliums*, BBB 30 (Bonn: Peter Hanstein, 1968), esp.
pp. 124-36.

^{32}On this, see further Chapter I, pp. 17-20, and
Chapter VI, pp. 151-54.

^{33}Against Bultmann, on p. 132 of his commentary,
who describes the contents of 3:1-8 thus: "The coming of
the Revealer is explained by the necessity of rebirth."
The necessity of "birth-from-above" rather follows from
the "coming from above" of the Revealer.

^{34}Cf. Matt 22:16 par. and Pap. Egerton 2, fol. 2^r
(given in Aland's Synopsis at Matt 22:15-22). The latter
text combines elements from John 3:2 with elements of the
pericope on paying the tribute money: διδάσκαλε Ἰησοῦ,
οἴδαμεν ὅτι ἀπὸ θεοῦ ἐλήλυθας· ἃ γὰρ ποιεῖς μαρτυρεῖ ὑπὲρ
τοὺς προφήτας πάντας.

^{35}Cf. Mark 10:17-31 par., with the connection between ζωὴ αἰώνιος (vs. 17) and βασιλεία τοῦ θεοῦ (vs. 23).
So also John 3:3 and 16:36.

^{36}See Meeks, *The Prophet-King*, pp. 42-61, 294-96.

[37]See also Pap. Egerton 2, fol. 2^r, quoted in n. 2, p. 349: ὑπὲρ τοὺς προφήτας πάντας.

[38]Like Jeremiah (Jer 1:19); further instances are mentioned by Schnackenburg, *The Gospel according to St John* I, p. 366, n. 61.

[39]See note 29.

[40]An illuminating excursus on ἀφ᾽ ἑαυτοῦ and comparable expressions in the Fourth Gospel is given by Blank, *Krisis*, pp. 112-13.

[41]See especially Meeks, *The Prophet-King*; P. Borgen, *Bread from Heaven. An Exegetical Study of the Concept of Manna in the Gospel of John and the Writings of Philo*, NovTSup 10 (Leiden: Brill, 1965); and idem, "God's Agent in the Fourth Gospel," in *Religions in Antiquity*, Essays in memory of E. R. Goodenough, ed. J. Neusner (Leiden: Brill, 1968), pp. 137-48. See further Chapter VI, pp. 141-49.

[42]On the typical Johannine ἐκ, denoting the origin which determines the nature of a person, thought, or action, see R. Schnackenburg, *Die Johannesbriefe*, Herders Theologischer Kommentar zum Neuen Testament (Freiburg-Basel-Wien: Herder, 1963), p. 131, and Blank, *Krisis*, pp. 194-96. Blank emphasizes: "Das scheinbar vorherrschende räumliche Schema 'oben-unten' ist hier wirklich nur Bild, in Wahrheit ist es aber einem personal-geschichtlichen Denken ein- und untergeordnet....Damit ist offenbar, dass das räumliche Schema nichts anders ist als eine bildhafte Wendung, die von ihrem sachlichen Hintergrund her verstanden werden muss." This is true, but it should not be forgotten that "die Sache" itself, for the author(s) of the Fourth Gospel, called for this two-level scheme of thought.

[43]See, again, Chapter VI, pp. 151-54.

CHAPTER III

JESUS AS PROPHET AND KING IN THE FOURTH GOSPEL

The words "king" and "prophet" are not used very
often in connection with Jesus in the Fourth Gospel. The
word "king" occurs twice in John's description of Jesus'
entry into Jerusalem in 12:12-19 and eleven times in the
Passion-narrative, especially in the dialogue between Jesus and Pilate in 18:33-38a and Pilate's discussion with
the Jews and Jesus in 18:39-19:16 (cf. 19:19-22). Apart
from these sections which show many points of contact with
the corresponding ones in the other three gospels we find
the title "king of Israel" in 1:49 used by Nathanael. In
6:15 we hear that Jesus goes off to the hills by himself
because he realizes that the people present at the feeding
of the five thousand will come and seize him to proclaim
him king. This is told by the evangelist after he has reported the statement of the crowd: "Surely this is the
Prophet who was to come to the world" (6:14).

The title "the Prophet" occurs five times in connection with Jesus: once in 6:14, just mentioned, twice
in the discussion between John the Baptist and the representatives sent by the Jews in Jerusalem in chapter 1 and
twice in the debates among the crowd and among the Jewish
leaders in Jerusalem in chapter 7. John the Baptist denies that he is ὁ χριστός, Elijah or ὁ προφήτης (1:21, cf.
vs. 25) and announces the arrival of ὁ ὀπίσω μου ἐρχόμενος
(vs. 26). In the discussions in Jerusalem some people call
Jesus ὁ προφήτης, others take him to be ὁ χριστός, a statement rejected with the argument that Jesus comes from Galilee and not from David's town of Bethlehem (7:40-44). "The
Christ" is obviously regarded as a royal figure from the
house of David. In the following section the Jewish leaders disqualify Jesus as "the Prophet," again because of
his Galilean descent (7:52).

In these four texts Jews make a distinction between the prophet and the--obviously royal--Christ. Does the evangelist himself show a preference for either of these two titles? It is clear that χριστός is a very important word for him to denote Jesus' dignity. In 4:19, e.g., the Samaritan woman expresses her admiration for Jesus' knowledge in the statement: "Sir, I can see that you are a prophet" (προφήτης is used here without the article). This is followed and superseded by her words in vs. 25: "I know that Messiah is coming" (cf. vs. 29), to which Jesus replies, "I am he, I who am speaking to you now" (vs. 26). This, again, is followed by the confession by the Samaritans at the end of chapter 4: "We know that this is in truth the Savior of the world" (vs. 42). Obviously "prophet" is neither the most suitable nor the final title for Jesus. The same is evident in chapter 9, where the blind young man first calls Jesus a prophet (vs. 18), but later confesses Jesus as the Son of Man--after a second meeting with Jesus (vss. 35-38). Here the word χριστός is only used in passing, though in the very significant statement that anyone who confesses Jesus as χριστός will be thrown out of the synagogue (vs. 22). This confession is obviously the breaking-point between the synagogue and the new community of believers in Jesus Christ.

Yet even ὁ χριστός is obviously not used as the final word to indicate the essential meaning of Jesus' mission in the world. In 1:41 ὁ Μεσσίας is only one of the titles used for Jesus by his first disciples who are beginning to discover who he is (cf. vss. 45, 49, 51); the last title used here is "Son of Man" (vs. 51) as in chapter 9:35. In chapter 4 ὁ Μεσσίας is followed by ὁ σωτὴρ τοῦ κόσμου, in 11:27 Martha answers Jesus with the confession: ἐγὼ πεπίστευκα ὅτι σὺ εἶ ὁ χριστὸς ὁ υἱὸς τοῦ θεοῦ ὁ εἰς τὸν κόσμον ἐρχόμενος. Also in the concluding words of chapter 20 where the author formulates the purpose of his gospel we find that ὁ χριστός is qualified by the immediately following ὁ υἱὸς τοῦ θεοῦ (20:31). "Son of Man"

and "Son of God," interpreted in a special Johannine way,[1]
are clearly the central titles in the Fourth Gospel, not
"king," "prophet" or even "the Christ."

      This, I think, is not brought out clearly enough by
W. A. Meeks in his useful and interesting book *The Prophet-
King*,[2] which deals with the subject at great length and is
particularly valuable because it gives a wealth of material
from Jewish, Samaritan and Mandean sources connected with
Moses, in order to illustrate some of the notions about
Jesus' prophethood and kingship in the Fourth Gospel. Because I shall have occasion to refer to Meeks' book several times it is perhaps wise to indicate briefly at what
point the present analysis differs from his.

      Meeks' book is an attempt "to clarify the way in
which the motifs represented by the two terms 'prophet'
and 'king' in the Fourth Gospel not only are interrelated,
but interpret each other."[3] His comment on the discourse
of the Good Shepherd in chapter 10 and on the dialogue between Jesus and Pilate in 18:33-38a brings out his main
thesis very clearly: "In both passages--and in the whole
Fourth Gospel--kingship is being radically redefined. The
remarkable thing is that it is being redefined in terms of
the mission of the prophet."[4] This links up with his conclusion after an analysis of the place of 6:14-15 within
the whole of chapter 6: "The identification of Jesus as
prophet-king is by no means denied by Jesus' 'flight' to
the mountain; only the time and the manner in which the
men seek to make him king are rejected."[5]

      These statements call for comment. Why, for in-
stance, does the Fourth Gospel avoid the word "prophet" in
its obvious redefinition of kingship in John 18? Was that
word not so suitable after all and is, perhaps, also the
notion of prophecy redefined in the course of the gospel?
Meeks rightly explains 18:37 with the help of 10:27, 28,
verses which speak about the sheep which hear Jesus' voice.
He overlooks the fact that in 10:25-30 the expression
"shepherd," so prominent in 10:1-16 and clearly referring

to Jesus' kingship, is replaced by "the Son" who lives in
unity with "the Father" (see especially vss. 25, 29, 30
and already vs. 15). In fact this little speech by Jesus
is a reply to the question of the Jews: "If you are the
Christ say so plainly" (vs. 24). If the essence of Jesus'
kingly authority in 18:33-38a is described in vs. 38 as
"to bear witness to the truth" this should be understood
against the background of the Son's coming into the world
in complete unity of words and work with the Father.

In short: *Jesus' kingship and his prophetic mission
are both redefined in terms of the unique relationship between Son and Father, as portrayed in the Fourth Gospel.*
This will, I hope, be clearly shown in the following discussion of the available evidence. In my analysis I shall
not deal with the possible Jewish or Hellenistic traditions
behind the Johannine views on Jesus' kingship and prophethood; I shall pay special attention to the structure of
the passages which interest us and to their function within the whole Gospel. I shall also make a clear distinction
between statements of believers and those of non-believers.
Casual critical or derogatory remarks and even formal
statements by people who, in the course of the narrative,
persist in their rejection of Jesus are not unimportant
but they always serve as a contrast to, or at the most as
a background for, the confession of people who believe.
Especially interesting are the cases where the statements
of people who are just beginning to believe are clearly
in need of further interpretation on the basis of deeper
insight into Jesus' true function and being, but are yet
accepted by the evangelist as first and promising steps on
the road towards a full understanding.

In 1:19-34[6] the activity of John the Baptist is described as "bearing witness to Jesus." This is clear
throughout this pericope (vss. 19, 32, 34) as it is in the
rest of the Gospel (see 1:7, 8, 15; 3:26; 5:33-36). John
says about himself: "I am a voice crying aloud in the
wilderness: Make the Lord's highway straight" (vs. 23).

He is nothing more than a witness and nothing less. He points forward to "one who is coming after him" (vs. 30, cf. vss. 15, 27); he does not know him, but the very reason why John came, baptizing in water, was that this man might be revealed to Israel (vs. 31). To *Israel*, not to the Jews! The true Israelite Nathanael hails him as the king of Israel (vss. 47, 49) but to the deputation sent by the Jews in Jerusalem the Baptist declares sternly: "Among you, though you do not know him, stands the one who is to come after me" (vs. 26). The pericope ends with John's words: "I saw it myself, and I have borne witness. This is the Son of God" (or, if we follow the variant reading, "God's Chosen One").[7] This is the one upon whom the Spirit came down to rest, and who will baptize with the Holy Spirit (vs. 33).

In this context John the Baptist's solemn negative declaration (see the pleonastic ὡμολόγησεν καὶ οὐκ ἠρνή- σατο, καὶ ὡμολόγησεν ὅτι... in vs. 20) has a double function. In the first place his denial that he is "the Christ" (vs. 20) points away from himself to Jesus who indeed may be called and is called ὁ χριστός. This is underlined by 3:28 which makes the Baptist refer to his earlier statement in the words: "I am not the Christ, but I have been sent before him." Secondly, the further questions put by the representatives of the Jews, "Are you Elijah?" and "Are you the Prophet?" (vs. 21, cf. vs. 25), and John's subsequent denials tend to underline the variety within Jewish messianic expectation, as viewed by the Fourth Gospel. The interesting question whether the evangelist gives a reliable picture of first-century Jewish ideas about messianic figures and especially the question in what way Elijah returning may be put on one level with the Christ and the Prophet will be discussed later.[8] It is clear that the Fourth Gospel regards "the Christ" as the most important figure; this is clear not only from 3:28 but also from 1:41 where the first of a number of confessions of faith in Jesus, that by Andrew, is: "We have found the Messiah." The evangelist, who translates this "Messiah" by "the Christ" wishes to show that he is aware of the fact that ὁ χριστός is a Jewish technical term with a certain meaning (cf. 4:25). As I said in the introduction, this term is interpreted anew in the course of the Gospel, nevertheless it is taken over as worthy of reinterpretation.

The term "Elijah" does not recur outside this pericope. Obviously John knew of an identification of the Baptist with Elijah, but he did not regard it worthwhile to give his opinion about a possible identification of Jesus and Elijah. The question whether Jesus may be the Prophet recurs in chapter 7:40-44 as we have seen, but only in the mouth of (admittedly sympathizing) people in the crowd in Jerusalem, not by believers in the full sense of the word, and this question is not answered affirmatively by Jesus himself, or by the evangelist; the same applies, *mutatis mutandis*, to 6:14, 15.

If we look at 7:40-44 somewhat more closely,[9] we notice that it belongs to the section of this chapter which begins with a solemn declaration by Jesus in vss. 37-38.[10] This declaration (the word ἔκραξεν, "he cried aloud," is used[11]) is connected with the last and greatest day of the Feast of Tabernacles and comes after a number of exchanges of opinion between the people in the crowd and Jesus in vss. 14-36, connected with "the middle of the feast" (vs. 14). It is important to note, I think, that in the last part of this chapter Jesus does not take part in the discussions but disappears from the stage, only to return in 8:12 with another solemn declaration, "I am the light of the world. No follower of mine shall wander in the dark; he shall have the light of life." This time a new debate follows, with various themes; we find it recorded in the long eighth chapter of the gospel.

Verses 40-44 in chapter 7 describe three parties among the crowd in Jerusalem. Two of these are sympathetic towards Jesus; the first party regards him as "the

Prophet," the second group calls him "the Christ." This
is denied by others who are of the opinion that the Christ
cannot come from Galilee; he is to be of the family of
David, and to come from David's town of Bethlehem. A
σχίσμα originates because of him as so often (see 9:16,
10:19) and this small section ends with a theme which recurs again and again in chapters 7-10--some wanted to
seize him (cf. vss. 30, 32; 8:20; 10:39)[12] but no one laid
hands upon him (cf. vs. 30; 8:59; 10:39) because, as it is
said elsewhere (vs. 30; 8:20 and cf. 2:4; 12:23; 13:1; 17:
1), his time had not yet come.

Much has been said about the possibility of typically Johannine irony in vs. 42.[13] These uninformed people
thought Jesus came from Galilee but those who really know
him also know that he, in fact, fulfilled the Jewish re-
quirements; Jesus was born at Bethlehem. I do not think
this interpretation is right. John, whether knowing about
Jesus' birth at Bethlehem or not, does not record it and
does not show himself interested in the question of Jesus'
earthly origin at all. In this very chapter he emphasizes
Jesus' heavenly origin quite clearly with words which he
puts into Jesus' own mouth (again ἔκραξεν is used): "Do
you really know me, and know where I am from? But I have
not come on my own. He who sent me, however, is true.
You do not know him, but I know him, for I come from him,
and he sent me" (vss. 28-29). Verses 40-44 only show that
people who do not know of Jesus' heavenly origin keep de-
bating about questions which are not essential. Verse 42
has its counterpart in vs. 52 where Nicodemus' critics
tell him plainly: "Are you from Galilee too? Study the
Scriptures and you will find that the Prophet does not
come from Galilee" (vs. 52).[14] The opposition between
Galilee and Judea/Jerusalem is quite marked in the Fourth
Gospel;[15] vs. 42 and vs. 52 give specimens of Judea-
centered thinking of Jesus' opponents among the crowd and
among the leaders.

What does that mean for the interpretation of vs. 40? It is clear that the title "the Christ" is accepted by the evangelist provided that all ideas connected with his earthly origin are dismissed. This is also very clear in vss. 25-30 where Jesus' words about his coming from the Father which I quoted a moment ago (vss. 28-29) are spoken in reply to the remark made by the crowd: "We know where this man comes from." But what about ὁ προφήτης? At this point I should like to draw attention to the very illuminating exegesis of vss. 14-24 in the present chapter given by Meeks.[16] According to him, these verses form an essential part of this chapter, notwithstanding the many links with chapter 5. The sudden reference to attempts to kill Jesus in vs. 19b can be explained by connecting this verse with vss. 16-18. Jesus' teaching is from God, *not from himself*, he is absolutely faithful to the One who sent him. Meeks refers to a remark by T. F. Glasson in his book *Moses in the Fourth Gospel*,[17] who found here a reference to the true prophet promised by Moses in Deut 18: 18-22, and especially to vs. 18: "and I will put my words in his mouth and he will speak to them all that I command him." If Jesus is the true prophet, he should be obeyed, if he speaks ἀφ' ἑαυτοῦ he is a false prophet and should be put to death (see Deut 18:20 and 13:5). The issue at stake in vss. 14-24 is whether Jesus is the true prophet like Moses; in the same way the following verses raise the question whether Jesus is the Christ.

This leads Meeks to speak of "Prophet" and "Christ" as ordering themes in John 7.[18] Wrongly, I think. No doubt Deut 18:15-22 is very important for an understanding of this pericope and of a number of other passages, quoted by Meeks and Glasson (3:34; 8:28, 40; 12:49-50; 14:10; 17: 8). Glasson rightly remarks "It is rather curious that commentaries on John do not always recognize the Old Testament undercurrents of these passages."[19] A little earlier, however, this same author makes the wise restriction that the connection with the conception of the true prophet "is only one element among several, but it is an important one."[20] Meeks, who is less cautious, overlooks the fact that 7:15-25 and the other passages mentioned adopt an important prophetic characteristic but do not connect it with the title "the Prophet." The title "the Christ" is taken over, and subsequently reinterpreted. The title "the Prophet" is not taken over though some elements of true prophecy form an integral part in the description of the unique relationship between the Son and the Father who sent him.

The statement of the Galilean crowd in 6:14: "Surely this is the prophet who was to come into the world," has the form of a confession. It should be understood against the background of the sign done by Jesus (see vs. 14a), the miraculous feeding in the desert recorded in vss. 1-13. The following discourse on the Bread from Heaven makes clear that the prophet meant here is the Prophet like Moses. At the same time it is evident that this identification of Jesus with the Mosaic Prophet, though perhaps pointing in the right direction, does not really explain the secret of Jesus' coming. Jesus' reaction towards the ideas of the crowd in the following discourse is entirely negative. In that chapter not the similarities but the dissimilarities receive all emphasis. These people have not really recognized the signs, they are out for ordinary bread (vs. 26), consequently they ask for a new sign, a repetition of Moses' manna-miracle (vs. 31). Jesus' answer is very emphatic: "It was not Moses who gave the bread from heaven, my Father gives you now the true bread from heaven" (see vs. 32), and he adds: "I am the bread of life" (see vss. 35, 48). This is not the place to give a detailed analysis of the whole of chapter 6;[21] it is clear, however, that the unique relationship between Jesus and God is underlined by means of the expression "my Father" (vss. 32, 37, 40, 44, and especially vs. 46) and the notion of "descent from heaven" (vss. 33, 41, 42, 50, 51); consequently--and this is important with

58

regard to 7:42--the fact that the Jews regard Jesus as the son of Joseph and think they know his father and mother (vs. 42) shows that they do not understand the real secret of his coming into the world; he is not simply a prophet like Moses as a second Moses, but the Son of God who came to do God's will (vs. 38), that is, to give eternal life to all who believe (vss. 39-40 and passim).

The following verse, 6:15, emphasizes Jesus' special knowledge; he understands what the crowd really means and what these people are going to do--they will make him king by force. The word "king" has a negative meaning here. To make someone king can obviously be compared with "working for perishable food" (vs. 27, cf. vss. 26, 34) as opposed to working the work which God requires, that is, to believe in the one whom God has sent (vss. 28-30). One should not *make* a man king, but accept the one who is more than a king in an earthly sense of the word, and who is sent by God from heaven.

In 1:49 and 12:13 (cf. vs. 15), the expression ὁ βασιλεὺς τοῦ Ἰσραήλ is used with a basically positive connotation. This in contrast with the expression ὁ βασιλεὺς τῶν Ἰουδαίων used by Pilate in his discussions with the Jews,[22] which has definite nationalistic overtones as we shall see presently. The simple βασιλεύς in 6:14 stands on one level with βασιλεὺς τῶν Ἰουδαίων but because of the fact that the story is situated in Galilee the term Ἰουδαῖοι could not be used.

Nathanael's confession in 1:49, "Rabbi, you are the Son of God, you are the king of Israel," follows on the recognition of Jesus as the Messiah by Andrew and an unknown disciple (vs. 41) and Philip's less specified statement, "We have met the man spoken of by Moses in the Law, and by the prophets, it is Jesus, son of Joseph, from Nazareth" (vs. 45). There is a clear connection also with vs. 31...ἵνα φανερωθῇ τῷ Ἰσραήλ (Nathanael is addressed by Jesus as the true Israelite in vs. 47) and with the μαρτυρία of John the Baptist in vs. 34...οὗτός ἐστιν ὁ υἱὸς τοῦ θεοῦ.[23]

Nathanael's words are the first confession of faith
(see also vs. 50 πιστεύεις) directly addressed to Jesus,
"you are...,"[24] and therefore very important. The title
ὁ υἱὸς τοῦ θεοῦ precedes βασιλεὺς τοῦ Ἰσραήλ; it has more
or less the same function as in 11:27 and 20:30, 31, where
it follows the title χριστός. In itself, ὁ υἱὸς τοῦ θεοῦ
may refer to the anointed king,[25] but in the context of
the Fourth Gospel, and certainly after 1:18, it must have
a deeper meaning. It is not quite certain to what extent
Nathanael is portrayed as living up to John's standards,
but in any case the deeper meaning is hinted at in Jesus'
reply, which emphasizes that Nathanael's faith should not
be based on astonishment about Jesus' superior knowledge
but on "greater things" which he will see. These "greater
things" are not specified[26] but it is clear that the evangelist connects them with Jesus' reference to the "Son of
Man" who will be in permanent contact with God in heaven.
John 1 starts in heaven and ends in heaven, God's unique
link with man being Jesus, the Son of God and the Son of
Man.[27]

These two titles which play an important role further on in the Gospel serve here, at the end of his first
introductory chapter, as an indication that Jesus' royal
authority over Israel should be interpreted against the
background of the unique relationship between Jesus the
Son and God the Father. This is borne out by the fact
that later on Jesus' knowledge of men is shown to have its
roots in his special relationship with the Father. Here
we may point again to 10:3, 4, 14, 15, 25-28[28] where the
royal shepherd who knows his sheep is said to be known by
the Father and to perform his deeds in the name of the
Father and in unity with the Father.

The short pericope which describes Jesus' entry
into Jerusalem, 12:12-19 (and which shows some points of
contact with the tradition preserved in the Synoptics[29]),
uses the title ὁ βασιλεὺς τοῦ Ἰσραήλ once, parallel with
the phrase "(blessed be he) who comes in the name of the

Lord," in the quotation from Ps 118:25, 26. This is a
Johannine addition, put into the mouth of the people that
have come to the Passover feast and gone out to meet Jesus. The fact that the expression εἰς ὑπάντησιν is used,
and that "palm branches" are waved by a large crowd shows
that John thinks of a triumphal entry into his capital as
the king of Israel.[30] Only after he has mentioned what
the people did he quotes Zech 9:9 where the words "your
king" occur again.[31] After vss. 12-15 which show points
of agreement with the Synoptics we get John's own comment
in vss. 16-19. Significantly the story of the entry is
linked to the preceding story of Lazarus. It was because
they had been told about the σημεῖον that the people had
gone out to meet Jesus (vs. 18). Twice before the evangelist has made clear that the raising of Lazarus aroused
sympathy and even led people to believe in Jesus (11:45-
48, 12:11). He does not add a negative comment either
here or at the earlier occasions, yet it is evident from
his negative opening statement in 12:23-25 and his equally
negative final judgment in 12:37, 42-43[32] that the action
of the people in Jerusalem and their ideas about kingship
are not adequate. The Pharisees who come to the scene in
vs. 19 speak a word which is more true than they suspect
themselves: "The world has run off after him." This King
of Israel is called to rule the world, and, indeed, in
following verses, 12:20ff., Ἕλληνές τινες, who are among
those who went up to worship at the festival, ask to see
Jesus.[33] Verse 16 indicates that the disciples at first
did not understand the true meaning of the triumphal entry. Only after Jesus had been glorified they remembered
what had happened and understood how this was announced by
Zechariah. Obviously the true meaning of Jesus' kingship
can only be understood after (and against the background
of) his glorification, that is, after his death, resurrection, return to his Father and the sending of the Spirit
(see 12:23; 7:1 and cf. 2:22; 7:39; 14:26; 16:13-15; 20:
9).[34] The title "King of Israel" is not rejected as un-
suitable but, again, reinterpreted.

Before we deal with the central passage about Jesus'
kingship, 18:28-19:16 (cf. also 19:19-22), we shall have
to devote some attention to chapters 4 and 9 where Jesus
is called προφήτης. Neither in 4:19 nor in 9:17 is the
definite article used, but this is of less importance than
one might suppose. On the one hand, the declarations "You
are a prophet" and "He is a prophet" presuppose that Jesus
is a *true* prophet and not a false one. On the other hand,
the title "the prophet" is never used as the final title
to define Jesus' mission. The discussion about Jesus'
prophetic activity, either as "a prophet" or as "the
Prophet," contributes only one element to the understanding of his real being.

The function of the use of the expression "prophet"
in 9:17 becomes evident when we analyze the structure of
this chapter.[35] In the introduction to and the description of the healing of the blind man in vss. 1-7, a few
Johannine phrases stand out clearly--"so that God's works
may be displayed" in vs. 3b and "We must carry on the
works of him who sent me so long as it is day" (vs. 4).
In vs. 5 the theme of 8:12, "I am the light of the world,"
returns and in fact the whole chapter is concerned with
the subject "Judgment by the Light."[36] In passing the
name Siloam is significantly translated as ἀπεσταλμένος, a
reference to Jesus' being sent by the Father (vs. 7). After vs. 7, Jesus disappears from the scene, only to return
after the blind man has been thrown out by the Jews. He
discloses to him his real nature by means of the title
"Son of Man," vss. 35-38, connected in vs. 39 with the
idea of the judgment of the world (see also the following
discussion between Jesus and the Pharisees, in which it
becomes clear that the Pharisees are blind because they do
not see the Light of the World, vss. 40-41). Verses 34-41
should be connected with vss. 1-7, as 5:19-30 show clearly:
the Son performs the works of the Father, that is, he gives
life and he executes judgment on behalf of the Father; 5:
27 specifies that the Son executes judgment as Son of Man,

and in this whole passage it is clear that man's attitude
towards Jesus *now* is a matter of eternal life and death.

"Son of Man," in its in-many-ways-typically-
Johannine setting,[37] is the final, central title in chapter 9. In the middle part of this chapter, however, which
consists of four different scenes, portraying the blind
man and his neighbors (vss. 8-12), the blind man and the
Pharisees (vss. 13-17), the Jews and the blind man's parents (vss. 18-23) and the Jews and the blind man (vss. 24-
34), this title does not occur. In Jesus' absence people
try to receive clarity as to who he is; the blind man evidently gradually discovers the truth concerning Jesus
though he, too, is dependent on Jesus' own final disclosure. In the second and the fourth scene, the point at
issue is whether Jesus is the true or the false prophet
predicted in Deuteronomy 18. Meeks, who recognized this
clearly, wrongly saw this as the central point of chapter
9 (as well as of 5:19-47) as a whole and not of the middle
part only, and therefore missed an important clue.[38]

According to Deut 13:1-5 and 18:15-22, the essential point in distinguishing between the true and the false
prophet is not simply whether the word spoken by the prophet becomes true (18:21, 22);[39] for even when the sign or
the portent predicted become true, the primary question is
whether this prophet serves the one, true God (13:2-5) and
whether he speaks the words put into his mouth by the God
of Israel (18:18-20). This is exactly the subject of the
discussion among the Jews in vss. 13-17 where another
σχίσμα occurs:[40] "Is this man παρὰ θεοῦ? He does not keep
the sabbath, yet how can a sinful man perform such σημεῖα?"
(vs. 16). The blind man declares that Jesus must be a
(true) prophet, and he has to defend his standpoint in the
discussion in vss. 24-34 where Jesus' opponents among the
Jews seem to have won, and where the Jews emphasize Jesus'
lack of obedience towards the Law of Moses (vs. 24). The
blind man refers equally persistently to the fact that he
is now able to see (vss. 25, 30-33). The disciples of

Moses stand over against this one disciple of Jesus (vs. 28). And the central difference is expressed by the Jews in the words of vs. 29: "We know that God spoke to Moses, as for that fellow we do not know where he is from." Of course *they* do not know πόθεν ἐστίν. He comes from God, as Son of Man, with the authority to perform God's works as a perfect servant of God like a true prophet and yet more than a prophet, more than Moses.[41] At the same time the discussion between the Jewish leaders and the blind man's parents in vss. 18-23 shows that the use of the title χριστός is the real breaking-point in the relations between the faithful members of the synagogue and those who are thrown out of the synagogue because of their loyalty to Jesus.[42] This title receives no further comment in the present chapter.

John 4:4-42, the story of Jesus' journey through Samaria, would deserve a far fuller treatment than it can receive here. I shall have to restrict myself to some remarks.[43]

First, we should see that there is a connection between stories of Nicodemus, representative of orthodox Jewry, and of Jerusalem (2:23-3:21), that of the Samaritan woman and the other people in her village, representatives of heterodox believers, in Samaria (4:4-42), and the royal official, very probably representative of Galilee, in Galilee (4:46-54). All three represent different reactions to the revelation presented by Jesus. Nicodemus' faith, based on "signs," is shown to be inadequate because he does not understand that Jesus is the Son sent by the Father,[44] the royal official believes first on Jesus' word (4:50) and afterwards he is said to believe with his whole family on the basis of word and sign together--and in this order (4:54).[45] The Samaritans' reaction will have to be defined more precisely, but should be studied in connection with that of Nicodemus and of the official.[46]

Secondly, the geographic element is not unimportant.[47] Samaria is situated between Galilee and Judea, as

64

4:3, 4 and 4:43 remind us, and this has a symbolical meaning. Jesus was rejected in his own country—clearly *Judea*
for the Fourth Gospel (4:44)—but gladly welcomed by the
Galileans though only because they had seen everything he
had done at the feast at Jerusalem (vs. 45)—a belief on
the basis of signs which is criticized later on (vs. 48).
In any case, though the reaction of the Galileans is not
adequate and comparable to that of the people of Jerusalem
in chapter 2, the first and the second sign which led the
disciples and the royal official to a true faith are explicitly situated in Galilee. Is the Samaritans' reaction
notably in vss. 41-42 considered to be somewhere "in between"? The woman's reactions to Jesus' message are not
quite adequate as we shall see presently, but the other
Samaritans of her village come to believe because of the
woman's word, ask Jesus to stay with them, and as a result
of that many more believe because of Jesus' own message:
"We believe now, not because of what you said, but because
we ourselves have heard him, and we know that he is really
the Saviour of the world" (vs. 42).

Thirdly, it should be noted that within chapter 4
there is a progression in thought, which is expressed in
the terms used successively to denote Jesus. In vs. 12
the woman asks, "Are you a greater man than our ancestor
Jacob?" In vs. 19 her reaction is, "Sir, I see that you
are a prophet."[48] In vs. 25 the statement, "I know that
the Messiah (that is, the Christ) is coming and when he
comes he will tell me everything," is still general and it
is up to Jesus to say, "I am he, I who am speaking to you
now" (vs. 26).[49] The result of this is the woman's announcement in the village, "Come and see a man who has
told me everything I ever did; could he be the Messiah?"[50]
It is only the villagers themselves who, after having
heard Jesus personally, declare, "We know that he is
really the Saviour of the world," a title used also in 1
John 4:14.

Lastly, it is possible that the woman's reactions, a prophet, a conception of Messiahship which emphasizes the revelatory aspects are meant to be understood against the background of Samaritan concepts known to the author(s) of the Fourth Gospel.[51] This is not said so explicitly in the present chapter. Some features in this story, however, deserve attention because they are clearly and explicitly of some importance. The woman's reactions[52] are hesitant and inadequate responses to Jesus' teaching about the life-giving water as true gift of God (vss. 10-15), his remarks about her personal life (vss. 16-17), and his discourse on worship in spirit and truth (vss. 19-24). Parallel passages in the Gospel clearly show that true insight into the meaning of Jesus' teaching presupposes insight into his descent from heaven and his return to the Father. See, e.g., 6:35 in the context of the discourse of the Bread from Heaven, "I am the Bread of Life. Whoever comes to me shall never be hungry, and whoever believes shall never be thirsty," and 7:37-38, Jesus' revelatory word about the living water which stands on its own between the discussions of chapter 7. The evangelist, in vs. 39, interprets this water as the Holy Spirit and makes the people in Jerusalem wonder whether this man is "the Prophet"--an inadequate designation as we have seen. The Spirit of truth is sent only after Jesus' return to the Father (14:17, 15:26, 16:13).[53] The Samaritan woman does not really understand Jesus' teaching (cf. the reactions of the Galilean crowd in chapter 6). Not even after Jesus' *own* disclosure in his ἐγώ εἰμι of vs. 26 does she come to a clear confession. Her μήτι οὗτός ἐστιν ὁ χριστός in vs. 29 stands in contrast to the blind man's πιστεύω, κύριε in 9:38 after Jesus' self-identification as Son of Man.[54]

But what about the other Samaritans? Admittedly their reaction is far more adequate than the woman's response or that of Nicodemus and the other people of Jerusalem. They believe after having heard Jesus' preaching and know that he is the Savior of the World (cf. 12:19).

And yet the Gospel indicates that there is "inside knowledge" of which they are not aware.[55] Very aptly John
moves the Samaritan woman to the back of the stage in order to discuss Jesus with the village-people, to give way
to the disciples returning from the village (vss. 8, 31),
in order to start a conversation with Jesus. The disciples are clearly in need of further instruction (vs. 33!)
and they get it, in private. Jesus' central statement is
obviously: "My food is to do the will of him who sent me
until I have finished his work" (vs. 34). The real secret
of his mission is his unity of will with God who sent him
(cf. 5:30, 6:38-40, and cf. 7:17, 9:31). This is made
clear in the conversation with the disciples, and the
Samaritans are not aware of it; it is a knowledge which
can be given to insiders only.[56]

There are a number of points which remain unclear
in this analysis. Yet we may say with some certainty, I
think, that the Fourth Gospel wants to show that Jesus'
teaching is the central point of reference in this chapter, that Jesus has to reveal himself as the Messiah who
ἀναγγελεῖ ἅπαντα (vs. 26), and that his own view on the
real meaning of the expression is given in the conversation with his disciples in vs. 34.

The central passage about Jesus' kingship is 18:28-
19:16, the story of Jesus' trial before Pilate,[57] together
with 19:19-22 which speaks about the inscription on the
cross. Here we find the only direct statement in the
Fourth Gospel on the nature of Jesus' kingship, in the
form of a proclamation of Jesus in the course of the in-
quiry conducted by Pilate.

In this whole section which can be subdivided into
seven units,[58] the title βασιλεύς plays an important part.
Pilate speaks persistently of "the king of the Jews" or
"your king," both inside the praetorium in the first of
his two conversations with Jesus (18:33-38a) and outside,
in his discussions with the Jews and their leaders.[59] Inside the praetorium he is the judge who gradually turns

out to be the accused, as representative of the unbelieving world; outside the praetorium he is Jesus' advocate
whose utterances have a deeper meaning than he realizes
himself. Besides maintaining Jesus' innocence (18:38; 19:
4, 6) he declares, "Look, here is the man" (19:5)[60] and
"Look, here is your king" (19:14); he has a notice made,
"Jesus of Nazareth, the king of the Jews," written in
three languages, nailed to the cross and read by many Jews,
and notwithstanding Jewish protests he does not alter or
remove the inscription (19:19-22).[61]

This man is "the king of the Jews," though the
evangelist prefers the title "King of Israel" as we have
seen in 1:49 and 12:13, and realizes that his kingship
concerns the world and not Israel alone (12:19, 19:20 and
18:37 to be discussed presently). This kingship is fittingly proclaimed by the representative of the Roman Em-
pire. The Jews themselves have a definitely earthly conception of kingship. They prefer Barabbas the ληστής[62] to
Jesus (18:39-40), they do not recognize Jesus, with his
crown and purple cloak, rightly hailed by the soldiers as
king of the Jews, as their king (19:1-3), they call a
claimant for Jewish kingship an enemy of Caesar (19:12)
and even declare, "We have no king but Caesar" (19:15), in
their zeal to have Jesus put out of the way. Indeed, those
who reject Jesus as king will have no king but the Roman
Emperor.[63]

The word "king" plays an important role in this
section, probably because this word was traditionally connected with Jesus' trial and crucifixion.[64] The evangelist gives a reinterpretation of the title, especially in
the first conversation between Jesus and Pilate, a Johannine version of a much shorter pericope in the Synoptics
(Mark 15:2-5, Matt 27:11-14, Luke 23:2-5), but also in the
other episodes of this section. I should like to point
here to vs. 32 which alludes to Jesus' "being lifted up,"[65]
and especially to the second conversation between Jesus
and Pilate which finds its starting-point in the Jewish

accusation in 19:7 that Jesus claimed to be the Son of
God. This claim implies a unity between God and his Son,
as parallel passages show,[66] and is regarded as blasphemy.
Pilate asks the question, πόθεν εἶ σύ, like many before
him.[67] The only true answer, ἄνωθεν, is not given,[68] except in connection with the origin of Pilate's own ἐξουσία
over Jesus.

In 18:33-38a a few things stand out. Pilate opens
the conversation with a statement which has the form of a
confession, "You are the king of the Jews."[69] Jesus' answer consists of two statements, one formulated negatively,
the other, after a hesitant question of Pilate, "You are a
king, then?" formulated positively. Jesus' kingly authority is οὐκ ἐκ τοῦ κόσμου τούτου (18:36), that is, οὐκ
ἐντεῦθεν; every reader of the Gospel knows that it is
ἄνωθεν.[70] Consequently this kingly authority does not
lead to armed resistance against the Romans and attempts
to save Jesus from arrest by the Jews. Positively it
means that Jesus came into the world[71] to bear witness to
the truth. Not everybody hears this witness--Pilate who
asks, "What is truth?" remains an outsider, but those who
are ἐκ τῆς ἀληθείας[72] listen to Jesus' voice.

The forensic term μαρτυρεῖν is very important here,
as elsewhere in the Gospel.[73] It is also clear that Jesus
as witness to the truth brings judgment upon the world.[74]
Meeks[75] connects the last part of vs. 37, "...listens to
my voice," with Deut 18:15 where people are admonished to
listen to the prophet like Moses who speaks God's words,
as Jesus does in his testimony to the truth. As we have
seen in the introduction, he also connects this with the
listening of the sheep to the voice of the good shepherd
in chapter 10. Not only in chapter 10, however, but also
here in the first and the second conversation between Jesus and Pilate, the fact that Jesus is sent from above,
from God, into the world and acts and speaks out of his
intimate relationship with the Father (cf. 3:31-36, esp.
vss. 32-33) receives more emphasis than the fact that he

fulfills the mission of a prophet. The reinterpretation
of Jesus' kingship is given in terms of divine Sonship,
understood in a typically Johannine way. Jesus is prophet
and king because he is the Son sent by the Father, and
only as Son of the Father.

CHAPTER III

[1]See also the discussion of 3:1-21 and 31-36 in Chapter II, pp. 37-42.

[2]Wayne A. Meeks, *The Prophet-King. Moses Traditions and the Johannine Christology* (Leiden: Brill, 1967). After the present chapter had been written, Meeks published his long and important article, "The Man from Heaven in Johannine Sectarianism," in *JBL* 91 (1972), pp. 44-72. I am glad to find myself in substantial agreement with much that 'has been written there, especially with what is said on p. 60: "Basic to the common definition of the apostolic prophet was the understanding that he did not speak his own words but the words of him who commissioned him, and that is a prominent motif in the Fourth Gospel. This notion could be underlined by the mythical picture of the apostle's assumption to heaven to receive the secret message, and that was doubtless a point of contact for the development of the Johannine picture of Jesus' descent and ascent, in connection with the Wisdom myths. But...the secret message which Jesus brings is virtually reduced to the statement of the descent and ascent, and of the relationship to God which that pattern implies. The content of his prophetic *martyria* is progressively more clearly identified with his knowledge of his own origin and destiny, which demonstrates his unique relationship to the Father."

[3]Meeks, *The Prophet-King*, p. 1.

[4]Ibid., p. 67.

[5]Ibid., p. 99.

[6]A very useful analysis of 1:19-51 is found in J. Willemse, *Het vierde evangelie. Een onderzoek naar zijn structuur* (Hilversum-Antwerpen: P. Brand, 1965), pp. 233-53. On the unity of chapter 1 as a whole, see also pp. 221-33 and 254-74.

[7]It is difficult to decide which reading is original. Nestle-Aland and *The Greek New Testament* print ὁ υἱὸς τοῦ θεοῦ, though Aland indicates a preference for ὁ ἐκλεκτός (since the 24th edition of the Nestle-Aland text); *The Greek New Testament* adds a (B) indicating that "there is some degree of doubt." One expects ὁ υἱὸς τοῦ θεοῦ in this verse which occupies a significant place in the Gospel (see also vs. 18, μονογενής; vs. 49, ὁ υἱὸς τοῦ θεοῦ) and therefore it is likely to be original; ἐκλεκτός may then be

explained as due to the influence of Isa 42:1 (cf. Luke 9:35, 23:35). On the other hand it is also possible that the unusual ἐκλεκτός was changed into the more familiar ὁ υἱός.

[8]See Chapter IV, pp. 85-90.

[9]See also Chapter II, pp. 34-37, and Chapter IV, pp. 93-94. John 7 gives a series of comments upon prevailing Jewish conceptions about the Messiah and refutations of Jewish objections against Jesus (see vss. 27, 31, 42, and cf. 12:34).

[10]This declaration has given many problems to the exegetes which need not detain us here. See the survey of recent opinion in the most recent commentary on this passage, R. Schnackenburg, *Das Johannesevangelium* II, Herders Theologischer Kommentar zum Neuen Testament (Freiburg-Basel-Wien: Herder, 1971), pp. 211-18.

[11]Cf. 1:15, 7:28, 12:44. In each case an important statement follows; see also W. Grundmann, art. κράζω, ἀνακράζω, κραυγή, κραυγάζω, *TDNT* 3, pp. 898-903, esp. p. 902.

[12]Compare the attempts "to kill" (vss. 1, 19, 20, 25; 8:37, 40) and "to stone" (8:59; 10:31, 32, 33; and also 11:8) Jesus.

[13]See, apart from the commentaries, E. D. Freed, *Old Testament Quotations in the Gospel of John*, NovTSup 11 (Leiden: Brill, 1965), pp. 39-59, and Chr. Burger, *Jesus als Davidssohn: Eine traditionsgeschichtliche Untersuchung*, FRLANT 98 (Göttingen: Vandenhoeck & Ruprecht, 1970), pp. 153-58. The exegesis given here agrees with that of Meeks, *The Prophet-King*, pp. 36-38; cf. his "Galilee and Judea in the Fourth Gospel," in *JBL* 85 (1966), pp. 159-69.

[14]The reading ὁ προφήτης seems to be generally accepted now; see Chapter II, pp. 36-37.

[15]See Meeks, *The Prophet-King*, pp. 35-41, 313-18, and Chapter II, p. 36.

[16]Meeks, *The Prophet-King*, pp. 42-47.

[17]T. F. Glasson, *Moses in the Fourth Gospel* (London: SCM Press, 1963), p. 30, in an interesting chapter devoted to "The Prophet," pp. 27-32.

[18]Meeks, *The Prophet-King*, p. 57.

[19]Glasson, *Moses in the Fourth Gospel*, p. 30; see, however, R. Bultmann, *The Gospel of John* (Philadelphia: Westminster, 1971), pp. 248-52, on 5:19, who gives a number of OT parallels before introducing the gnostic myth as more important background. "Thus the terminology of the

myth provides John with a means of describing the person and the word of Jesus in a way which takes him beyond the OT idea of prophecy" (p. 252). This, of course, is by no means universally accepted--see, e.g., R. Schnackenburg, *The Gospel according to St John* I, Herder's Theological Commentary on the New Testament (New York: Herder and Herder; London: Burns & Oates, 1968), pp. 543-57, Excursus VI, "The Gnostic Myth of the Redeemer and the Johannine Christology."

[20] Glasson, *Moses in the Fourth Gospel*, p. 30.

[21] See, e.g., Meeks, *The Prophet-King*, pp. 91-98; P. Borgen, *Bread from Heaven. An Exegetical Study of the Concept of Manna in the Gospel of John and the Writings of Philo*, NovTSup 10 (Leiden: Brill, 1965), and J. L. Martyn, *History and Theology in the Fourth Gospel* (New York-Evanston: Harper & Row, 1968), pp. 112-19 (see especially his conclusion on p. 119: "Far from being predicated on certain exegetical patterns, such as the Moses-Messiah typology, faith has only one essential presupposition: the presence of Jesus and his self-authenticating word").

[22] See 18:33, 39; 19:19, 21; cf. also ὁ βασιλεὺς ὑμῶν in 19:14, 15, and the soldiers' greeting, ὁ βασιλεὺς τῶν Ἰουδαίων in 19:3.

[23] On 1:35-51, see Willemse, *Het vierde evangelie*, esp. pp. 237-51, and Schnackenburg, *The Gospel according to St John* I, pp. 507-14, Excursus III, "The Titles of Jesus in John 1."

[24] Cf. 4:19, 6:69, 11:27 (and 1:19, 21, 25; 8:25; 10:24; 18:33; 21:12) and the οὗτός ἐστιν-formulas (1:30, 33, 34; 4:29, 42; 6:14, 50; 7:26, 40, 41).

[25] See, e.g., Ps 2:7!

[26] Cf. 5:20, 14:12.

[27] Important is Willemse's thesis of two christologies in John in general and in John 1:1-18 and 1:19-51 in particular. 1:1-18 stands in the Wisdom-tradition and emphasizes the "vertical" connection between heaven and earth. 1:19-51 emphasizes the "horizontal" messianic line. The two conceptions are brought together in 1:49-51 (as well as in 11:27, 20:30-31). See Willemse, *Het vierde evangelie*, pp. 264-71.

[28] Cf. Meeks, *The Prophet-King*, pp. 82-83, who speaks, however, of "prophetic kingship."

[29] See Freed, *Old Testament Quotations in the Gospel of John*, pp. 66-81 (and also *JBL* 80 [1961], pp. 329-38); D. M. Smith, "John 12:12ff and the Question of John's Use of the Synoptics," *JBL* 82 (1963), pp. 58-64; and Schnackenburg, *Das Johannesevangelium* II, pp. 474-76.

[30]See E. Peterson, "Die Einholung des Kyrios," in
ZST 7 (1930), pp. 62-66, and (recently) B. A. Mastin, "The
Date of the Triumphal Entry," *NTS* 16 (1969-70), pp. 76-82.

[31]The words about the king's humility are *not* taken
over (they are quoted in Matt 21:5). The first line of
vs. 15 is often connected with Zeph 3:14-17.

[32]See Chapter II, p. 32.

[33]See also Meeks, *The Prophet-King*, pp. 83-87.

[34]See Chapter I, pp. 7-10.

[35]See Martyn, *History and Theology in the Fourth
Gospel*, pp. 1-16, 131-32.

[36]See C. H. Dodd, *The Interpretation of the Fourth
Gospel* (Cambridge: Cambridge University Press, 1953), p. 354.

[37]See, e.g., Schnackenburg, *The Gospel according to
St. John* I, pp. 529-42, Excursus V, "The 'Son of Man' in
the Fourth Gospel."

[38]Meeks, *The Prophet-King*, pp. 294-95. See also
the commentaries of C. K. Barrett, *The Gospel according to
St. John* (London: Macmillan, 1955), and R. E. Brown, *The
Gospel according to John (i-xii)*, The Anchor Bible 29
(Garden City, NY: Doubleday, 1966), on 9:16.

[39]Though, of course, the fact that it does not become true is itself proof that the word was not spoken in
the name of God.

[40]Cf. 7:43, discussed above.

[41]See also Chapter II, pp. 39-41.

[42]See Martyn, *History and Theology in the Fourth
Gospel*, pp. 17-41.

[43]See also Chapter IV, Appendix.

[44]See Chapter II.

[45]See Chapter V, pp. 123-24.

[46]See Willemse, *Het vierde evangelie*, pp. 302-8,
and I. de la Potterie, "Structura primae partis Evangelii
Johannis (capita III et IV)," in *VD* 47 (1969), pp. 130-40.
Both authors call the christology of chapter 3 "vertical"
and that of chapter 4 "horizontal" (for this terminology,
see n. 27, above). This is too one-sided, both as a char-
acterization of chapter 3 and of chapter 4.

[47]See also Meeks, *The Prophet-King*, pp. 39-41, 313-18.

[48]Cf. 9:17 and also Luke 7:39!

[49]On possible overtones in ἐγώ εἰμι, see Schnackenburg, *The Gospel according to St John* I, pp. 441-42. In
the second volume of his commentary, p. 61, discussing 4:
26 and 8:18(23), Schnackenburg remarks: "Sprachlich und
formell gehören diese Stellen nicht zur eigentlichen For-
mel; aber theologisch haben sie die gleiche Bedeutung."

[50]Μήτι in questions generally implies a negative
answer (see BDF 427.2) but there are some instances where
a more positive notion ("es scheint aber doch so zu sein")
may be implied; see John 4:26, 33; 7:26; Matt 12:23.

[51]See Chapter IV, Appendix.

[52]See, e.g., Brown's analysis of 4:17-26 and his
excursus on "living water" and "worship in spirit and
truth" on pp. 176-81 of his *The Gospel according to John
(i-xii)*. Brown very closely follows F. Roustang, "Les
moments de l'acte de foi et ses conditions de possibilité,"
in *RSR* 46 (1958), pp. 344-78.

[53]See Chapter I, pp. 9-12.

[54]C. L. Porter, "John IX.38, 39a: a Liturgical Addition to the Text," in *NTS* 13 (1966-67), pp. 387-94, has
tried to show that vss. 38-39a, omitted in some ancient authorities, are a later liturgical addition. Yet some final
positive reaction of the blind man seems to be needed.

[55]See also Dodd, *The Interpretation of the Fourth
Gospel*, pp. 315-16.

[56]It is, of course, quite useless to speculate on
the conversations between Jesus and the Samaritans in the
two days Jesus spent in the village.

[57]Much has been written recently on this section of
the Gospel or parts of it. I should like to mention especially J. Blank, "Die Verhandlung vor Pilatus Joh 18,28-19,
16 im Lichte johanneischer Theologie," in *BZ*, Neue Folge 3
(1959), pp. 60-81; I. de la Potterie, "Jésus roi et juge
d'après Jn 19,13," in *Bib* 41 (1960), pp. 217-47; Meeks, *The
Prophet-King*, pp. 61-81; F. Hahn, "Der Prozess Jesu nach
dem Johannesevangelium," in EKKNT, *Vorarbeiten*, Heft 2
(1970), pp. 23-96; and H. van der Kwaak, *Het proces van
Jezus* (Assen: van Gorcum, 1969), pp. 178-87.

[58]18:28-32, 33-38a, 38b-40; 19:1-3, 4-7, 8-12, 13-16.

[59]See n. 22, above.

[60]The meaning of ὁ ἄνθρωπος here is a matter of dis-
pute. For a survey of recent opinion, see R. E. Brown, *The
Gospel according to John (xiii-xxi)*, The Anchor Bible 29A
(Garden City, NY: Doubleday, 1970), pp. 875-76.

[61]Blank, "Die Verhandlung vor Pilatus," p. 62: "So-
dann ist das Ganze als 'Königs-Epiphanie' dargestellt: 1.

mit Königsproklamation (durch Jesus vor Pilatus), 2. mit Königsinthronisation und Investitur (Verspottungsszene), 3. mit Königsepiphanie vor dem Volke (im Purpurmantel und Dornenkrone), 4. mit Königsakklamation durch das Volk (σταύρωσον, σταύρωσον)."

[62]On the meaning of ληστής and its use by Josephus to denote Jewish "rebels," see M. Hengel, *Die Zeloten* (Leiden: Brill, 1961), pp. 25-46.

[63]Meeks, *The Prophet-King*, p. 76: "Rejecting the 'King of the Jews,' 'the Jews' cease to be 'Israel,' the special people of God, and become only one of the ἔθνη subject to Caesar."

[64]See, e.g., Meeks, *The Prophet-King*, p. 79, esp. n. 1 on that page.

[65]Verse 32 must refer to 12:32, 33.

[66]See 5:18 and 10:33, and cf., of course, Mark 14: 61, Matt 26:63, and Luke 22:70.

[67]Cf. 4:11; 7:27, 28; 8:14; 9:29, 30.

[68]Cf. 3:27, and n. 69, below.

[69]A statement, not a question; see the alternative translation in the *NEB*, and esp. van der Kwaak, *Het proces van Jezus*, p. 178, n. 2. The formula does not differ from that in the Synoptics, but there it is introduced by the verb ἐπηρώτησεν (Matthew, Mark) or ἠρώτησεν (Luke). In vs. 37 we have a real question (provided we accent οὐκοῦν, not οὔκουν!); here Jesus gives an answer which is best understood as a qualified assent (on the much debated question of the meaning of σὺ λέγεις, see Brown, *The Gospel according to John (xiii-xxi)*, pp. 853-54). With the use of ἀφ' ἑαυτοῦ in vs. 34, compare 11:51, 52.

[70]Cf. 3:3, 7, 31; 8:23; and 6:31-58 passim.

[71]See the emphatic ἐγὼ εἰς τοῦτο γεγέννημαι καὶ εἰς τοῦτο ἐλήλυθα εἰς τὸν κόσμον, and cf. 1:14, 17.

[72]Cf. 1 John 2:21, 3:19, and parallel expressions like ἐκ τοῦ πνεύματος (3:6) and ἐκ τοῦ θεοῦ (7:17, etc.). See Bultmann, *The Gospel of John*, p. 161, n. 3.

[73]See esp. 3:32; 5:31-40; 8:13, 14, 18; 10:25.

[74]See, among others, de la Potterie, "Jésus roi et juge d'après Jn 19,13," who defends vigorously the thesis that ἐκάθισεν should be understood transitively. Of course, there are other arguments to find here the conception of Jesus as judge (in pp. 240-47 de la Potterie rightly points to 5:21-30; 9:39; 12:31, 48; 16:11). Particularly in 5:19-38 and 8:12-30 the themes of witness and judgment are interrelated (thus Meeks, *The Prophet-King*, p. 65).

[75]Meeks, *The Prophet-King*, pp. 63-67.

CHAPTER IV

JEWISH EXPECTATIONS ABOUT THE "MESSIAH"
ACCORDING TO THE FOURTH GOSPEL

I. Introduction

cl. 7

1. This chapter will deal with a number of passages in the Fourth Gospel in which Jews express Jewish beliefs concerning the Messiah. Three of these are found in the debates among various groups in Jerusalem which are recorded in chapter 7; they all deal with the *coming* of the Messiah.

7:27   ὁ δὲ χριστὸς ὅταν ἔρχηται, οὐδεὶς γινώσκει
         πόθεν ἐστίν.

7:31   ὁ χριστὸς ὅταν ἔλθῃ, μὴ πλείονα σημεῖα
         ποιήσει ὧν οὖτος ἐποίησεν;

7:41b, μὴ γὰρ ἐκ τῆς Γαλιλαίας ὁ χριστὸς
42   ἔρχεται; οὐχ ἡ γραφὴ εἶπεν ὅτι ἐκ τοῦ
         σπέρματος Δαυίδ, καὶ ἀπὸ Βηθλέεμ τῆς
         κώμης ὅπου ἦν Δαυίδ, ἔρχεται ὁ χριστός;

To these three must be added the statement in 12:34, ἡμεῖς ἠκούσαμεν ἐκ τοῦ νόμου ὅτι ὁ χριστὸς μένει εἰς τὸν αἰῶνα, adduced as an objection to Jesus' announcement ὅτι δεῖ ὑψωθῆναι τὸν υἱὸν τοῦ ἀνθρώπου.

Besides these direct statements there is an allusion to Jewish beliefs concerning the Messiah in 1:19-34 where John the Baptist is questioned by representatives of the Jews. On the question "Who are you?" there seem to be three possible answers: "the Christ," "Elijah" and "the Prophet," obviously in accordance with known variants in Jewish expectation. There is a clear connection (apart from the Elijah-concept) between this section and 7:40-44 where there are two options: "the Prophet" or "the Christ."

Next, 1:35-51 should be mentioned, because in this passage Jesus' first disciples confess their faith in

Jesus in terms which are obviously meant to represent
various aspects of Jewish expectation. Andrew speaks of
ὁ Μεσσίας (translated explicitly as "the Christ," 1:41);
Philip announces "him about whom Moses in the Law and the
Prophets have written" (1:45, note the emphasis there and
here on εὑρήκαμεν!) and Nathanael in his confession speaks
of ὁ υἱὸς τοῦ θεοῦ, ὁ βασιλεὺς τοῦ Ἰσραήλ (1:49).

Similarly, 4:25 points to the Samaritan expectation
of (again) the *coming* of the Messiah, οἶδα ὅτι Μεσσίας
ἔρχεται...ὅταν ἔλθῃ ἐκεῖνος, ἀναγγελεῖ ἡμῖν ἅπαντα.

2. In all these cases the Fourth Gospel clearly
wishes to confront Jesus' own statements about himself, or
pronouncements of others concerning him, with current Jewish (and Samaritan) expectations. Our primary task,
therefore, is to investigate how these references to Jewish (or Samaritan) beliefs function in the setting in
which they occur, and within the Gospel as a whole.

Secondly, we must ask from what source(s) the evangelist derived his information concerning these expectations about "the Messiah," and we must try to assess his
reliability in reproducing them. Are there parallels in
Jewish (or Christian) documents which may corroborate or
supplement the statements made by the Jews (and the Samaritans) in the Fourth Gospel, so that we can understand why
and how they are introduced in the Gospel? If not, do the
statements in the Fourth Gospel supplement what we know
from other sources and do they help us to sketch a more
coherent picture of Jewish beliefs concerning the Messiah
at the time the Fourth Gospel was written? I should like
to stress that we cannot deal with the second problem until we have discussed the first. We cannot use the Johannine material without taking into account that the Jews,
whose opinion is expressed in the Gospel, appear on a scene
set by a Christian evangelist. They are portrayed as "representative Jews" and are obviously introduced in the Gospel because it was important to compare John's views on
Jesus the Christ with Jewish expectations concerning the
Messiah.

If statements made by Jewish opponents or sympathizers in the Fourth Gospel do not agree with expressions
or conceptions found in Jewish sources, or show only par-
tial agreements, we may not exclude the possibility that
the Gospel, as only source, has preserved truly Jewish notions and beliefs. After all, the Jewish material is
variegated, and very scanty and haphazard. Yet the Johannine material can only be used to fill in the gaps or
to correct the picture after due allowance has been made
for its function within the Fourth Gospel.

II. The Function of the Jewish Statements Concerning "the Messiah" in the Gospel--Some General Characteristics[1]

Before turning to a more detailed treatment of the
individual passages, some more general remarks, relating
to all passages, may be useful.

1. In an important excursus in his commentary on
the Fourth Gospel,[2] R. Schnackenburg has emphasized that
the entire passage 1:19-51 is purposely centered on the
question of the fulfillment of Jewish messianic expectations in Jesus. The Baptist refuses to ascribe any messianic dignity to himself and points to the One who comes
after him; the first disciples understand right from the
start that various aspects of Jewish messianic expectation
converge in this Jesus whom they have met. They need further instruction leading to a deeper insight--and this instruction is given in the later chapters of the Gospel--
but clearly this chapter is meant to give a survey of messianic titles and designations and to emphasize that they
find their true meaning and fulfillment in Jesus.

In the same way in 4:1-42 some typical Samaritan
reactions are recorded and here again Jesus is portrayed
as the one whom the Samaritan woman expects (vs. 26) and
whom the villagers hail as the Savior of the world (vs.
42).[3] In chapter 7 the evangelist deals with various reactions in the crowd and in the leading circles in Jerusalem, and in this framework he brings up one tentative

question in favor of Jesus and a number of Jewish objections against his Messiahship--the last of these being reserved to a later occasion, in 12:34.[4] A similar treatment of the question of Jesus' true identity by means of a report of a debate taking up one theme from various points of view we find in chapter 9, where, however, the title Messiah (Christ) does not occupy a central position. All this, of course, is well known; I mention it here because I want to emphasize the literary character of the treatment of the problem of Jesus' Messiahship. Representative people (disciples, ordinary people--the crowd, Jewish leaders, Samaritans) express representative beliefs and raise representative objections.

2. Though the persons mentioned in the various stories are meant to be representative, they are more like actors in a play, whose utterances help along the course of events and, even more, the development of thought, than identifiable individuals belonging to clearly defined groups, even if we look at the Fourth Gospel by itself, regardless of its links with history. This may be illustrated by a very short survey of the dramatis personae in 7:10-52.[5]

Here we find in vss. 10-13 two groups among the crowds over against the Jews whom they fear (vs. 13). The hostility of "the Jews" is quite marked here, as it is elsewhere in the Gospel (see, e.g., 7:1, 19 and 5:16, 18; 10:31; 11:8). Yet in vs. 11 (as in vs. 35), a broader and not specifically hostile group may be meant. In vss. 14-24 "the Jews" are Jesus' opponents in a discussion which ends with a rabbinical argument, so we might suppose that this term indicates the Jewish leaders in Jerusalem.[6] Yet in vs. 19, ὁ ὄχλος has already appeared again. Moreover, where Jewish leaders are mentioned explicitly in this chapter they are never called "the Jews"; vs. 32 speaks of "the Pharisees" and "the chief priests and the Pharisees"; in vss. 45-52, where we are told of the discussions in the council-chamber, the term "rulers" is also introduced (vs.

48, cf. vs. 26). ὁ ὄχλος or οἱ ὄχλοι are never clearly
defined or divided groups; the evangelist is clearly not
interested in the description of different parties, but
contents himself with outlining different reactions (see
vss. 10-12, 31, 41-43); the picture is further complicated
by the introduction of "some of the people of Jerusalem"
in vss. 25-30 who stand over against "the rulers" (vs. 26).
It is not clear whether they belong to the crowd or not,
and whether they or a different undefined group (cf. vs.
25) try to kill Jesus (vs. 30).

This subject would deserve further treatment, but
for the purpose of this study, these illustrations taken
from one chapter may suffice. Yet, however vague the description may be, it is useful to note *who* are said to express Jewish messianic beliefs. In 7:27 the speakers are
"some of the people of Jerusalem." In 7:40-44 we meet
various groups in the crowd, one of which makes the objection about the Messiah's Davidic descent and his birth in
Bethlehem. In 12:34 it is ὁ ὄχλος that is speaking. In
7:31 we are told that "many believed in him"; these believers put the question (to be answered negatively!):
"When the Messiah comes, is it likely that he will perform
more signs than this man?" It is after their reaction
that the Pharisees decide to take action.

People who are sympathetic towards Jesus occur
several times in the Gospel. Sometimes they belong to
common people (2:23-25; 6:2; 7:40-41; 8:31; 10:42; 11:45,
47-48; 12:11). Sometimes they belong to the leaders
(Nicodemus, 3:1-2, 7:50-52, 19:38-42; Joseph of Arimathea,
19:38-42; many of the ἄρχοντες, 12:42-43; some of the
Pharisees, 9:16). Often this sympathy is called faith
(2:23-25; 7:31; 8:31; 10:42; 11:45, 48; 12:11, 42) and
Joseph of Arimathea is called a disciple (19:38). This
faith is often connected with the signs performed by Jesus
(2:23-25; 11:45, 47-48; 12:10-11, 42; cf. 6:2, 10:42) as
it is in 7:31. In Chapter V we shall say more about the
function of signs in the Fourth Gospel and about the

Gospel's effort to define correctly the relationship between faith in Jesus and the signs and works performed by
him. It is sufficient to note here that the people meant
here eventually fall under a negative verdict. Their
faith needs a fundamental correction; 2:23-25, the first
passage to mention this category of Jewish believers,
tells quite plainly: "Jesus for his part would not trust
himself to them. He knew men so well, all of them, that
he needed no evidence from others about a man, for he
himself could tell what was in a man."[7]

3. Next, I should like to point out that there is
no real discussion about the Jewish statements. In 7:25-
30 Jesus' reaction is significantly introduced by ἔκραξεν
ἐν τῷ ἱερῷ διδάσκων (cf. 7:37).[8] Jesus takes up the πόθεν,
explains it in terms of his special mission, which presupposes a unique relationship between Father and Son, but he
does not use the word χριστός himself. There is no reaction from Jesus whatever after 7:31; we are obviously expected to make the necessary adjustments by comparing this
statement with the outcome of the discussion between Jesus
and Nicodemus in chapter 3, the discourse on the Bread
from Heaven in chapter 6 and elsewhere. The debate in 7:
40-44 is a typically inner-Jewish discussion in which Jesus himself does not take part; once the problem where he
comes from is answered in 7:25-30, there is no need for
further comment on matters like Davidic descent and birth
at Bethlehem. In 12:34 the objection voiced by the crowd
concerning Jesus' pronouncement that the Son of Man must
be lifted up, and the following question about the identity of this Son of Man, are not answered. Here as in the
previous cases the Jewish statements point to a more or
less fundamental misunderstanding.[9]

4. In this connection it may be useful to point
out that 1:19-51, where various messianic designations,
including the word "Messiah" itself, occur successively,
ends with a reference to the Son of Man, his contact with
heaven by means of ascending and descending angels. This

is not the place to speak about the ascent-descent pattern
in the Fourth Gospel. I should like to refer here to W.
A. Meeks' fundamental contribution to Johannine studies in
his recent article, "The Man from Heaven in Johannine
Sectarianism."[10] It may be useful to emphasize that 1:19-
50 stands between 1:18 and 1:51, both dealing with the
heavenly status of the One to whom all the designations in
the intermediate section point in their own way. The same
is true of chapter 3 where the term "a teacher sent by
God, performing signs" in vs. 2 is corrected and superseded by the expressions (only) Son, Son of God, and Son
of Man which designate Jesus' heavenly origin and ultimate
authority. We may also mention here chapter 9 where the
discussion is concerned with Jesus' authority conceived in
terms of true prophecy, and where Jesus in a private final
conversation with the blind man introduces the term "Son
of Man" in connection with his own mission--as in 1:51 and
3:13, 14. Titles like "prophet," "teacher sent by God,"
"king" or even "Messiah" do not correspond completely with
the real status and authority of Him to whom they point.
The terms are not wrong but insufficient; they may be used
in a wrong context and are, therefore, in need of further
definition.

In the case of the use of χριστός, this further
definition is given with the help of the terms Son of Man
and Son of God. So 1:51 comes after 1:41; 7:28, 29 implying Jesus' being Son of the Father come after 7:27 and
correct this basically so that by implication the discussion in 7:40-44 becomes superficial and superfluous.[11]
Also, in 12:34, it is clear that the Jews introduce the
term "Messiah" in a context where Jesus prefers the term
"Son of Man" and connects this Son of Man concept with the
notion of "being lifted up."

5. The results of II. 3 and 4 are fully borne out
by a study of the statements about "the Christ" which have
not yet been mentioned. Again there is only room for some
short comments.[12]

It is clear that the evangelist realizes that ὁ χριστός is a Jewish designation; we have seen that he uses the transliteration ὁ Μεσσίας and translates it in 1:41. In 9:22 he tells his readers that a confession of Jesus as ὁ χριστός will necessarily be followed by expulsion from the synagogue. The Fourth Gospel wishes to stress that the use of the title ὁ χριστός for Jesus is the real issue in the debate between synagogue and Christian community. This is also the reason why this term occupies such a prominent place in the arguments used by Jews. Yet the evangelist himself regards the title ὁ χριστός as inadequate and in need of further comment.

The section on John the Baptist in 1:19-34 ends with John's witness to Jesus as the Son of God,[13] not to Jesus as the Christ, though that is the central designation used by the representatives of the Jews (3:28 referring to 1:21-23). In his reply to the question of the Jews in 10:24, "If you are the Messiah say so plainly," Jesus refers to the acts performed by him in the name of the Father (10:25). This passage ends with a very penetrating discourse and debate on the nature of Jesus' sonship and of his unity with the Father (10:25-30, 31-39). When Martha confesses her faith in 11:27 she says to Jesus: "I am convinced (πεπίστευκα) that you are the Messiah, the Son of God, who was to come into the world." The title ὁ χριστός and the use of the verb ἔρχεσθαι in connection with it are well-known features of Jewish statements in John, as we have seen. But the Christian confession ὁ χριστός is interpreted by the addition ὁ υἱὸς τοῦ θεοῦ. This is also the case in 20:30, 31, the well-known "first ending" of the Gospel. A number of the signs which Jesus performed in the presence of his disciples were recorded in this book in order that the readers might believe that Jesus is the Christ, the Son of God, and that through this faith they might have life in his name. This shows the inadequacy of the formulation and, therefore, of the faith of the believers among the crowd in 7:31 who held that the signs performed by Jesus pointed to his Messiahship. They were right and yet not right, because they did not pay sufficient attention to the fact that this Jesus is the Son of God.

6. This rather rapid and general survey has made clear, I think, that the Jewish statements about the Messiah *either* point to a complete misunderstanding (7:27, 41b-42; 12:34) and are therefore ignored (7:41b, 42; 12:34) or reinterpreted fundamentally (7:27); *or* they represent an inadequate formulation of belief in Jesus (7:31) which is subsequently implicitly corrected.[14] Christian believers may use and do use "the Christ" as designation for Jesus (1:41, cf. 7:41)--it is the central point in the debate between Jews and Christians--but this title needs to be interpreted. The Gospel interprets it by the title Son of God, pointing to the unity between Jesus and the Father who sent him.

We shall now try to fill in this general picture with the help of the results of a more detailed treatment of the passages concerned and of a comparison of the statements which concern us with data known from other sources.

III. Treatment of Individual Passages

1. The Witness of John the Baptist (1:19-34)

The first passage to be dealt with is 1:19-34, a section of the Gospel which did not receive much attention in the preceding part of the chapter, because it presupposes Jewish beliefs rather than mentioning or correcting them explicitly.[15]

John's explicit and solemn negative confession (vs. 20: καὶ ὡμολόγησεν καὶ οὐκ ἠρνήσατο, καὶ ὡμολόγησεν!) spoken in front of official representatives of the Jews (vss. 19, 22, 24)[16] is an important part of his μαρτυρία. John is portrayed as the ideal witness to Christ (vss. 19, 32, 34 and 7-8; 3:26 and 5:33-36).[17] There is no doubt that he is ἀπεσταλμένος παρὰ θεοῦ (1:6, 3:28) and that he

witnesses to the truth (5:33). That is why the section
devoted to his preaching is made to end with the perfectly
adequate statement, "He (Jesus) is the Son of God." Yet
John is no more than a witness to the truth, whose testimony is important and essential for those for whom he
preached--some of his disciples become disciples of Jesus,
and if the Jews whom Jesus addresses in chapter 5 had accepted John's testimony, they would have been saved (vs.
34)--yet Jesus himself, though announced by John, does not
really need him. In 5:34-37 he points to the direct witness of the Father on his behalf; the very works he performs witness to his being sent by the Father.[18] This may
be the reason why Jesus' baptism by John is not mentioned
in 1:29-33. John came baptizing with water ἵνα φανερωθῇ
τῷ Ἰσραήλ (vs. 31). This passive implies God himself as
actor. John himself could only *announce* the one who was
to come,[19] he could not *reveal* him, because he did not
know who he was. This explicit statement in vs. 31 is repeated in vs. 33; God, who sent John to baptize with water,
had announced that his successor, who would baptize with
the Spirit, could be recognized by the fact that the Spirit
descended upon him and remained on him. Only because God
had told him this could John identify Jesus when he saw
this happen (vss. 32-33).[20]

In vss. 20-22 we hear first of all that John is not
the Christ, though John himself chooses the title "Son of
God" to designate Jesus, clearly in accord with the evangelist's deepest intentions. "The Christ" clearly is the
main title in vss. 20-22; it is the first to be mentioned
in 1:21 (and 1:25), and in 3:26-30 which refers to the
episode related in chapter 1 it is the *only* title.[21] Why,
however, does John also deny that he is Elijah or the
Prophet? Jesus is identified with the Prophet by people
in the crowd (6:14, 7:40-44) and prophetic notions are
very important for the delineation of the Gospel's christology[22] so that the statement of John concerning the
Prophet may have been considered necessary. But Jesus is

never identified with Elijah! One has pointed to Mark 6:
14-16 par. and 8:27-29 par. which mention Elijah and "one
of the prophets" besides "the Christ" as possible "messianic" options in connection with Jesus.[23] One has even
tried to connect the three figures mentioned in 1:20-21
with the three figures expected in 1QS 9.2.[24] In doing so
one overlooks first of all that Elijah is not mentioned
anywhere else in this Gospel and that, for example, 7:40-
44 mentions only "the Prophet" and "the Christ"; secondly,
that the three are mentioned here as Jewish "messianic
possibilities" without any implication that they should
appear together at the same time.

The fact that the identification of John the Baptist with Elijah is denied categorically must have something to do with earlier Christian views which found their
expression in Mark and Matthew, and to some extent also in
Luke. But why would the Fourth Gospel want to contradict
this identification while it took over many other things
from the tradition concerning John the Baptist, and why
did it identify John with "the voice in the wilderness who
helped to prepare the way of the Lord" (in agreement with
Mark 1:3), thereby emphasizing John's function as the
herald? One can say John is merely "a voice," a witness;
he no longer conforms to any known figure within the
framework of Jewish expectation.[25] But this theory does
not explain the explicit denial of John's identification
with Elijah.

Now this denial must have christological significance, just like John's denial that he is the Christ and
the Prophet. Are we in a position to prove this? I think
we are. In 1:26 John tells the people who listen to him
that the one who comes after him stands already among
them--though they do not know him. The phrase μέσος ὑμῶν
στήκει ὃν ὑμεῖς οὐκ οἴδατε is only found in the Fourth
Gospel. The Jews who are addressed do not know him, because they do not accept him; 1:10-11 has already made
clear that this is a matter of basic misunderstanding and

rejection. When 1:31 speaks of a revelation to Israel, it is clear that the true believers among the Jewish people are meant, not just the Jews.[26]

The terminology used here is that of the Fourth Gospel, but there is a link with other traditions concerning an unknown Messiah. Much has been written on the subject; by far the best treatment of it is found in chapter 2, "Der verborgene Messias im Judentum," in Erik Sjöberg's *Der verborgene Menschensohn in den Evangelien*.[27] Our earliest sources witness to two types of expectation. The one is found in 1 Enoch, 4 Ezra and 2 Apoc. Bar., where a pre-existence of the Messiah (or, in the case of Enoch, the Son of Man) in heaven is presupposed. He will appear at the appointed time and it is certain that he will come, for he is already there, though hidden from mortal eyes.[28] Besides that, there is the conception that the Messiah is already on earth, incognito and even himself not knowing who he is.[29]

Now it is important to note that in both conceptions mentioned the essential point is the fact that the Messiah *appears*, *is revealed*, that is, is seen by the people, though not acknowledged by all of them. Speculations about the place where he is hidden, or (in other terms) is preserved by God are clearly of secondary importance.[30] John 1:26 seems to presuppose the second conception, for which Trypho in Justin's *Dialogus cum Tryphone* seems to be the first witness. This is interesting because the same passages in the *Dialogue* (8.3, 49.1, 110.1) provide the earliest evidence for Jewish expectations concerning Elijah as the forerunner, who anoints the Messiah.[31]

The important elements in the picture given in the *Dialogue* are the following. Even if the Christ has already been born, he is ἄγνωστος; he does not know himself and has no power until Elijah anoints him and φανερὸν πᾶσι ποιήσῃ (8.4). Justin refers to this belief in 110.1, telling Trypho that he is aware of the fact that Jewish teachers are of this opinion. He uses the phrases οὐ γινώσκεται ὅς

ἐστιν, ἀλλ' ὅταν ἐμφανὴς καὶ ἔνδοξος γένηται, τότε γνωσθή-
σεται ὅς ἐστιν.[32] It is important also that in 49.1
Trypho connects this with the expectation of a χριστός as
ἄνθρωπος ἐξ ἀνθρώπων who is anointed κατ' ἐκλογήν by
Elijah and becomes Christ in this way. This is a conception which is also found in Christianity, as Justin tells
us (*Dialogue* 48)[33]--a view which he respects though he
does not share it.

It seems clear that John knows Jewish conceptions
like that defended by Trypho and his colleagues, and that
he opposes them because the Messiah (a) is not aware of
his own mission, (b) is dependent on Elijah for his being
revealed to men, and (c) is a mere ἄνθρωπος ἐξ ἀνθρώπων.
Of course Jesus is not ἐξ ἀνθρώπων; the Fourth Gospel is
at great pains to assert that he is ἄνωθεν, ἐκ τοῦ θεοῦ,
ἐκ τοῦ οὐρανοῦ (3:31; 8:23, 42; 16:28; 18:36) and it
stresses the fundamental opposition between heaven and
earth (see 3:31-36, 8:21-29). Therefore Jesus the Christ
cannot be dependent on Elijah; the decisive act of φανέρω-
σις is ascribed to God himself, John is only a witness.
The gift of the Spirit is set over against John's baptizing with water; the pouring out of the Spirit could have
been called anointing,[34] but then ὁ χριστός is not the
most important title in John as we have seen. And of
course it is quite inconceivable that Jesus would not have
been aware of his own mission. John the Baptist cannot
have been Elijah if his being Elijah implies the functions
ascribed to him by Trypho and his colleagues. *My hypothesis is that in the view of the Fourth Gospel calling John
Elijah did imply that.*

I realize, of course, that it is difficult to ad-
duce mid-second-century evidence in order to illustrate
the possible background of the Fourth Gospel. Yet if the
"criterion of dissimilarity" may be applied, it gives us a
strong case. Justin is certainly not dependent on the
Fourth Gospel here; he is much more explicit and uses
terms the Gospel does not use, and in *Dialogue* 88 he gives

an entirely different view on the activity of John the
Baptist though he does emphasize that John denied that he
was the Christ and identified himself with the voice crying aloud.[35] And if we ask whether Justin has christian-
ized Trypho's views, the answer must be that this is unlikely,[36] because Trypho's objections here do not really
serve Justin's argument either positively or negatively.
So, if in Justin's Dialogue we have genuine evidence for
the existence of Jewish beliefs in the middle of the second century with regard to Elijah's function in the revealing of the Messiah, it may not be too rash to conclude
that the Fourth Gospel presupposes similar notions and
criticizes them implicitly but effectively.[37]

Yet we should remember that the Jewish beliefs presupposed or expressed in John 1:19-34 and the passages in
Justin's Dialogue are found in Christian writings and
function within the context of the debate between Judaism
and Christianity. If the Fourth Gospel opposes Jewish notions it may have known them only through the medium of
written or oral tradition, the *Sitz im Leben* of which was
the Jewish-Christian debate.[38]

2. The Statement in 7:27

It is possible that the tradition of "the hidden
Messiah" is also hinted at in 7:27. We have seen that in
the two earliest forms of this tradition no stress is laid
on the place where the Messiah is hidden. In 7:27 the
central word πόθεν is clearly used in order to lead up to
Jesus' reaction. Those who think that they know where
Jesus comes from do not really know. Jesus' answer to the
πόθεν is: ἐκ τοῦ οὐρανοῦ, i.e., directly sent by the Father.[39] The objection, τοῦτον οἴδαμεν πόθεν ἐστίν, refers
to Jesus' supposed earthly origin; we may compare here 6:
42, "Surely this is Jesus son of Joseph; we know his father and his mother; how can he now say: 'I have come down
from heaven'?"[40] We cannot prove conclusively that the
statement οὐδεὶς γινώσκεται πόθεν ἐστίν refers to the

heavenly origin of the Messiah; 6:42 points in this direction and it is quite possible that the evangelist, with
his usual irony, makes the Jerusalemites think of a Messiah of the type found in 4 Ezra (and 2 Apoc. Bar.). They
expect their royal Messiah from heaven[41] and indeed that
is where Jesus comes from--only they do not realize this.
There is no reason to think that the specific form of the
tradition voiced by Trypho is presupposed here.

The essential point in both forms of the tradition
of "the hidden Messiah" was the contrast between "first
hidden"/"finally revealed."[42] In this connection we may
point to 7:3 where Jesus' unbelieving brothers urge him
φανέρωσον σεαυτὸν τῷ κόσμῳ--a fundamental misunderstanding
in John's eyes because the revelation takes place in the
world but not to the world (17:6!). We should note that
the dialectic between "openness" and "concealment" is quite
marked in chapters 7 and 8 (7:4, 10, 13, 26; 8:59). Outsiders cannot really know who Jesus is.[43]

3. The Question in 7:31

Many authors have already pointed out that according to the available Jewish evidence the Messiah is not
expected to perform miracles. There is no need to dwell
on this subject at great length, because the situation has
been summed up admirably by J. L. Martyn.[44] God's future
salvation will include miracles, and there are a few references in Josephus to wonder-workers who led crowds of
people into the wilderness and promised the occurrence of
signs, but these people are not called Messiahs. In Tan-
naitic literature the situation is not essentially different. Klausner's remark, "*The Messiah*--and this should be
carefully noted--*is never mentioned anywhere in the Tan-
naitic literature as a wonder-worker* per se," is often
quoted.[45]

Therefore we cannot escape the conclusion that the
terminology used in 7:31 is Christian;[46] we should remember that the statement is said to be made by many people

from the crowd *who began to believe in Jesus*! In the NT
we may point first of all to Matt 11:2-6 (par. Luke 7:18-
23) where Jesus' reference to his miracles in his message
to John the Baptist is placed under the heading τὰ ἔργα
τοῦ χριστοῦ.[47] Next there is Mark 13:22 (par. Matt 24:24)
where σημεῖα καὶ τέρατα are ascribed both to pseudo-
Messiahs and pseudo-prophets (cf. 2 Thess 2:9).[48] Martyn
points out "that the figures expected by Jews to play
roles in the eschatological future...were allowed to coa-
lesce in the most varied ways,"[49] and he assumes that
"prophetic elements" have been connected with the figure
of the Messiah. In the second part of his book he assumes
that the debate between Church and Synagogue centered on
the notion of "the expectation of the Prophet-Messiah"
like Moses as opposed to that of "the presence of the Son
of Man."

Now Martyn is right in emphasizing the merging of
various messianic conceptions in Jewish expectation,[50] in
11QMelch 18 we have even explicit proof that a prophetic
figure could be called "anointed by the Spirit."[51] In the
Fourth Gospel, however, the prophet and the Messiah are
kept separate--also in one of the following episodes in
this same chapter, 7:40-44! The notion of a prophet like
Moses is often in the background where Jesus' signs are
mentioned (most notably in 3:2, chapter 6, chapter 9) but
the only text which connects σημεῖα with the designation
ὁ χριστός is the central statement, 20:30. There, as we
have seen, the statement of 7:31 is supplemented and corrected by the assertion that Jesus is the Christ, *the Son
of God.*[52]

Our conclusion must be that the Fourth Gospel refers here to the views of sympathizing Jews which it corrects further on. Because, however, the terminology used
by these Jews is Christian, we may just as well say that
the Fourth Gospel refers here to the views of Christians
of Jewish descent which it criticizes.[53]

4.   The Debate in 7:40-44

This pericope has been mentioned several times already. I have tried to show that the Gospel itself regards the problems raised here as superficial; they are not concerned with the real issue because they are dealt with on an earthly level. Yet the evangelist evidently assumes that objections against Jesus' Messiahship were raised on account of doubts concerning his Davidic descent and his coming from Bethlehem. Now--as many others have pointed out--it is not in the least difficult to find evidence for the Davidic descent of the royal Messiah,[54] but the statement that the Messiah comes from David's village Bethlehem presents us with difficulties. The key passage often quoted here is Targ. Mic. 5:1,[55] which connects the appearance of the Messiah with Bethlehem. This passage is, of course, also quoted by commentators in connection with Matt 2:6, where parts of Mic. 5:1 and 3 are adduced in connection with the birthplace of the Messiah by "the chief priests and the scribes of the people." Matt 2:5, 6 point to an early date of the tradition preserved in the Targum and, on the other hand, this targumic tradition proves that Matthew could be aware of the existence of such a view in Judaism. Yet it is impossible to prove that John in 7:42, 43 shows knowledge of Jewish views about the Messiah's coming from Bethlehem apart from what he knew of the arguments put forward in the Jewish-Christian debate. It is clear that, by assigning to 7:40-44 the place in the structure of chapter 7 which he did assign to it, he not only indicates that an inner-Jewish discussion of prophethood and messiahship connected with Jesus does not penetrate into the real secret of Jesus' mission, but also that the matter of Jesus' Davidic descent and the question of his birthplace are not of essential importance. We should not overlook that this implicit criticism is not only concerned with Jewish contributions to the Jewish-Christian debate, either negative, hesitant or positive, but also with those Christians who

try to counter the arguments put forward in 7:44 on the
level of their opponents.[56]

This does not mean, of course, that the Fourth
Gospel would deny that texts from Scripture can be quoted
as proof. It quotes them often and the Johannine Jesus
tells quite clearly that "the Scriptures witness to him"
(5:39). The Gospel also shows acquaintance with typical
Jewish argumentation--see for example the midrashic exposition in the discourse on the Bread in chapter 6 or the
reasoning in accordance with the Jewish principle of *qal-
waḥomer* in 7:19 (to mention only a few examples in the
immediate neighborhood of our passage). And yet, if
Scripture is not read and interpreted with the center of
Johannine theology as starting-point, one will never discover the truth revealed by God. That is why not only
hostile but also sympathetic Jews are considered outsiders, and why Christians who use Jewish arguments from
a wrong starting-point are subject to John's criticism.
It is clear that John is critical towards argumentation
regarding Bethlehem as Jesus' birthplace, his Davidic descent and his divine Sonship as this is found in the birth-
stories in Matthew and Luke. By such an approach one will
never reach the heart of the matter.

5. The Objection in 12:34

The question asked by the crowd in 12:34 is really
an objection. It is not answered and is clearly inserted
here in order to show how little the people who listened
to Jesus understood what he meant. The sentence πῶς λέγεις
σὺ ὅτι δεῖ ὑψωθῆναι τὸν υἱὸν τοῦ ἀνθρώπου; does not bear
upon any statement by Jesus in the immediate context,
though he has stated in vs. 23, ἐλήλυθεν ἡ ὥρα ἵνα δοξασθῇ
ὁ υἱὸς τοῦ ἀνθρώπου, and has spoken of his being lifted up
(ὑψωθῶ) from the earth. There is a clear reference to
3:14, οὕτως ὑψωθῆναι δεῖ τὸν υἱὸν τοῦ ἀνθρώπου, and a less
clear one to 8:28. Putting 12:34 directly behind 8:28-29[57]
does not give any solution; 12:34 is not intended to

function within a coherent picture of a debate between
Jesus and people from the crowd--it serves as a further
clarification of Johannine christology directed at the
reader of the Gospel. In 12:31-33 Jesus explains the true
meaning of his ὑψωθῆναι: it is connected with the victory
over ὁ ἄρχων τοῦ κόσμου τούτου, it means that he will draw
all people unto him and, paradoxically, it means death on
the cross (18:32).[58]

The people in the crowd are not able to follow him.
They appeal to Scripture[59] which says that the Messiah is
to remain for ever; the nearest scriptural parallel to be
found is Ps 89:37, as Van Unnik has shown,[60] but we do not
find here a direct quotation. Like 7:42, this text gives
a general statement about expectations connected with the
king to be born from the seed of David. The crowd does
not explicitly connect the Messiah-title with Jesus, but
the evangelist, after 7:42 and 10:24, clearly implies that
it means to say: If one is to think of you as the Messiah
and if Scripture tells us clearly that the Messiah remains
for ever, how can you say that the Son of Man must be
lifted up? The crowd is aware of the fact that Jesus refers to himself when he uses the expression "Son of Man,"
and evidently regards ὑψωθῆναι as the opposite of μένειν
εἰς τὸν αἰῶνα--whatever it is supposed to understand exactly. The question therefore is not only, How can you
say that?, but also, Whom do you mean if you cannot mean
yourself?, τίς ἐστιν οὗτος ὁ υἱὸς τοῦ ἀνθρώπου;[61]

At this point of our investigations, a full discussion of the "Son of Man" problem would be desirable, though
I doubt whether it could really shed much light on our
text. John wants to make clear that the Jewish Messiah-
concept is fixed--it is connected with the expectation of
the Davidic King. "Son of Man" is only used by Jesus himself,[62] and to the Jews who refer to it in 12:34 this expression does not convey a clear picture. They ask, What
do you mean and whom do you mean--didn't you mean yourself?
In Jewish literature we find a number of cases where the

expressions Messiah and "Son of Man" occur together, but
the combination is brought about in different ways[63] and
we cannot speak of any fixed concept. The nearest parallel is--again--provided by Justin's *Dialogus cum Tryphone*
where Trypho, in 32.1, speaks of the expectation of "one
who is great and glorious, and takes over the everlasting
kingdom from the Ancient of Days as Son of Man." Trypho
implies that this one is the Messiah, for he goes on, "But
this your so-called Christ is without honour and glory, so
that He has even fallen into the uttermost curse that is
in the Law of God, for he was crucified."[64] Trypho clearly
uses expressions taken from the Son of Man chapter in Dan-
iel as illustrations for the coming of the Messiah. It is
by no means certain that the Fourth Gospel presupposes the
presence of such ideas in the minds of the interlocutors
of the crowd. It is only interested in Jesus' singular
use of the expression "Son of Man" and in the fundamental
difference between his teaching and current expectations
connected with the Messiah.

6. Some Conclusions

Our further study of the passages concerned has, I
think, brought out a few things very clearly.

(a) Not only are these statements entirely subordi-
nate to a clearer exposition of Johannine christology--
this was already clear in the use made of them in chapter
7 and has now become evident also in our analysis of 1:19-
34--but also the very terminology put into the mouth of
Jewish interlocutors often has a Johannine flavor. So the
πόθεν in 7:27 leads up to the typically Johannine statement which follows; in 12:34 the traditional Messiah-
concept comes out clearly, but no possible connections between this view on the Messiah and Jewish exegesis of Dan
7:13-14, 27. In 1:26 there is at least a typical Johannine ambiguity.

(b) Consequently these statements of "Johannine
Jews" add little or nothing to our knowledge of Jewish

expectations concerning the Messiah known from other
sources. Where there is disagreement in wording or conception there is always Johannine influence to be considered. Comparison with non-Johannine material proved to be
useful, because it brought out more clearly what the
Fourth Gospel wanted to emphasize; this is equally true of
the passages where direct parallels were found and of
those where the Jewish statements in the Fourth Gospel
have obviously been adapted to serve its purpose better.

We should note that the tradition concerning the
hidden Messiah, attributed by Justin to Trypho and other
Jewish teachers, was shown to exist before the middle of
the second century, because the Fourth Gospel presupposes
and opposes it.

(c) It became clear that the Fourth Gospel criticizes earlier Christian thinking, for example that concerning the σημεῖα--see 7:31 as compared with 20:30, 31.
In 7:40-44 and 1:19-34 there is reason to think of a reaction of the Fourth Gospel on issues in earlier or contem-
porary Christian-Jewish controversies.[65] In both cases it
brings out its own theological viewpoint very clearly, not
only in opposition to current Jewish beliefs but, in the
case of 12:42, also with clear implicit criticism of other
Christian attempts to answer this Jewish objection.

IV. Some Remarks on the Purpose of the Fourth Gospel

1. R. Schnackenburg's treatment of the messianic
question in the Gospel of John ends with a discussion of
the implications of our views on Johannine christology for
our view on the purpose of the Gospel. Against W. C. van
Unnik and John A. T. Robinson, who advocate the theory of
the Fourth Gospel as a missionary document, he defends the
thesis that the Fourth Gospel was written for inner-Church
use.[66] Its primary concern is with the christological
self-revelation of Jesus and it wants to show all aspects
and implications of that revelation. A secondary aim will
have been to fortify Christians of Jewish descent in their

faith by showing them what they could reply to objections
raised by the Jews outside the Church--and the same applies to non-Jewish Christians who are confronted with
Jewish opposition. The present investigation leads to the
same conclusion (see particularly section II. and conclusion (a) in III. 6). Schnackenburg also rightly emphasizes
that the objections are not just literary "inventions"
used solely to carry the debate a step further--like so
many other instances of misunderstanding in the Fourth
Gospel. They have that function but they do take into account existing differences of opinion in the Jewish-
Christian debate at the time.

   2. As I tried to show in Chapter I, the Fourth
Gospel is not only written for inner-Church use, it also
presupposes the community of believers as the place where
true insight and real knowledge are granted, preserved and
deepened through the activity of the Spirit. This is emphasized very strongly in chapters 13-17 which occupy an
important place in the present Gospel. Within the community of believers the true "view" on the facts of Jesus'
life, death and glorification is communicated, the true
interpretation of his words is given, and consequently
also the right interpretation of Scripture (see, apart
from the so-called "Paraclete-passages," also 21:22; 12:
16, 17; 20:9). In chapters 1-12, true believers are mentioned besides and over against unbelievers. Faith is the
unconditional acceptance of Jesus as the One who is sent
by the Father (see, for example, 5:36-38, 6:29). Only
very seldom do we find explicit reflection on the question
why certain people (among these "the disciples" and "the
twelve") were able to accept Jesus and others rejected
him. In the last resort, faith is a gift from God, believers are dependent on the divine initiative (1:12, 13;
3:3, 5, 8--here again the Spirit is mentioned!--6:37, 44,
65). The "twelve," who do not leave Jesus unlike so many
other disciples (6:60-71), have been chosen by Jesus (vs.
70).

The Gospel was written from the point of view of
the community of believers led by the Spirit. It, no
doubt, intends to present the truth to the entire Church
and on behalf of the entire Church. Yet the results
reached above in sections II. and III. compel us to say
that the Fourth Gospel *de facto* presents the theology of a
particular group within the Church. Here I agree fully
with W. A. Meeks' important article "The Man from Heaven
in Johannine Sectarianism,"[67] who calls the Fourth Gospel
a book for insiders who belong to the Johannine community.
"One of the primary functions of the book, therefore, must
have been to provide a reinforcement for the community's
social identity..." he writes.[68] I am not sure that Meeks
is right when he supposes that this social identity was
largely negative, but I do agree with him that theological
and social identity presuppose one another and that Johannine theology is a typical in-group theology. Meeks follows J. L. Martyn who has shown "that the actual trauma of
the Johannine community's separation from the synagogue
and its continuing hostile relationships with the synagogue come clearly to expression here."[69] But I doubt
whether this is quite true. Of course, Meeks is right
when he thinks that for the Fourth Gospel the true faith
in Jesus presupposes membership of the Johannine community
and breaking away from the world, particularly the world
of Judaism--but the actual situation must have been more
complicated.

3. I differ from Schnackenburg and Meeks, in that
I would put more emphasis on the fact that Johannine
christology is developed not only in contrast with Jewish
thinking but also with other christological views. The
Johannine community does not only assert its identity by
pondering over the true reason for its being separated
from the synagogue and by developing christological motifs
in explanation of that; it also tries to formulate its own
standpoint over against christological discussions in the
Church, particularly over against Christian arguments adduced in the debate between Christians and Jews.

Moreover, the fact that the interlocutors remain vague (II. 2) and that there is no real discussion on christological issues (II. 3) combined with the Gospel's criticism of current Christian argumentation shows, I think, that the Gospel gives theological reflection on the real issues in the debate between Christians and Jews rather than provides arguments in an acute struggle.[70] The very emphasis on the typical Johannine christology which is sometimes set off against Jewish objections but more often is developed quite independently (though presupposing [other] Jewish ways of thought)[71] also points in that direction. In this connection it should be remembered that "the Jews" in the Fourth Gospel are not only Jews, but also typical representatives of the outside world, of "*the* World."[72] No doubt the Fourth Gospel was written in a particular situation, but not necessarily *for* that situation; it wants to stress the essential points.[73]

4. A few concluding remarks about texts referring to people who reacted favorably to Jesus' preaching, at least in the beginning (see II. 2, end), but who are criticized severely and regarded as outsiders[74] may make my position a bit clearer. They are all Jews, there is no doubt about that; but one might ask whether we should call them Jewish sympathizers or Jewish Christians. In many of the instances listed under II. 2 the Gospel uses the expression πιστεύω εἰς (αὐτόν, τὸ ὄνομα αὐτοῦ, τὸν ᾿Ιησοῦν) and this is the expression also used for the real Christian faith.[75] Joseph of Arimathea is called a μαθητὴς [τοῦ] ᾿Ιησοῦ (19:38) though in secret, because he was afraid of the Jews. This added phrase rules him out as a true believer as 12:42-43 shows unmistakably. The same applies to Nicodemus, his companion at the burial of Jesus (19:38-42). Though sympathetic towards Jesus and coming to him with a statement of faith, the discussion in 3:1-21 shows him as a man who cannot understand and does not believe the real secret of Jesus' mission. He belongs to the group mentioned in 2:23-25 consisting of believers to

whom Jesus would not trust himself. Now the Gospel's references to Nicodemus *cum suis*, Joseph and other Jewish
leaders[76] all come under the verdict expressed in 12:42-
43. Notwithstanding the use of πιστεύω and μαθητής *we*
would call them sympathizing Jews. The same applies to
the enthusiastic crowd in 6:1-15 which hails Jesus as "the
prophet who was coming into the world" but is shown to
have only an imperfect understanding of his real being.
The discourse on the Bread, and particularly vss. 60-71
following it, bring to light that much faith in Jesus was
not real faith; many of Jesus' disciples leave him. Are
we to think of the people mentioned in vss. 60-71 (cf. 7:3)
as Jewish Christians and distinct from the sympathizers in
vss. 1-15?[77] And what about the crowds impressed by what
happened to Lazarus and hailing Jesus when he entered
Jerusalem (11:45; 12:11, 18)? In 7:31 we are inclined to
call the people who speak about the signs of the Messiah
Jewish Christians because of their Christian terminology.
In 8:30-31 this would also be right, I think. Here we
have people who have come to believe in Jesus and who are
admonished to remain in his word (cf. 5:38; 15:7, 14) in
order that they may truly be disciples of Jesus. I am not
going into the particular difficulty caused by the fact
that there is no indication of a change of scene after vss.
30-32, so that in the present set-up of the Gospel the
vehement debate between Jesus and the Jews before vs. 30
goes on after vs. 32 between Jesus and Jewish Christians.[78]

       Whatever the solution of this problem may be, I
think that the very confused picture which emerges from
our rather rapid survey of these passages shows that our
approach is wrong. Only one thing is certain: all these
people are outsiders, they do not really understand Jesus,
their faith is, therefore, imperfect and insufficient; they
do not belong to the group of true believers. Seen from
the standpoint of the Johannine group and its theology,
there is no real difference between sympathizing Jews and
Jewish Christians if the latter are still thinking along

what what the Fourth Gospel considers to be purely Jewish
lines.[79] The vagueness of the Fourth Gospel's description
of Jewish groups corresponds with its vagueness in describing non-Johannine Christianity of Jewish descent.
Everything in the Gospel is centered on its consistent and
persistent search for the right terms and conceptions to
express the truth about Jesus the Son of God, the Son of
Man.

APPENDIX

In 4:25, a representative Samaritan statement concerning the coming of the Messiah is recorded. An encounter between Jesus and the Samaritans is stated in order to confront Jesus' message with typical Samaritan beliefs.

The attitude of the Samaritans towards Jesus is, at
least at the end, very friendly--as vss. 39-42 show. And
Jesus' reply to the statement οἶδα ὅτι Μεσσίας ἔρχεται...
ὅταν ἔλθῃ ἐκεῖνος, ἀναγγελεῖ ἡμῖν ἅπαντα is positive. In
fact, he declares ἐγώ εἰμι, ὁ λαλῶν σοι. Is it because of
the addition "he will announce all things to us" that Jesus accepts this title for himself--whatever overtones ἐγώ
εἰμι may have because of its use further on in this Gospel?

This is not the place to give a full analysis of 4:
1-42, but some remarks can be made which may, perhaps,
carry the problem a little further.[80] The woman's reaction, "I see that you are a prophet," in vs. 19 and the
statement concerning the Messiah in vs. 25 are reactions
to previous teaching of Jesus--about the life-giving water
as a gift of God (vss. 10-15) and about the woman's personal life (vss. 16-17) and to Jesus' discourse on
worship in spirit and truth (vss. 19-24). Here we do not
find Jesus directly or indirectly reacting to statements
made by the other partners in the discussion, he conducts
the discussion in his own terms and is interrupted by remarks made by the Samaritan woman. It is interesting to
note that she is portrayed as being able to say "you are

a (true) prophet," but does not identify Jesus as the Messiah. It is Jesus who has to disclose himself as such (cf. 9:37, 10:25). And even after this the woman does not go any further than a hesitating, "Could this be the Messiah?" (vs. 29). Next, we should note that neither prophet nor Messiah is the final title used in this section. The Samaritans who have come to believe--after the woman's words about Jesus' disclosure of her past and present--and who have deepened their faith and insight in the course of a two-day stay of Jesus in their village, finally profess their faith in the words, "We have heard him ourselves and we know that he is the Saviour of the World" (vs. 42). These Samaritans, one would say, are at least at the same level as the disciples of 1:35-51 who stayed with Jesus (vs. 39) and were convinced by his teaching. Yet these disciples appear on the scene, after the woman has run off to her village and before the villagers profess their faith, in order to receive inside information in a special conversation with Jesus. They need it, because they misunderstand completely a word of Jesus concerning the food he has to eat, but they receive it and Jesus' instruction introduces a theme which will be developed further in chapter 6. The essential expression here is "to do the will of him who sent me" which also recurs several times in the Gospel. In 5:30-36, 6:38-40, it becomes clear that the unity of will between Jesus and the One who sent him is the unity of will between Son and Father.

Somehow the Samaritans (of whom we hear nothing further on in the Gospel) do not belong to the inner circle of οἱ μαθηταί who receive special instruction and accompany Jesus on his travels, receiving further initiation in the true nature of his message and mission, including that given in the Farewell Discourses (chapters 13-17) announcing the guidance of the Spirit after Jesus' glorification. In any case, "Messiah" is not the final title and the woman who uses it does not fully grasp the real meaning of this designation as applied to Jesus.

Returning to 4:25f., we cannot deny that Jesus accepts here the title Messiah as a self-designation. He does so, however, inclusive of the phrase ἀναγγελεῖ ἡμῖν ἅπαντα and, clearly, with his own interpretation of the term Messiah and of this additional phrase, as the context of the chapter shows. Commentators usually do not discuss the meaning of this ὅταν ἔλθῃ ἐκεῖνος, ἀναγγελεῖ ἡμῖν ἅπαντα in the context of the Fourth Gospel, because they are anxious to compare 4:25 with known Samaritan concepts. W. A. Meeks,[81] however, rightly points to 13:19, 18:4, 14:29, and 16:4 where Jesus announces what is surely to come. Meeks regards this as a sign of prophetic authenticity to be viewed against the background of Deut 18:18-22.[82] Jesus is more than a prophet, but what is essential for prophecy is also essential for his teaching.

This, of course, leads to the question whether the Samaritans are rightly depicted as expecting a "prophetic Messiah." Here we are confronted with a difficult situation. Much has been written lately on the Samaritans and their beliefs. I should like to mention above all J. Macdonald's *The Theology of the Samaritans*,[83] the fifth chapter, "Moses as King and Prophet in Samaritan Sources," in W. A. Meeks' *The Prophet-King*[84] and, most recently, H. G. Kippenberg, *Garizim und Synagoge. Traditionsgeschichtliche Untersuchungen zur samaritanischen Religion der aramaischen Periode.*[85] However, the non-specialist notes with regret that there is no agreement between the specialists with regard to their views on Samaritan eschatological beliefs in the first century A.D. Nearly all our sources are much later and evidently it is not easy to decide which traditions are old and which not. At one point there is no disagreement--the title משיח is not used in Samaritan sources before the sixteenth century.[86] W. A. Meeks is right, therefore, in saying "that the title Μεσσίας has even been put in the mouth of the Samaritan woman (4:25) is a clear sign of the levelling of different terminologies."[87] But if John is guilty here of "levelling the

different terminologies," like Justin Martyr after him who
tells us that both Jews and Samaritans expect τὸν χριστόν,[88]
he did so in order to show that Jesus fulfilled Jewish and
Samaritan expectations.

It is also clear that the expectation of the Prophet
like Moses occupied a very important place in Samaritanism,
because the Samaritan Pentateuch adds Deut 5:28-29, 18:18-
22, and 5:30-31 immediately after Exod 20:21, that is, after the Decalogue. There are indications that this expectation is early.[89] Do we have to connect this with John
4:19 or with 4:25? Kippenberg connects it with vs. 19[90]
but overlooks the fact that in 4:19 the article is omitted.
Jesus is called *a* prophet (and of course a real, *true* prophet is meant) but not *the* prophet who is always called ὁ
προφήτης.[91] If there is any connection between the Samaritan expectation of *the* prophet and John's presentation of
it, we should look to 4:25 and assume that it was John who
introduced the term "Messiah," while adding the "prophetic"
phrase ἀναγγελεῖ ἡμῖν ἅπαντα.[92]

Traditions regarding the coming of Moses and the
Taheb are very variegated and it is not quite clear how
they are interrelated and connected with the expectation
of the Mosaic prophet;[93] consequently, there is also difference of opinion as to the earliest form of these expectations. H. G. Kippenberg states quite clearly: The
Taheb is simply the prototype of those who return (to the
Lord) and who receive God's compassion. The Taheb is a
"vague" figure and that is the reason why so many different traditions could be connected with it--also prophetic
and Mosaic notions. It remains to be asked, however,
whether Kippenberg's result--originally strictly divided
concepts of prophet like Moses and Taheb, and the return
of Moses only as an anti-Dosithean variant of the former
one[94]--is not due to his method. His "Traditionsgeschichte"
is mainly a "Begriffsgeschichte" and he presupposes evidently a development from simplicity to complexity.[95] This
presupposition may well be wrong; Samaritan expectation may

have been far more complex right from the beginning than
Kippenberg thinks. If this is true, the background of
John 4:25 may well be more complex too--it may be of im-
portance that we find no less than three times in Memar
Marqa that the Taheb "will reveal the truth."[96]

Finally, it may be remarked that 4:21-24 dealing
with true worship may be a reaction to Samaritan beliefs
regarding the restoration of the true worship on Mount
Gerizim. Here we have the well-known story in Josephus'
Ant. 18.85-89 about a Samaritan "uprising" under Pilate.
In the background, there is the expectation that in future
the Mosaic tabernacle would be restored on Mount Gerizim.[97]
In the story told by Josephus, there is a connection with
Moses-traditions and the leader of the action is a Moses-
like figure.

NOTES

CHAPTER IV

[1]Most of the points raised in this section are dealt with in Chapters II and III.

[2]R. Schnackenburg, *The Gospel according to St John* I, Herder's Theological Commentary on the New Testament (New York: Herder and Herder; London: Burns & Oates, 1968), pp. 507-14, Excursus III, "The Titles of Jesus in John 1." See also his "Die Messiasfrage im Johannesevangelium," in *Neutestamentliche Aufsätze* (Festschrift J. Schmid) (Regensburg: F. Pustet, 1963), pp. 240-64.

[3]See further the Appendix to this chapter.

[4]See esp. Schnackenburg, "Die Messiasfrage," pp. 249-52, and C. H. Dodd, *The Interpretation of the Fourth Gospel* (Cambridge: Cambridge University Press, 1953), pp. 89-92 and p. 346, where Dodd says, "The evangelist has brought together here most of what he has to say in reply to Jewish objections against the messianic claims made for Jesus."

[5]See also M. de Jonge, "Onbegrip in Jeruzalem. Jezus en de Joden in Johannes 7," *Rondom het Woord* 15 (1973), pp. 61-80.

[6]Cf., for example, the alternation between οἱ Ἰουδαῖοι (vss. 18, 22) and οἱ Φαρισαῖοι (vss. 13, 15, 16, 40) in chapter 9.

[7]See also Chapter II and section IV. 4 of the present chapter.

[8]κράζω occurs also in 7:28, 1:15, and 12:44. It is used especially of inspired utterances; see R. Bultmann, *The Gospel of John* (Philadelphia: Westminster, 1971), p. 75, n. 1, who refers to Rom 8:15, 9:27; Gal 4:6.

[9]See further Chapter III, and "Onbegrip in Jeruzalem," mentioned in n. 5, above.

[10]W. A. Meeks, "The Man from Heaven in Johannine Sectarianism," *JBL* 91 (1972), pp. 44-72.

[11]See Chapter III.

[12]See Schnackenburg, "Die Messiasfrage," pp. 240-44, 254-56, and M. de Jonge, "The Use of the Word ΧΡΙΣΤΟΣ in

108

the Johannine Epistles," in *Studies in John* presented to
Professor Dr. J. N. Sevenster, NovTSup 24 (Leiden: Brill,
1970), pp. 66-74, esp. 71-74. In 1:17 and 17:3, the expression ʾΙησοῦς Χριστός occurs, both times in a context
which emphasizes the unity between Father and Son.

[13]The title "Son of God" is exactly like the one we
would expect in 1:34, and therefore it is likely to be
original. On the other hand, it can be argued that the
unusual ἐκλεκτός (variant found in ℵ*, some Old Latin and
the two Old Syrian versions and in Ambrose) was changed
into the more familiar υἱὸς τοῦ θεοῦ. See also Chapter
III, n. 7.

[14]Cf. 4:25. See Appendix to this chapter.

[15]A useful survey of recent opinion is found in
chapter 5, "John the Baptist in the Fourth Gospel," in
Walter Wink's *John the Baptist in the Gospel Tradition*,
SNTSMS 7 (London: Cambridge University Press, 1968), pp.
87-106.

[16]It is not clear whether in the present text vs. 24
refers back to vs. 19 or introduces a new deputation. On
theories of interpretation and redaction regarding vss. 22-
24, see Schnackenburg, *The Gospel according to St John* I,
pp. 280-81, and R. E. Brown, *The Gospel according to John
(i-xii)*, The Anchor Bible 29 (Garden City, NY: Doubleday,
1966), pp. 67-71.

[17]Wink, *John the Baptist in the Gospel Tradition*,
pp. 105-6, calls μαρτυρεῖ in 1:15 and ἀπεσταλμένος·εἰμι "a
timeless present"; cf. the use of the perfect in 1:34 and
5:33; see also R. Schnackenburg, *Das Johannesevangelium* II,
Herders Theologischer Kommentar zum Neuen Testament
(Freiburg-Basel-Wien: Herder, 1971), p. 172, on vss. 33-35.

[18]Verse 37 does not introduce a new μαρτυρία but
refers back to vs. 36 and to the opening statement in vss.
31-32; see Schnackenburg, *Das Johannesevangelium* II, p. 174.

[19]Of course John was not a real "forerunner," because the one whom he announces was already before him and
is, therefore, higher in rank (see 1:15, 27, 30).

[20]See also 3:27, a general statement clearly referring to the special case of Jesus.

[21]Cf. also Luke 3:15 and Acts 13:25.

[22]See Chapter III.

[23]So, e.g., J. A. T. Robinson, "Elijah, John and
Jesus. An Essay in Detection," *NTS* 4 (1957-58), pp. 263-
81, esp. p. 270.

[24] See especially G. Richter, "Bist du Elias? Joh. i.21," *BZ*, Neue Folge 6 (1962), pp. 79-92, 238-56; and 7 (1963), pp. 63-80. On possible parallels from Qumran, see *BZ* 6 (1962), pp. 85-92; on other possible Jewish parallels according to which Elijah might stand on the same level as the Messiah and the Prophet, see *BZ* 7 (1963), pp. 70-76. In both cases, no evidence is adduced which helps us to understand 1:20-22.

[25] So, e.g., Wink, *John the Baptist in the Gospel Tradition*, pp. 89-90, following C. K. Barrett and R. E. Brown.

[26] See 1:49 and 12:13, where Jesus is called ὁ βασιλεὺς τοῦ ᾿Ισραήλ; cf. Nathanael as ἀληθῶς ᾿Ισραηλίτης, and 3:10, Nicodemus as ὁ διδάσκαλος τοῦ ᾿Ισραήλ (who, because of this position, should know better).

[27] Erik Sjöberg, *Der verborgene Menschensohn in den Evangelien* (Lund: Gleerup, 1955), pp. 41-98; see also Str-B 2, pp. 339-40, 488-89; E. Stauffer, "Agnostos Christos. Joh. ii 24 und die Eschatologie des vierten Evangeliums," in *The Background of the New Testament and its Eschatology*, ed. W. D. Davies and D. Daube (Cambridge: Cambridge University Press, 1954, [2]1964), pp. 281-99, and U. B. Müller, *Messias und Menschensohn in jüdischen Apokalypsen und in der Offenbarung des Johannes*, SNT 6 (Gütersloh: Mohn, 1972), pp. 147-54.

[28] See 1 Enoch 48:6-7; 62:7; 2 Apoc. Bar. 29:3; 39:7; 73:1; 4 Ezra 7:28; 12:32; 13:26, 32, 52; 14:9. Müller, *Messias und Menschensohn*, p. 152, sees a difference between 1 Enoch (emphasis on a special heavenly abode and preexistence before creation of the Son of Man) and 4 Ezra (emphasis on "preservation" of the Messiah, expressing the fact that what is going to happen is determined by God). See also M. de Jonge, art. χρίω, κτλ., *TDNT* 9, p. 516.

[29] A third, and later, conception that the Messiah lives on earth, knowing who he is but awaiting God's time, need not occupy us here.

[30] So, e.g., Sjöberg, *Der verborgene Menschensohn*, pp. 44-51, 54-56.

[31] See Str-B 4.2, pp. 779-98; J. Jeremias, art. ᾿Ηλ(ε)ίας, *TDNT* 2, pp. 928-41; and Richter, "Bist du Elias? Joh. i.21," *BZ* Neue Folge 7, pp. 70-76.

[32] Cf. Justin, *Apol.* 35.1--ὡς δὲ καὶ λήσειν ἔμελλε τοὺς ἄλλους ἀνθρώπους γεννηθεὶς ὁ χριστὸς ἄχρις ἀνδρωθῇ, ὅπερ καὶ γέγονεν, ἀκούσατε.... Compare also the relation between David and Samuel in Ps. Philo, *Lib. Ant.* 59.4, "et cum veniret propheta non clamaverunt me et quando nominatus est christus obliti sunt me."

[33]See also *Dial.* 67.2.

[34]In Luke 4:18 and Acts 10:38, Jesus is portrayed as the Anointed by the Spirit; see further M. de Jonge and A. S. van der Woude, "11Q Melchizedek and the New Testament," *NTS* 12 (1965-66), pp. 301-26, esp. pp. 309-12, and the literature mentioned there. 1:26-27 and 1:31-33 compare a baptism with the Spirit and one with water; here John clearly uses an earlier Christian tradition in his own way. In 1:25 a connection is made between baptism and the coming of the Messiah, Elijah, of the Prophet--Jews are the speakers here, and no clear parallels have yet been found (Richter, "Bist du Elias? Joh. i.21," *BZ* Neue Folge 7, p. 67: "Die Vorstellung einer messianischen Taufe ist bis jetzt nicht bezeugt..."). In any case, no connection is made between baptism and anointing; cf., however, Luke 3:16 after 3:15.

[35]See *Dial.* 88.7, combining references to John 1:20, 23 and Matt 3:11. In *Dial.* 49 the conception of two advents of the Christ is combined with that of two advents of Elijah. The Spirit of God which was in Elijah was also in John (49.3 and 49.6, 7; cf. Luke 1:17).

[36]See esp. Sjöberg, *Der verborgene Menschensohn*, p. 82. On the general question of the reliability of Justin's *Dialogue* as source for Jewish belief, see A. von Harnack, *Judentum und Judenchristentum in Justins Dialog mit Trypho*, TU 39.1 (Leipzig: Hinrichs, 1913), pp. 47-98, esp. pp. 54 and 61-78.

[37]A polemical attitude toward followers of John the Baptist may also have been of importance for the shaping of this section of the Gospel, but it should not be overrated (so Wink, *John the Baptist in the Gospel Tradition*, pp. 98-105). In our case it is important to note that there is no evidence that the Johannine sect ever regarded John as Elijah (so also Brown, *The Gospel according to John (i-xii)*, pp. 47-48).

[38]It may be useful to emphasize a few points in Justin's argumentation in chapter 48. At Trypho's remarks that he considers it strange and even foolish to believe προϋπάρχειν θεὸν ὄντα πρὸ αἰώνων τοῦτον τὸν χριστόν (§1), Justin replies that the matter seems to be strange especially to those of Trypho's race, who prefer to believe and to practice what "your teachers" teach rather than what God asks (τὰ τῶν διδασκάλων ὑμῶν--τὰ τοῦ θεοῦ, implicit reference to Isa 29:13; cf. Matt 15:9) (§2). Also with regard to Jewish Christians who maintain that the Christ is an ἄνθρωπος ἐξ ἀνθρώπων, he states that the Christ himself commanded not to follow ἀνθρωπείοις διδάγμασι, but τοῖς διὰ τῶν μακαρίων προφητῶν κηρυχθεῖσι καὶ δι' αὐτοῦ διδαχθεῖσι (§4). Yet Justin concedes that Divine Sonship, including preexistence and virgin birth, are not

necessary prerequisites for Messiahship. One cannot deny that Jesus is the Christ--ἐὰν φαίνηται ὡς ἄνθρωπος ἐξ ἀνθρώπων γεννηθείς, καὶ ἐκλογὴ γενόμενος εἰς τὸν χριστὸν εἶναι ἀποδεικνύηται.

[39]See, again, 3:31-36; 8:14, 21-29; 9:29-30.

[40]In the background of 6:42 and 7:27, we may suppose the tradition preserved in Mark 6:1-6 (par. Matt 13: 53-58; cf. Luke 4:15-30). See also Mark 11:27-30 (par. Matt 21:23-27, Luke 20:1-8). In John, however, this is entirely recast in terms of the ascent-descent theme--on which see Meeks, "The Man from Heaven in Johannine Sectarianism," esp. pp. 59-60, where he assumes the influence of Jewish Wisdom myths on the conception of the apostolic prophet.

[41]The principal texts are listed in n. 28, above.

[42]See p. 88, above.

[43]In 1 Enoch, 48:6, 7 and 62:7 speak of a revelation of the hidden Son of Man to the holy and righteous (elect). It is not clear whether this revelation takes place at the end of timè or at an earlier period; see Müller, *Messias und Menschensohn*, pp. 47-51, against Sjöberg, *Der verborgene Menschensohn*, p. 46.

[44]J. L. Martyn, *History and Theology in the Fourth Gospel* (New York-Evanston: Harper & Row, 1968), pp. 81-88.

[45]J. Klausner, *The Messianic Idea in Israel*, trans. W. F. Stinespring (New York: Macmillan, 1955), p. 506, quoted, e.g., by Martyn, *History and Theology in the Fourth Gospel*, p. 506, and by F. Hahn, *Christologische Hoheitstitel* (Göttingen: Vandenhoeck & Ruprecht, 1963), p. 360, n. 2.

[46]So Schnackenburg, *Das Johannesevangelium* II, pp. 205-6.

[47]One should note that the question is σὺ εἶ ὁ ἐρχόμενος; (also in Luke 7:19).

[48]Miracles are also connected with the Son of David (Mark 10:46-52, par. Matt 20:29-34; Matt 9:27-31; 12:22-24; 15:21-28; 21:14-16). This tradition is to be explained differently; there seems to be a connection with Solomon, cf. Wis 7:17-21; Josephus, *Ant.* 8.44-49; Testament of Solomon. Contra Chr. Burger, *Jesus als Davidssohn: eine traditionsgeschichtliche Untersuchung*, FRLANT 98 (Göttingen: Vandenhoeck & Ruprecht, 1970). See K. Berger, "Die königlichen Messiastraditionen des Neuen Testaments," *NTS* 20 (1973-74), pp. 1-44.

[49]Martyn, *History and Theology in the Fourth Gospel*, pp. 87-88.

[50]A. S. van der Woude and the present author tried to show that the word Messiah is connected with different figures which play a role in Jewish expectation and also that we cannot speak of "fixed concepts"--see their contribution, "Messianic Ideas in Later Judaism," *TDNT* 9, pp. 509-27 (in the article χρίω, κτλ.).

[51]See de Jonge and van der Woude, "11Q Melchizedek and the New Testament," pp. 306-7; cf. CD 2.12, 6.1 and 1QM 11.7.

[52]In 6:14, the indirect connection between σημεῖα and (a Jewish view on) kingship runs via the προφήτης-title. 12:18 is (part of) a redactional link between the pericope of the Entrance into Jerusalem and the preceding Lazarus-episode. Thereby also an indirect connection is made between the title ὁ βασιλεὺς τοῦ Ἰσραήλ and the σημεῖον. There is no reason to suppose that this was important for the evangelist, nor that he wanted to suggest that this was "theologically" important for the crowd.

[53]On the question of the right terminology (Jewish sympathizers or Christians of Jewish descent), see below, section IV. 4.

[54]Schnackenburg, *Das Johannesevangelium* II, p. 219, n. 3, follows B. van Iersel, "Fils de David et Fils de Dieu," in *La Venue du Messie*, RechBib 6 (1962), pp. 113-32, in calling ἐκ σπέρματος Δαυίδ a typically Christian phrase. Van Iersel regards ἐκ σπέρματος Δαυίδ as a Christian "reduction" of υἱὸς Δαυίδ, in connection with the use of the title "Son of God" (Rom 1:3-4). It should be noted, however, that a phrase very similar to ἐκ σπέρματος Δαυίδ occurs in all but the Latin versions of 4 Ezra 12:32 and is likely to be original (see de Jonge, *TDNT* 9, p. 515, following the editions of B. Violet and L. Gry, and Müller, *Messias und Menschensohn*, p. 152).

[55]The assertion of the Jews is said to be warranted by Scripture. On this see E. D. Freed, *Old Testament Quotations in the Gospel of John*, NovTSup 11 (Leiden: Brill, 1965), pp. 39-59. It is interesting to note that the Targum interprets Mic 5:1b as referring to the calling of the name of the Messiah from the beginning; cf. 1 Enoch 48:3 and further instances in Sjöberg, *Der verborgene Menschensohn*, p. 58, nn. 2 and 3.

[56]Burger, *Jesus als Davidssohn*, pp. 153-58, is too one-sided when he regards this as a completely inner-Christian controversy in which John's opponents are disqualified as Jews.

[57]So Bultmann, *The Gospel of John*, pp. 354-57.
Cf. Schnackenburg, *Das Johannesevangelium* II, p. 495: "Ihm
genügt die Anknüpfungsmöglichkeit im Kontext, im übrigen
formuliert er nach seinem Kerygma 3, 14...."

[58]See I. de la Potterie, "L'Exaltation du Fils de
l'homme," *Greg* 49 (1968), pp. 460-78.

[59]νόμος with the wider meaning of "Scripture," cf.
10:34, 15:25, and W. Bauer, *A Greek-English Lexicon of the
New Testament and Other Early Christian Literature* (Chicago: The University of Chicago Press, 1957), s.v. νόμος
4b, p. 545.

[60]W. C. van Unnik, "The Quotation from the Old Testament in John 12:34," *NovT* 3 (1959), pp. 174-79.

[61]So also R. Leivestad in his discussion of this
passage on pp. 250-51 of his article, "Exit the Apocalyptic Son of Man," *NTS* 18 (1971-72), pp. 243-67.

[62]In 9:35-38 Jesus identifies himself as Son of Man;
the blind man has to ask τίς ἐστιν, κύριε, ἵνα πιστεύσω
εἰς αὐτόν; before he confesses his faith in the Son of Man,
as Jesus requests.

[63]See de Jonge, *TDNT* 9, p. 514 (on 1 Enoch) and pp.
515-16 (on 4 Ezra). In 4 Ezra and *2 Apoc. Bar.*, a distinction is made between the days of the Messiah and the
Age to Come. We should note, however, that, nevertheless,
in *2 Apoc. Bar.* 40.3, the reign of "my Messiah" is said to
last "forever," "until the world of corruption is at an
end and until the times aforesaid are fulfilled."

[64]Translation by A. Lukyn Williams in his *Justin
Martyr. The Dialogue with Trypho*, Translation, Introduction and Notes (New York-Toronto: Macmillan, 1930). The
last sentence presupposes Gal 3:13 referring to Deut 21:
23. See also Schnackenburg, *Das Johannesevangelium* II, p.
252.

[65]Schnackenburg, "Die Messiasfrage," pp. 251-52,
would put here also 12:34. Because we cannot prove that
the Jews here identify Messiah and Son of Man, a comparison with Justin, *Dialogue* 32.1 remains hazardous. Schnackenburg himself remarks, "Stärker getrieben aber wird er
sicher wieder von seinem positiven christologischen Inter-
esse an die 'Erhöhung des Menschensohnes' und den damit
gegebenen 'Weggang' des Sohnes zum Vater" (p. 252).

[66]Schnackenburg, "Die Messiasfrage," pp. 257-64.

[67]See note 10.

[68]Meeks, "The Man from Heaven in Johannine Sectarianism," p. 70.

[69] Formulation by Meeks, "The Man from Heaven," p. 69, of the general purport of Martyn's *History and Theology in the Fourth Gospel*.

[70] The same would seem to apply *mutatis mutandis* to the Gospel of Matthew. On the whole, the way from a literary document like the Gospel of John to a reconstruction of the actual situation in which it was written is much longer and much more difficult than some authors seem to realize.

[71] This would have to be shown first of all in an analysis of the use of the titles Son, Son of God, Son of Man, and of the ἄνω-κάτω scheme. See also Chapter VI.

[72] See, particularly, E. Grässer, "Die antijüdische Polemik im Johannesevangelium," *NTS* 9 (1964), pp. 74-90, esp. pp. 88-90.

[73] Here we should remember that the Fourth Gospel in its present form shows signs also of the beginning of a struggle against docetism; see Chapter VIII.

[74] See section II. 2, above, with the reference to Chapter II.

[75] See 1:12; 2:11; 13:16, 18, 36; 6:29, etc.

[76] See also 9:16, where some Pharisees react positively without really taking Jesus' side, as the sequel shows.

[77] The reaction of the μαθηταί in vs. 61 is called γογγυσμός, like that of the Jews in vss. 41, 43. The reaction of the "disciples" comes, however, after the last part of the discourse (6:51b-58) with its anti-docetic emphasis on the flesh and blood of Jesus. From the Johannine point of view, Judaism and docetism, in different ways, deny the same truth, i.e., that Jesus is the Messiah, the Son of God--see, e.g., the statement in 1 John 2:22, 23, and the present author's comment on it in his *De Brieven van Johannes* (Nijkerk: Callenbach, 1968, [2]1973), pp. 116-24. See also P. Borgen, *Bread from Heaven. An Exegetical Study of the Concept of Manna in the Gospel of John and the Writings of Philo*, NovTSup 10 (Leiden: Brill, 1965), pp. 183-92, and N. A. Dahl, "Der Erstgeborene des Satans und der Vater des Teufels (Polyk. 7:1 und Joh. 8:44)," in *Apophoreta. Festschrift E. Haenchen*, BZNW 30 (Berlin: Töpelmann, 1964), pp. 70-84, esp. pp. 79-81.

[78] On this verse, see especially C. H. Dodd, "A l'arriere-plan d'un dialogue johannique," *RHPR* 37 (1957), pp. 5-17, and a forthcoming publication by B. E. Schein, "The Seed of Abraham. John 8:31-59." See Meeks, "The Man from Heaven in Johannine Sectarianism," p. 67, n. 76. Mr. Schein kindly sent me a typescript of his paper.

[79] See also E. Allen, "The Jewish Christian Church in the Fourth Gospel," *JBL* 74 (1955), pp. 88-92, and R. M. Grant, "The Origin of the Fourth Gospel," *JBL* 69 (1950), pp. 305-22. On the Fourth Gospel's anti-Jewish attitude, Grant remarks: "The circumstances under which such an attack would seem advisable would be those in which Jewish Christians insisted that the synoptic gospels (any one of them) were adequate representations of the ministry of Jesus, or in which Jews outside the Church pointed to the Jewishness of Jesus. Naturally Jews outside the Church would influence Christians only slightly unless there were Jewish Christians inside who would be moved by Jewish arguments" (p. 320).

[80] See also Chapter I, p. 15 with n. 53, and Chapter III, pp. 63-66.

[81] W. A. Meeks, *The Prophet-King. Moses Traditions and the Johannine Christology* (Leiden: Brill, 1967), p. 46, n. 2.

[82] We may also point here to the activity of the "Spirit of truth" in 16:12-15. He will lead the believers εἰς τὴν ἀλήθειαν πᾶσαν. Like a true prophet he will not speak ἀφ᾽ ἑαυτοῦ but will speak what he hears καὶ τὰ ἐρχόμενα ἀναγγελεῖ ὑμῖν (vs. 13; see also vss. 14, 15).

[83] M. Macdonald, *The Theology of the Samaritans* (Philadelphia: Westminster, 1964). For our purpose, Part Four, "Eschatology," pp. 357-90, is especially important.

[84] Meeks, *The Prophet-King*, pp. 216-57.

[85] H. G. Kippenberg, *Garazim und Synagoge. Traditionsgeschichtliche Untersuchungen zur samaritanischen Religion der aramäischen Periode*, Religionsgeschichtliche Versuche und Vorarbeiten 30 (Berlin-New York: W. de Gruyter, 1971). See especially chapter 11, "Der Taheb," pp. 276-305, and chapter 12, "Der Prophet wie Mose," pp. 306-27.

[86] Ibid., p. 303, n. 218, refers to Abraham haq-Qabbāṣî.

[87] Meeks, *The Prophet-King*, p. 318, n. 1. Macdonald, *The Theology of the Samaritans*, p. 361, says rather more vaguely on 4:25: "...though Messiah is hardly the right term in the Samaritan case, for their concept of the one who is to come is not quite like that of Judaism and Christianity."

[88] *Apol.* 53.6. Justin adds that they did so ἔχοντες τὸν παρὰ τοῦ θεοῦ λόγον διὰ τῶν προφητῶν παραδοθέντα αὐτοῖς!

[89] See Kippenberg, *Garazim und Synagoge*, chapter 12.

116

[90]Ibid., p. 313 and pp. 115-17 (on John 4), 324-27 (on "the prophet," especially in John). Kippenberg's treatment of Johannine texts is, on the whole, disappointing.

[91]So rightly Meeks, *The Prophet-King*, p. 34. This distinction is not important for the use of the prophet-title as starting-point for Johannine christology.

[92]Besides the Johannine parallels mentioned by Meeks, compare also 1 Macc 4:46, where one stores the stones of the defiled altar somewhere until a prophet comes τοῦ ἀποκριθῆναι περὶ αὐτῶν (cf. 14:41). See also CD 6.10-11 (the coming of a יורה הצדק with new instructions), and 1QS 9.10-11 (where the prophet and the anointed one[s] of Aaron and Israel have this function); on these and other texts see M. de Jonge, "The Role of Intermediaries in God's Final Intervention in the Future according to the Qumran Scrolls," in O. Michel et al., *Studies on the Jewish Background of the New Testament* (Assen: van Gorcum, 1969), pp. 44-63, esp. pp. 54-55.

[93]See Meeks, *The Prophet-King*, pp. 246-54, and Macdonald, *The Theology of the Samaritans*, pp. 362-71.

[94]So Kippenberg, *Garazim und Synagoge*, chapter 12.

[95]See ibid., pp. 27-29.

[96]Memar Marqa 2.44.31-32; 4.108.6-7; 4.111.13-14; see Kippenberg, *Garazim und Synagoge*, pp. 289-93, and his n. 159 on p. 293: "Offensichtlich die wichtigste Tätigkeit des Taheb, da sie zum drittenmal erwähnt wird."

[97]See Kippenberg, *Garazim und Synagoge*, pp. 113-14, and chapter 9, pp. 234-54.

CHAPTER V

SIGNS AND WORKS IN THE FOURTH GOSPEL

Introduction

The purpose of the present chapter is to analyze
the function of the stories about and comments upon the
"signs" and "works" within the argument and structure of
the Fourth Gospel. Much has been written lately on the
existence of a Signs- or Miracles-source or even of a
Signs-Gospel,[1] and James M. Robinson has argued that "the
surprisingly strong survival record of the 'miracles-
source' (σημεῖα-Quelle) made familiar by Bultmann" is in
itself an argument for taking his source seriously.[2]

This chapter does not intend to analyze or criti-
cize the existing source- and redaction-theories. One
cannot exclude the possibility that the Fourth Gospel reflects more than one stage in the development of the theology of the Johannine communities which produced the Gospel and the Epistles of John.[3] It is also likely that the
Fourth Gospel incorporates narrative and discourse material
belonging to pre-Johannine stages and non-Johannine strands
in the tradition. But the arguments in favor of the existence of a pre-Johannine (or even early Johannine) Signs-
source or Signs-Gospel with a clearly defined number of
stories and a definite theology of its own are not conclu-
sive. The question must be asked whether the distinction
between the present Johannine redaction and the supposed
presentation in the source really helps to explain the
way in which the signs-stories and the statements about
Jesus' works function in the present Gospel.

All theories concerning a Signs-source have to assume that "John" criticized his source, and yet incorporated it substantially in his own work. The evangelist
is always supposed to have been far more subtle than the
people whose work he used: he rewrote considerable parts

of the source(s) before him and yet did not do his work thoroughly enough. He left a clear Johannine stamp everywhere and yet we are able to reconstruct the state of his material before it received this stamp.

Now if it is difficult to believe that the Johannine redaction left sufficient pre-Johannine traces to enable us to explain Johannine theology in terms of an explicit criticism of theological tendencies in earlier writings, we must make an attempt to explain tensions and apparent inconsistencies in John's picture of Jesus' acts first and foremost on the level and within the framework of the very complicated (and at the same time carefully balanced) theology of the Johannine community as reflected in the Gospel itself. As Barnabas Lindars puts it: "The impression that Jesus is a wonder-worker [the Christology commonly attributed to the source] is intentional at the stage in the argument to which they belong, i.e., the opening of it. It cannot be taken for granted that, before John rewrote them, they would have given this impression."[4] This chapter attempts to show that Lindars' thesis is a useful starting-point for an analysis of the function of "signs" and "works" in the present Gospel. It is worthwhile to look at the passages concerned from this angle, even if within the compass of our chapter many aspects cannot be dealt with or can only be mentioned in passing.

John 20:30-31

We should return for a moment to 20:30-31, the well-known "first ending" of the Gospel.[5] Here the author makes clear that he has described a number of σημεῖα in order to promote and strengthen faith in Jesus. More precisely it is stated that the signs were performed by Jesus ἐνώπιον τῶν μαθητῶν. The Gospel records what these μαθηταί saw, understood, and interpreted.

Next, faith in Jesus is faith in Jesus the Christ, the Son of God. *Fides qua* and *fides quae* are closely

connected in the Fourth Gospel as I have tried to show in
Chapters I-IV. Here it may be sufficient to emphasize
that Johannine Christology centers around the mystery of
the unique relationship between the Father and the Son
sent by the Father, expressed in various terms and represented by various titles--among these "the Son, "the Son
of God," "the Son of Man." These titles indicate, for
John, the unique otherness of Jesus, over against designations as prophet, priest, king, and even Christ, which
are expressions of man's highest expectations. They are
not entirely discarded; elements of the expectations connected with them are taken up within a larger framework
and receive a deeper meaning, and consequently the titles
as such are reinterpreted in a fundamental way. In 20:31,
"Son of God" interprets "the Christ." Basic to the σημεῖα
is that they lead to faith in Jesus, commonly called the
Christ, as Son of God. In this faith the believers receive true *life* in his name. Signs give *life* to those who
are willing and able to believe in Him who presents life
through these signs.

John 20:30-31 shows, in connection with the preceding vss. 28 and 29, how the disciples believed because
they really saw what was revealed to them, but that generations after them are dependent on the word, i.e., on
the apostles' testimony. In order to transmit this testimony, the Gospel was written (cf. 1 John 1:1-4). Thomas,
in a way, is a borderline case. He could and should have
believed the words of his fellow-disciples, justly commissioned by Jesus through the Spirit (20:19-23), but he
is still in a position in which his request to see and to
feel can be granted. He becomes a believer and confesses
his faith in words reminiscent of the opening sentences of
the Gospel. Those who come after him have to listen to
and to rely on the record of the deeds performed by Jesus
in the presence of the disciples.

A true understanding of the signs during Jesus'
sojourn on earth implies seeing, faith in Jesus sent by

120

God his Father as the giver of Life, and discipleship.
The Gospel describes how a number of people received that
understanding, and how many people started on their way to
Jesus but did not attain that full understanding. It also
emphasizes that discipleship means being led to a yet
fuller understanding by the Spirit operating within the
Christian community after Jesus' departure to the Father.[6]

This, I think, is shown clearly in a number of passages, taken on their own and particularly if considered
in their interdependence, within the framework of the entire Gospel.

Two Concluding Redactional Passages Comparable to 20:30-31

Two passages which are obviously redactional because they serve as conclusion to larger units of the Gospel now call for some consideration.
The first is 10:40-42. Jesus returns to where it
all started, the place across the Jordan where John had
been baptizing earlier. Many come to believe in him
there, after having acknowledged that all that John had
said about this man was true. John's witness in 1:19-34
ends with the statement that Jesus is the Son of God. He
denies explicitly that he himself is the Messiah, the
Prophet, or Elijah (1:21, 25). He is a mere "voice" (1:
23).[7] Consequently, 10:41 states that John did not perform signs but yet spoke the truth. John was a typical
witness, a man of *words*. Jesus is a man of words *and
signs*; in 5:31-36, where Jesus contrasts his own witness
to that of John, he says, "I rely on a testimony higher
than John's. There is enough to testify that the Father
has sent me, in the works my Father gave me to do and to
finish--the very works I have in hand" (vs. 36).[8]
The second passage is very important for our purpose. At the conclusion of Jesus' public ministry (12:36),
at the transition to the instruction directed to the disciples in chapters 13-17, the evangelist states, "In spite
of the many signs which Jesus had performed in their

presence they would not believe in him" (vs. 37). The
ἔμπροσθεν αὐτῶν in the present verse stands over against
the ἐνώπιον τῶν μαθητῶν of 20:30.[9] The outsiders did not
believe and could not believe, as the evangelist assures
us with a reference to Isa 6:9, 10. I pass over this use
of Scripture but want to underscore the following comment,
"Isaiah said this because he saw his *glory* and spoke about
him" (vs. 41). Isaiah saw what the unbelieving Jews did
not see, the divine glory revealed in Jesus.[10]

In vss. 42-43, the believers among the Jewish leaders appear on the scene--representatives of the many,
among the leaders and among the crowds, who believed in
Jesus, but not in a way that is acceptable to the Gospel.
They cannot be regarded as true believers, because they do
not dare to confess Jesus openly for fear of the Pharisees.
They valued τὴν δόξαν τῶν ἀνθρώπων more highly than τὴν
δόξαν τοῦ θεοῦ (cf. 5:34).[11]

The real meaning of Jesus' words and signs remained
hidden to outsiders. The οὐκ ἐπίστευον εἰς αὐτόν (vs. 37)
and the οὐκ ἠδύναντο πιστεύειν (vs. 39) state the Gospel's
position very clearly. The passage 12:36b-43 refers back
to 2:23-25, the first passage to speak about signs done by
Jesus in Jerusalem. Although Jesus refuses to perform a
sign on request, when "the Jews" ask for divine legitimation of his words and action (2:18; cf. 6:30, 7:31, 9:16,
11:47), and refers to his coming death and resurrection
(2:19--they are *not* explicitly called signs!), he is said
to perform signs during the Passover feast in Jerusalem.
The result is that many believe in his name. The expression found here is used in 1:12 to denote the positive reaction to Jesus of the children of God--yet there is something wrong with the people in Jerusalem: Jesus did not
trust himself to them. Why not? The following example of
Nicodemus shows that, for all their enthusiasm and sympathy for Jesus, the people in Jerusalem, represented by
Nicodemus, did not penetrate into the real secret of Jesus'
coming.[12] The σημεῖα are demonstrations of Jesus' special

power and authority, but can only be understood and interpreted rightly by people who are initiated into the mystery of the relationship between Son and Father.

There can be no question of legitimation, in the
sense that evidence is supplied that will convince any
neutral observer. A σημεῖον is a demonstration which asks
for reaction. In the case of positive reaction, the principal question is, however, What power and authority do
you believe to be demonstrated here? Again *fides qua* and
fides quae are closely related. The inner circle of the
disciples receive the true faith; this group of people is
commissioned and empowered to hand on the message of life
to future generations. All others, including sympathizers
and half-believers, are out.[13]

The First Two Signs

The first two signs, recorded in 2:1-11 and 4:46-
54, are both connected with Cana in Galilee. In concluding comments they are called "the beginning of the signs"
(2:11)[14] and "the second sign" (4:54). They may well have
belonged to a pre-Johannine collection of stories. We can
easily connect 2:12a with 4:46b, and the enumeration of
the signs (which is not continued further in the Gospel)
may well stem from the original collection. Moreover,
there is clearly some discrepancy between 2:11 and the
preceding story, if only because the disciples do not
really play a part in the story (they are only mentioned
in vs. 2) and yet occupy a central position in the summing
up in vs. 11. And, as synoptic parallels to 4:46-54
clearly show, the second story embodies traditional material.[15]

The (probably complicated) pre-history of these two
pericopae cannot be discussed here. If we try to define
their function within the present Gospel, we may make the
following observations:

     a. The enumeration of the signs may have been
taken over from a source, but why did the evangelist keep

it? It is possible that he wanted to connect the two
signs in Galilee which lead to true faith--over against
the many signs in Jerusalem (2:23-25; cf. 4:45) which did
not.

      b. The concluding comment in 2:11 connects signs
with the revelation of δόξα, leading to belief on the part
of Jesus' disciples. The second story centers around the
word of Jesus, "Your son will live," spoken in 4:50, underlined in vs. 53, and taken up by the people who meet the
father on the way (vs. 51). Jesus' word is effective--
water is changed into wine, the boy is healed; in his
signs Jesus reveals his glory and grants Life. This is in
keeping with the Prologue, where the Logos is connected
with the Life and the Light (1:4-9). It is accepted by
those who receive the ἐξουσία to become children of God
(1:11-12). They are able to say, "*We* saw his glory" (1:
14), a glory described as a glory which befits the Father's
only Son, full of grace and truth.

      c. The βασιλικός in the second Cana-story is not
explicitly called a disciple, yet he obviously believes in
the right way. Verse 48 is commonly thought to be a typically Johannine remark and it no doubt is. It characterizes the belief in Galilean circles (vs. 48 uses the second person plural and should be connected with vs. 45) as
a belief in σημεῖα καὶ τέρατα.[16] Jesus' answer is not so
much a reproach as a challenge; it is certainly not a dis-
qualification of signs as such. The man is challenged to
believe Jesus as the giver of Life on his word, and he
does so (vs. 50). The repetition in vs. 49 of what was
already said in vs. 47 is not (or not only) the result of
the insertion of vs. 48; it makes clear that the man per-
sists in expecting help from Jesus and it places Jesus'
promise of life against the dark background of the son's
expected imminent death. Faith in Jesus' word is followed
by faith on the basis of word plus sign, not only of the
man, but also of his whole house; vs. 53 serves as a concluding remark to the whole story. The sign follows

124

necessarily, as demonstration of Jesus' life-giving power, after Jesus' word has been accepted. First the word, then the sign--this order is also presupposed in the Thomas-story.

d. 2:11 seems quite straightforward. It emphasizes the central position of the disciples, provides a fitting conclusion to the whole section 1:35-2:11,[17] and should certainly be connected with 20:30-31. Yet it becomes clear from the context that even the disciples did not fully understand what they saw until after Jesus' death and resurrection. First, there is the typically Johannine οὔπω ἥκει ἡ ὥρα μου in 2:4. In view of 7:30; 8:20; 12:23, 27; 13:1 and 17:1, we cannot escape the conclusion that here the hour of Jesus' suffering, death, and resurrection (seen as a unity) is meant.[18] The evangelist, therefore, in one way or another, views the whole passage 2:1-11, including the reaction of the disciples in 2:11, from a post-resurrection perspective.

This is also evident in 2:13-22. We have already seen that Jesus refuses a sign which might serve as legitimation for his action in the temple, and refers to his death and resurrection. This interpretation of Jesus' word recorded in vs. 19 and significantly misunderstood by the Jews in vs. 20 is given in a redactional comment in vs. 21. To this is added that the disciples also did not fully understand what Jesus meant until after his resurrection: "After his resurrection his disciples recalled what he had said, and they believed the Scripture and the words that Jesus had spoken" (vs. 22).

The statement in 2:11, therefore, stands "between brackets"--the brackets being provided by 2:4 and 2:21. This arrangement is intentional, as was shown in Chapter I.

The Last Sign: The Raising of Lazarus in Chapter 11

The last sign is appropriately again concerned with the giving of life. John 11 is a well-known crux for all scholars who want to distinguish here between the theology

of the source and the redaction of the evangelist.[19] Some
have thought that in this chapter the signs are reinterpreted so drastically that they are, in fact, disqualified; after the conversation between Jesus and Martha in
vss. 20-27 the actual raising of Lazarus seems to be
superfluous.[20] This interpretation is clearly wrong; here
again the word which calls for faith is followed by the
sign which demonstrates the truth and the power of the
word.

In the context of the present study, we should
note in particular vs. 4 which speaks of the glory of God,
vs. 25 which mentions the ἐγώ εἰμι connected with ἀνάστασις and ζωή, and vs. 40 which refers back to vs. 25 with
the words, "Did I not tell you that if you have faith you
will see the glory of God?"--just before the actual miracle takes place.

Resurrection and the giving of life are closely
connected, here and in 5:25-29. In the latter passage it
is made clear that giving of life as well as judgment are
a divine prerogative granted to the Son by the Father. It
is also good to emphasize that both in chapter 11 and in
chapter 5 present and future life are mentioned together
(cf. 6:39-40, 47-51, 54, and 3:16, 8:51). The risen
Lazarus is an example of what was announced in 5:25, "A
time is coming, indeed is already here, when the dead
shall hear the voice of the Son of God, and all who hear
shall come to life."[21] We should note that the conversation between Jesus and Martha appropriately ends with a
confession by Martha which gives expression to the full
Christian faith, in terms reminiscent of 20:31, "I now believe (or: I am convinced, πεπίστευκα) that you are the
Messiah, the Son of God, who was to come into the world."

Faith is also mentioned in vs. 15, where Jesus says
to his disciples, "Lazarus is dead. I am glad not to have
been there; it will be for your good and for the good of
your faith" (δι᾽ ὑμᾶς, ἵνα πιστεύσητε). Next, there is
vs. 42, where the prayer (to the Father, vs. 41) which

accompanies the miracle is said to be spoken for the sake
of the ὄχλος standing around, that they may believe that
God sent Jesus.

In fact, this story about the final sign shows
(again!) that there are three possible reactions to the
signs of Jesus. There is, first, the hostile reaction of
the Jewish leaders who start planning Jesus' death (11:47-
54, 57; 12:19). Yet, with sublime Johannine irony, the
high priest is portrayed as prophesying unwittingly the
meaning of this death (11:51, 52), and in the discourse
immediately following the story of the entry into Jerusalem (12:20-36) Jesus reveals that the hour of his death
is the hour of his glorification (vss. 23, 27, 28).

Next, there is the reaction of the sympathizers
among the crowd, mentioned in 11:45; 12:9-11, 17-18. Here
Jews who come to belief in Jesus because of what they have
seen (11:45; 12:11, 17; cf. also 11:42) acclaim Jesus as
the king of Israel (12:13). This is not, in itself, a
wrong designation, but it needs further interpretation--
an interpretation in the light of Zech 9:9, quoted in vs.
15, discovered by the disciples, but only "after Jesus had
been glorified," as vs. 16 tells us. The sympathizers in
the crowd seek in the right direction, but like the people
mentioned in 2:23-25 they do not possess the true faith,
or real insight.[22]

Full insight is granted only to the disciples, including Martha (even before the sign was performed), who
see the glory of God and accept the power of Jesus as Life-
giver sent by God, and who express their faith in the appropriate Christological terminology. Yet there is the
significant proviso in 12:16 which has its parallel in 2:
22, a verse already discussed. And Jesus' opening statement in 11:4, "This illness will not end in death; it has
come for the glory of God, to bring glory to the Son of
God," is at least ambiguous. The ἵνα δοξασθῇ ὁ υἱὸς τοῦ
θεοῦ has two aspects--cf. 12:23 and, particularly, 12:28--
καὶ ἐδόξασα καὶ πάλιν δοξάσω.[23]

In 7:39 we are told that the Spirit could only be given after Jesus' glorification, and according to the Paraclete-passages in the farewell discourses it is the Spirit which will teach the disciples everything and will remind them (cf. 2:17, 22; 12:16) of all that Jesus has told them (14:26; cf. 16:12-15). Evidently the disciples occupy a central position in the process of understanding the truth about Jesus during his life on earth. But only after his glorification will their understanding be deepened and strengthened; the Spirit will operate in them and through them and enable them to transmit the message concerning Jesus to following generations.

In connection with this, another observation may be pertinent. One of the arguments in favor of the Signs-source hypothesis has always been the isolated position of 20:30, a verse which again characterizes Jesus' deeds as σημεῖα, although that word has not been mentioned since 12:37. Moreover, καὶ ἄλλα σημεῖα are spoken of, although the resurrection appearances are nowhere classified as signs. The usual explanation is that the evangelist took over the concluding section of the Signs-source with some corrections.

A far more likely theory, however, is that the evangelist could only adequately present the Gospel as a record of signs after he had told how the Risen Lord had given the Spirit to the disciples who had seen the signs. In giving the Spirit, Jesus not only commissioned them as agents, but he also guaranteed the truth of their message. Moreover, if the δόξα shown forth in the signs has any connection with the δόξα of Jesus in his being lifted up from the earth and his return to the Father, it is only to be expected that the revelation of life and glory in the signs is mentioned in retrospect, *after* cross and resurrection and the giving of the Spirit--*all* moments in the glorification process--have been recorded.[24]

Brief Remarks on Chapters 5, 6, 7, and 9

The picture given above may be supplemented by a few remarks on some words and passages in chapters 5, 6, 7, and 9.

In chapter 5, the word σημεῖον is not used, either in the story or in the following discourse which is only loosely connected with it. As by afterthought the healing is set in the context of a sabbath conflict (vss. 9 and 16). Jesus' central answer to the objections of the Jews is found in vs. 17: "My Father has never ceased his work and I am working too." The terms used are ἐργάζεσθαι and ἔργα, and these denote the unity of intention and action between Son and Father; this is made very clear in vss. 19-20, 30, and 36.[25] The divine actions performed by Jesus are, above all, the giving of life and the exercise of judgment. The real issue at stake in the interpretation of the healing on the sabbath is whether Jesus is a man who wrongly claims equality with God, or whether he is the Son, sent and commissioned by the Father.

This also becomes clear in chapter 9, where the blind man is portrayed as the believing counterpart of the cripple of chapter 5. He confesses Jesus as the Son of Man in vss. 35-38, after long discussions with the Jews ending in his expulsion from the synagogue: the cripple does not come to any sort of confession (5:10-15). The word σημεῖον occurs only in passing, in vs. 16, in a context which is essentially concerned to answer the question whether Jesus is a true prophet or not. Again his relationship to the sabbath law is the main issue (vss. 14, 16).[26] The reader of the Gospel who comes to chapter 9 after chapter 5 knows that this question cannot be answered on the level of a discussion about prophecy and obedience to the law of Moses. This is made clear by the evangelist in the beginning and the end of this chapter. Verses 1-5 emphasize that Jesus carries out the work of God who sent him (see especially vss. 3-4) and that he does so as the light of the world. The result is that

blind people are <u>allowed to see the light</u>, and that others
who think that they are seeing discover that they are
blind (vss. 39-41). Light means Life, but at the same
time it discloses darkness as darkness--as was already
made clear in 3:19-21. Therefore the final discovery of
the <u>blind man</u> is that Jesus is the *Son of Man*, and he confesses him as such. This discovery is not his own; it
comes only after Jesus reveals himself as Son of Man: "Indeed, it is he who is speaking to you" (vs. 37). This
revelation is given to a man who is truly "a disciple of
Jesus" (vs. 28) and acts like one, defending Jesus against
the disciples of Moses, even to the extent of accepting
expulsion from the synagogue.[27]

In chapter 6 we have, again, a story--or rather,
two stories--with a following discourse which gives the
Johannine interpretation of the meaning of the event(s)
reported in the stories. Again only a few remarks.

First we should note that the people who see the
sign interpret it in terms of a <u>reference</u> to the prophet
like Moses who is expected to come into the world (vs. 14;
cf. vs. 2). In the discussion at the beginning of the
discourse the Jews refer again to what *Moses* did in the
desert (vss. 30-31). To the evangelist it is self-evident
that people with a Jewish background would connect signs
with prophecy, particularly with prophecy after the manner
of Moses. This is clear here, in 9:13-17 (and 24-34), and
particularly in 3:2. Jesus realizes that this is a high-
handed attempt to make him king in a human way. He is
king according to the Fourth Gospel, but in his own very
special, God-oriented way (12:15 and 18:33-38).[28] Jesus
withdraws again to the hills by himself (vs. 15).

Before the real meaning of the multiplication of
the loaves is disclosed in the discourse, the story of
Jesus' walking on the lake is told; in its present, not
specifically Johannine, context it serves a particular
Johannine purpose. It is the <u>revelation of Jesus</u> to his
disciples, and to his disciples *only*, through the word
ἐγώ εἰμι (vss. 16-21).

Verses 24-29 serve as a transitional passage to the
great homily in vss. 32-58.[29] The title Son of Man is
substituted for that of prophet (vs. 27), and the unity of
this Son of Man with God the Father is emphasized. The
perishable food is discarded and people are exhorted to
work for the food that lasts, the food of eternal life
which can only be given by the Son of Man.[30] In the following homily a number of phrases recur repeatedly, underlining the essential points of Johannine Christology: The
true bread comes from heaven (vss. 32 and 33 as interpretation of vs. 31); Jesus is the bread descended from
heaven (vss. 41, 50, 51, 58) because he may say that he
has descended from heaven (vss. 38, 42). He is the living
bread (vs. 51), that is, the bread of life (vss. 50, 51b-
58; cf. vss. 40, 47). Several times the unity of intention and action between the Father and the Son is emphasized with different expressions (vss. 38, 40, 44, 45, 46,
57); see particularly vs. 38: καταβέβηκα ἀπὸ τοῦ οὐρανοῦ
οὐχ ἵνα ποιῶ τὸ θέλημα τὸ ἐμὸν ἀλλὰ τὸ θέλημα τοῦ πέμψαντός
με. The essential difficulty for the Jews is their convic-
tion that Jesus is a man whose father and mother they know
and who, therefore, cannot claim to have come from heaven
(vs. 42; cf. vs. 52). In the last part of the chapter
(vss. 60-65), we hear that the difficulty of the Jews is
also the difficulty of the great majority of Jesus' disciples.[31] In the end only "the twelve" are left; on their
behalf Peter testifies that Jesus' words are the "words of
eternal life" and he calls him "the Holy One of God."
Again the disciples, this time the inner circle of the
disciples (those who were present when Jesus walked on the
lake and addressed his disciples[32]) are the only true believers.

On chapter 7, two remarks should be made. The
first is on the introductory passage, vss. 1-9. Here the
unbelieving brothers of Jesus advise him to seek publicity
in Jerusalem in order that his disciples may see his
"works" (vs. 3). They are right about the relation

between seeing, disciples, and "works" (evidently identical with the signs in 20:30, 31); they are wrong, however,
in connecting this with a revelation *to the world* (vs. 4).
The world hates Jesus, who unmasks the works of the world
as evil (vs. 7). Moreover, Jesus' time has not yet come
(vss. 6, 8; cf. 2:4). If he goes to Jerusalem it is οὐ
φανερῶς ἀλλὰ ὡς ἐν κρυπτῷ (vs. 10).

The second comment is on 7:31, where believers in
the crowd ask, "When the Messiah comes, is it likely that
he will perform more signs than this man?" The connection
between "signs" and the title "Messiah" is found only in
Christian writings. John does not comment on this question directly, but in other places, notably in 11:27 and
20:31, passages we have already discussed, he clearly supplements and corrects the statement of these believers by
adding the phrase "the Son of God"--and this is entirely
in keeping with the main line of the Christological argumentation in the present chapter.[33]

Signs and Works

Looking back upon the passages in the Fourth Gospel
where σημεῖον is used, we may recapitulate as follows:

a) Seven times the word is used by Jews, either belonging to the crowd or to the authorities. Twice a sign
is requested for legitimation (2:18, 6:30); Jesus refuses
because he does not accept the frame of reference presupposed by the demand. In the five other cases also the
word is used without a full understanding of Jesus' real
being (3:2, 7:31, 9:36, 10:41, 11:47).

b) The same is true in four cases where the evangelist describes reactions of Jews: 2:23; 6:2, 12; 12:18.
Yet

c) the Gospel wants to make clear that Jesus' signs
could elicit true faith, and in fact did so in the case of
the disciples (and of the βασιλικός, not explicitly called
a disciple: 2:11, 4:54, 12:37, 20:30).

d) Only twice do we find the word on the lips of
Jesus himself, and both times with a critical connotation
with regard to the reaction of people in Galilee (4:48, 6:
26).

The signs point to Jesus' special power and authority, but by no means unequivocally. They may lead to
faith, but also to rejection; often they lead to an imperfect understanding which is, in fact, misunderstanding.
The evangelist, writing from the perspective of a Christian community relying on the word of the disciples/apos-
tles, is quite clear and adamant about that.

If we turn now to the word ἔργον, which we have already had occasion to refer to a few times,[34] we notice
that in two texts it is certainly used on the same level
and with practically the same meaning as σημεῖον. In 7:3
the use of τὰ ἔργα σοῦ is parallel to that of σημεῖα in
20:30. In 6:30 the expression τί ποιεῖς σὺ σημεῖον is
used alongside τί ἐργάζῃ (following on a discussion of τὸ
ἔργον/τὰ ἔργα τοῦ θεοῦ). In 7:3 the word ἔργα is used in
antithesis to the "words of the world" in 7:7. In the
second case mentioned it is used in order to connect the
works wrought and inspired by God in men with the works
wrought by God in and through Jesus (6:21-28, 3:19-21; cf.
8:39-41).

With the exception of the texts just mentioned, the
word ἔργον is only used in connection with Jesus by Jesus
himself.[35] In all cases Jesus uses it in order to give
expression to his unity in intention and action with God.
The words "Son" and "Father" occur in this context and the
term ἔργα is clearly regarded as more suitable to denote
the inner meaning of Jesus' actions than the word σημεῖα.
Jesus' works are God's works performed by and through
Jesus. Once that is clear, all ambiguity is removed and
only one reaction is possible; study of the ἔργα passages
leads us to the heart of the matter and the center of Johannine Christology and theology. We may, very briefly,
point to the following aspects of the use of ἔργον.

First, there is the use of ἔργον in the singular in
4:34 and 17:4, the first and the last text where the word
is used in connection with Jesus. The terminology is very
similar; in 4:34 we read: "It is meat and drink for me to
do the will of him who sent me until I have finished his
work," and in 17:4: "I have glorified thee on earth by
completing the work which thou gavest me to do." Essentially the works are one work, done on the initiative of
God and in obedience to the Father.[36] The work comprises
more than just a number of acts which can be described as
σημεῖα; it is all that Jesus did (and said) on earth.

God's initiative is expressed in the terms ὁ πέμψας
με (4:34) and ὁ δέδωκάς μοι (17:4). Both expressions recur in similar contexts (respectively in 6:38-39, 9:4;
cf. 17:3, just before vs. 4, and in 5:36). Jesus' works
are also said to be performed "in the name of the Father"
(10:25). Therefore they may also be called God's works
(9:3, 10:37-38).

Jesus' obedience is expressed by ποιεῖν τὸ θέλημα
τοῦ πέμψαντός με (4:34, 5:30, 6:38-39). In 5:30 this presupposes a continuous listening to the Father (καθὼς ἀκούω
κρίνω) which is, again, parallel to "looking to the Father"
in 5:19. Jesus' work can only be God's work in a unity of
intention and action between Son and Father (5:17, 19-20,
30). If in this context also a perfect is used (as in vs.
22, τὴν κρίσιν πᾶσαν δέδωκεν τῷ υἱῷ; cf. 5:36, 17:4 and
12:50), or in similar passages an aorist (8:25, ἃ ἤκουσα
παρ' αὐτοῦ; cf. 8:40, 15:15, 5:28, καθὼς ἐδίδαξέν με),
this serves to emphasize that God took the initiative for
this continuous "cooperation." The Son is completely and
uniquely dependent on the Father. Besides in the expressions just mentioned, this is brought out in the ἐν ἐμοὶ ὁ
πατὴρ κἀγὼ ἐν τῷ πατρί of 10:38, and the ὁ πατὴρ ἐν ἐμοὶ
μένων ποιεῖ τὰ ἔργα αὐτοῦ in 14:10, connected with the ἐγὼ
ἐν τῷ πατρὶ καὶ ὁ πατὴρ ἐν ἐμοί of vs. 11.

Thirdly, because Jesus' works are the works of the
Father they can be said to provide convincing evidence

with regard to Jesus' relation to God (5:36, 10:25; cf.
10:37, 14:11, 15:24). We cannot discuss this in detail,[37]
but it should be remarked that the whole question of legitimation returns here. Once one accepts that Jesus has
the right to claim that his works are those of the Father,
one should believe in his unique mission; no other reaction is possible. But in order to accept this, one needs
faith. The identification of Jesus' ἔργα with God's ἔργα
is only possible and convincing within the circle of the
believers: to outsiders it remains an impossible conclusion, as 5:18; 8:13-19, 26-29, 40-42; and 10:31-39 show
clearly.

Fourthly, it should be remarked that Jesus' work,
although said to be completed at his return to the Father
(17:4, 4:34), is continued. The programmatic μείζω τούτων
ὄψη in 1:50 probably refers to all the Son of God/Son of
Man will do from that moment onwards, during his sojourn
on earth and later. In 5:20 the present healing points to
future μείζονα ἔργα, in the context: the giving of life
and the final judgment. Clearly all activity of the Son
in unity with the Father is meant, from the present moment
till the last judgment and the raising of the dead inclu-
sive--before and after his return to the Father. In 14:
12-14, Jesus tells his disciples that he who has faith in
him, because of the works done by the Father in and through
Jesus, "will do what I am doing; and he will do greater
things still because I am going to the Father." In fact
the Son will do these greater things himself, "so that the
Father may be glorified in the Son."[38]

Nowhere do we hear that the disciples perform signs;
clearly the word most suited to denote their activity and
their Master's continuing activity is ἔργα. What they do
he does, just as their word is his word (17:8, 14, 17, 18,
20; and 20:21, 24-31).

This brings us to a last point. All that Jesus did
and said on earth is summed up in the word ἔργον, and in
the instances where ἔργα is used, the word refers, in all

likelihood, not only to the σημεῖα proper, but also to a wide range of activities, just because God is active in the Son, and the Son is completely obedient to the Father. If this is true, what then is the relation between "works" and "words"? Two things should be emphasized here.

There is a clear parallelism between seeing and hearing, works and words, and, to some extent, there is interchangeability also. As to the relation between Son and Father, 5:19, with its emphasis on βλέπειν and ποιεῖν, is followed by 5:30, with its emphasis on ἀκούειν and κρίνειν, as an illustration of this ποιεῖν.[39] The same applies *mutatis mutandis* to 5:37, 38, after 5:36 and 8:28. The very use of the term τὰ ἔργα...μαρτυρεῖ περὶ ἐμοῦ in 5:36 (cf. 10:25) shows how closely works and words are related; the same is clear in the passing remark in 10:21. Yet works and words are never identified. 15:24 stands parallel to 15:22; after the temporarily concluding passage 12:37-43, dealing with the impact of Jesus' signs, we get a new concluding reference to Jesus' witness in complete unity with the Father in vss. 44-50, ending with the statement, "What the Father has said to me, therefore-- that is what I speak." Verses 44-50 come unexpected after vs. 36b and have no organic link with the preceding chapters. They consist of a number of statements which, in other forms, have already occurred in other contexts; these verses add nothing new and they are not meant to add anything new. In the present composition of the Gospel they give a summing up of the real intention of Jesus' preaching, after the preceding vss. 37-43 which look back on Jesus' signs.

Secondly, we have already noticed that the Gospel has a preference for belief in Jesus' word preceding belief in him on the strength of his signs. This is clear in the case of the βασιλικός in chapter 4, and in that of Martha in chapter 11, while the Thomas-story in chapter 20 points in the same direction. The demonstrative character of the signs is apt to be misinterpreted; but nowhere does the

Gospel disqualify the signs as superfluous or "second
best." R. Bultmann's often quoted saying, "The works of
Jesus (or, seen collectively as a whole: his work) are his
words" (occurring in §48, "The Revelation as the Word," of
his *Theology of the New Testament*),[40] is one-sided and
wrong.

The passages just mentioned link up with 10:32-38
and 14:8-12 which, while underlining the unity between
Father and Son, connect *and* distinguish what Jesus speaks
and does. Jesus' acts are essential; 10:37, referring
back to 5:36, gives the word of Jesus, "If I am not acting
as my Father would, do not believe me." To this, vs. 38
adds, "But if I am, accept the evidence of my deeds, even
if you do not believe me...." Jesus' words could and
should be convincing; his works irrefutably demonstrate
his unity with the Father. This is said to non-believing
Jews. Their misunderstanding and rejection of Jesus may,
in the last resort, be attributed to God's initiative (12:
37-43! just like the faith of the believers), yet they
have no excuse (15:22-25; cf. 9:40-41).

This passage, like the next, clearly does not aim
at discrediting the value of Jesus' deeds. 14:10 is usually adduced as the final proof-text for the identification of ἔργα and ῥήματα; it cannot be used as such, because in vs. 11 these two are again distinguished, and related to one another in the same way as in 10:32-38.
Moreover, the verse should be seen against the background
of the discourse on the unity of the Father and the Son in
chapter 5, where there is no identification but thoroughgoing parallelism. In vs. 11 we find "believe me" alongside "accept the evidence of the deeds themselves," this
time not as an argument for Jewish outsiders but as one
directed to disciples. Again the deeds are not mentioned
as "second best," but as finally convincing evidence. Jesus' words are effective, and his ἔργα give a reliable testimony. For those who are able to believe in it, there is
a surprising unity of event and proclamation in *all* that God
works in and through Jesus--but no identity.

NOTES

CHAPTER V

[1]See the useful survey in G. van Belle, *De Semeia-bron in het vierde evangelie. Ontstaan en groei van een hypothese* (Leuven: Universitaire Pers, 1975). R. T. Fortna's *The Gospel of Signs*, SNTSMS 11 (Cambridge: Cambridge University Press, 1970), and W. Nicol's *The Sēmeia in the Fourth Gospel*, NovTSup 32 (Leiden: Brill, 1972), have drawn much attention lately (see van Belle, *De Semeia-bron in het vierde evangelie*, pp. 111-48, on their books and the subsequent discussion). On Bultmann's earlier theory of a σημεῖα-Quelle, see particularly D. M. Smith, *The Composition and Order of the Fourth Gospel* (New Haven and London: Yale University Press, 1965).

[2]J. M. Robinson's article, "The Johannine Trajectory," in J. M. Robinson and Helmut Koester, *Trajectories through Early Christianity* (Philadelphia: Fortress, 1971), p. 235.

[3]I return to this question in Chapter VIII.

[4]Barnabas Lindars, *Behind the Fourth Gospel* (London: SPCK, 1971), p. 39. On the possible historical background of the argumentation, see Chapter IV, sections II, 3 and 6, and IV.

[5]See Chapter I, pp. 1-3.

[6]See Chapter I, pp. 7-12.

[7]On John the Baptist, see Chapter IV, pp. 85-90.

[8]On this verse, see above, pp. 133-34.

[9]As has often been remarked, the word σημεῖον does not occur between 12:37 and 20:30.

[10]The evangelist probably means that Isaiah saw the glory of the preexistent Son; see W. Thüsing, *Die Erhöhung und Verherrlichung Jesu im Johannesevangelium*, NTAbh 11, 1/2 (Münster: Aschendorff, [2]1970), pp. 218-19.

[11]On this, see Chapter II, esp. pp. 30-31.

[12]See Chapter II, esp. pp. 37-42.

[13]The Gospel not only closely relates *fides qua* and *fides quae*, but takes it for granted that true faith is possible only within the inner circle of those who are

instructed by Jesus (particularly in chapters 13-17, where they are prepared for his departure) and who submit themselves to the guidance of the Spirit after Jesus' glorification--see Chapter I.

[14]B. Olsson, who, in his *Structure and Meaning in the Fourth Gospel. A Text-linguistic Analysis of John 2:1-11 and 4:1-42*, ConB, NT Ser. 6 (Lund: Gleerup, 1974), consistently approaches the Gospel as a structured and meaningful whole, rightly argues that ἀρχή means more than just "first." What happened in Cana is "a primary sign, somehow representative of the creative and transforming work of Jesus" (pp. 67-69; see also p. 64).

[15]On this, see, e.g., R. Schnackenburg, *The Gospel according to St John* I, Herder's Theological Commentary on the New Testament (New York: Herder and Herder; London: Burns & Oates, 1968), pp. 464-75.

[16]This combination of words is found in the Fourth Gospel only here. It is rather frequently used in Acts and in the OT, particularly in Deuteronomy and other passages influenced by deuteronomistic theology; see K. H. Rengstorf, art. σημεῖον, in *TDNT* 7, pp. 200-61, esp. 216-17, 221, and 240-43. Here the addition of καὶ τέρατα seems to emphasize the miraculous aspect of the signs.

[17]So Olsson, *Structure and Meaning in the Fourth Gospel*, p. 77.

[18]See, again, ibid., pp. 43-45.

[19]Fortna also admits this, quoting words of Dodd: "Nowhere in the gospel have attempts to analyse out a written source, or sources, proved less convincing" (*The Gospel of Signs*, p. 74).

[20]So, e.g., J. Becker, "Wunder und Christologie," *NTS* 16 (1969-70), pp. 130-48, esp. pp. 146-47: "Durch seine Stellung degradiert Joh. xi 25f. das eigentliche Wunder zu einer nachhinkenden Sinnlosigkeit," and p. 147: "Das nämlich ist die Ironie in Joh. xi: Die Ungläubigen denen der Sinn von Joh. xi 25f. verborgen ist, sehen das Äussere und stossen sich am Wundertäter, der dieser Wunder genau zuvor seine theologische Relevanz genommen hatte."

[21]Besides this, it is clear that his resurrection, recorded just before the Passion (and, in fact, leading up to the Passion), presents to the reader "a preview of the wonder which lies beyond the passion, to be held in his mind as he reads the solemn passion narrative, and to guide his interpretation of it" (Lindars, *Behind the Fourth Gospel*, p. 55).

[22]See also Chapter III, pp. 59-60.

[23] The concept of "glorification" cannot be treated here; see, particularly, Thüsing, *Die Erhöhung und Verherrlichung Jesu im Johannesevangelium*, pp. 229-30. On pp. 193-98 he includes Jesus' obedience to death in his earthly work and sets it over against the further glorification after his return to the Father; we should speak here of two stages in God's revelation and work of salvation through the Son (and the Paraclete). See, however, p. 203 also: "So ist das verherrlichende Heilswerk in seinen beiden Stadien eine *Ganzheit*. Das Offenbarungsgeschehen des Erdenlebens Jesu und das des Parakleten sind nicht zwei verschiedene Werke, sonder das Werk Jesu selbst in seinen beiden Verwirklichungsphasen." Compare also R. Schnackenburg, *Das Johannesevangelium* II, Herders Theologischer Kommentar zum Neuen Testament (Freiburg-Basel-Wien: Herder, 1971), pp. 498-512, Exkurs 13, "Erhöhung und Verherrlichung Jesu." On what follows in this section, see, again, Chapter I, pp. 7-12.

[24] We are reminded here of 2:18-22; the first time death and resurrection are mentioned explicitly in the Gospel, it is in reply to a request of the Jews for a sign. They are not, however, themselves called a sign. This may be because, from the evangelist's post-resurrection viewpoint, the signs bear a preliminary character, whereas death and resurrection mark the beginning of a new period. See R. E. Brown, *The Gospel according to John (i-xii)*, The Anchor Bible 29 (Garden City, NY: Doubleday, 1966), p. 530: "Thus, the miracle is a sign, not only qualitatively (a material action pointing toward a spiritual reality), but also temporally (what happens before *the hour* prophesying what will happen after the hour has come). That is why, as we have explained, the signs of Jesus are found only in the first half of the Gospel (chs. i-xii)." Compare also Olsson, *Structure and Meaning in the Fourth Gospel*, p. 69.

[25] See further, above, pp. 133-34.

[26] Again the fact that the healing was performed on a sabbath is mentioned very late in the story.

[27] See further Chapter III, pp. 61-63.

[28] Chapter III, passim, and esp. pp. 57-58.

[29] On the following, see particularly P. Borgen, *Bread from Heaven. An Exegetical Study of the Concept of Manna in the Gospel of John and the Writings of Philo*, NovTSup 10 (Leiden: Brill, 1965).

[30] See vss. 26-27, and also 31 and 49. In vs. 26, Jesus even denies that his interlocutors have seen signs (notwithstanding vss. 2 and 14). Those who do not relate the signs to the gift of the true life have not really seen anything--compare here the same tension and ambiguity in the notion of faith elsewhere in the Gospel!

[31]On vss. 52-58 and 60-65, see Chapter VIII, pp. 208-9.

[32]The designation "the Twelve" is used only here and in 20:24, and is obviously regarded as known to the readers; it is not used in vss. 16-21 but occurs in vs. 67 to distinguish the faithful few from the many who have gone away.

[33]See Chapter IV, pp. 90-94.

[34]On this word, see now the monograph by J. Riedl, *Das Heilswerk Jesu nach Johannes*, Freiburger Theologische Studien 93 (Freiburg-Basel-Wien: Herder, 1973). In *Zeichen und Werke. Ein Beitrag zur Theologie des 4. Evangeliums in Erzählungs- und Redestoff*, ATANT 55 (Zürich: Zwingli Verlag, 1969), W. Wilkens has tried to explain the differences between signs and works by means of a theory of two forms of the Gospel, both written by the same author. A signs-gospel would have been expanded with discourse material and redacted; characteristic of the second stage is the use of the word "works." Wilkens finds it difficult to explain why the word "sign" does not occur in chapter 5, and only once in chapter 9. He also tends to maximize the differences in use and meaning between the two central words.

[35]In 10:33 it is used by the Jews, because they pick up the word used by Jesus in vs. 32.

[36]On this and related aspects of the relation between Jesus and God, see Chapter VI, pp. 142-49.

[37]See J. Beutler, *Martyria. Traditionsgeschichtliche Untersuchungen zum Zeugnisthema bei Johannes*, Frankfurter Theologische Studien 10 (Frankfurt: Knecht, 1972), particularly pp. 259-60, 272-73, and 293-98.

[38]Because of 4:34, 17:4, and 9:4, it is clear that there is not only continuity but also discontinuity between the works of the earthly Jesus and the exalted Son; one may compare here the two stages observed in connection with glory and glorification. See again Thüsing, *Die Erhöhung und Verherrlichung Jesu im Johannesevangelium*, particularly pp. 58-63.

[39]See also 3:32, "He who comes from heaven bears witness to what he has seen and heard."

[40]R. Bultmann, *Theology of the New Testament* II (New York: Scribner, 1955), p. 60.

CHAPTER VI

THE SON OF GOD AND THE CHILDREN OF GOD

"The reinterpretation of Jesus' kingship is given
in terms of divine Sonship, understood in a typically Johannine way. Jesus is prophet and king because he is the
Son sent by the Father, and only as Son of the Father."[1]
This conclusion at the end of the third chapter, "Jesus
as Prophet and King in the Fourth Gospel," expresses what
has proved to be important in all the other chapters as
well. The real heart of Johannine Christology is found in
a typically Johannine emphasis on the unique relationship
between Father and Son. At the same time we have often
had occasion to note that this innermost secret of Jesus
is revealed only to a small group of insiders. As was
noted in the study of "Nicodemus and Jesus," "Only the
children of God, of whom it may be said that they were
born from God (ἐκ θεοῦ ἐγεννήθησαν, John 1:12, 13; 1 John
3:1, 2, 10; 5:2), are able to understand and to follow
the unique Son of God."[2]

This leads us in this chapter to some further remarks on Jesus' divine Sonship, and to an investigation of
the relation between the Son of God and the children of
God. I concentrate again on the connection of ideas within the framework of the present Gospel, against the background of a number of stimulating studies in which the
relation between God and Jesus is viewed in the light of
general Oriental and Hellenistic ideas as well as particularly Jewish ideas of agency.[3] The concept of agency
covers a whole range of messengers and representatives
(including the son of the house) and has juridical aspects
(very important in the Fourth Gospel!) as well. In the
case of commissioning by God it includes prophets, angels,
personified Wisdom, the Son.

Before we analyze the expression "the Father who sent me," which is central against this background, we shall do well to discuss a number of related terms that illustrate aspects of Jesus' mission which are essential to John's argument.

Whence?

In the disputes between Jesus and the Jews in John 7[4] the question "Whence?" is first posed with respect to Jesus' teaching and then with respect to Jesus himself. "Where did he get this?" is connected with "Where does he himself come from?" Jesus' very being and his origin are discussed in the light of what he says and what he does. In 7:16 Jesus says: "What I am teaching you I do not have of myself, but it comes from him who sent me. He who wishes to do what God wills shall be able to discern whether my teaching comes from God or from myself." In vss. 27-29, referring to the Jewish position that "When the Messiah comes, no one will know whence he is" and the comment of the bystanders that they know very well whence Jesus comes, Jesus says: "So you know me, and you know whence I come? Yet I have not come on my own initiative; I am sent by him who is the true one; you do not know him. I know him, for I come from him. He has sent me."

Thus we see that the question, "Whence?", is answered with terms such as "not from myself," "from the Father," "sent." We find the same kind of response in 8:13-19 and 9:24-34. Anyone who does not know whence Jesus comes, such as his Jewish opponents, cannot recognize his authority. Pilate too is groping in the dark. After the Jewish accusation that Jesus has made himself God's Son (19:7), he asks the accused, "Whence do you come?" The fact that he still must ask proves that he does not know, and indeed he never will know. That had already earlier become evident, in the conversation that is set forth in 18:33-38. Jesus' kingdom is not of this world (or, to put it in another way, not from here); therefore his servants do not fight, and Jesus goes to the cross. Jesus' task is to be a witness to the truth; to this end he was born and has come into the world. And just as it is said in 7:16, that in order to understand Jesus one must will to do what God wills, in 18:37 it is stated that "everyone who is of the truth listens to my voice." Then Pilate asks, "What is truth?" thus betraying his own ignorance. And yet it may be said of him, "You would have no power over me at all if God had not given it to you" (19:11).

Thus the question as to "whence?" is the question of the source and authorization of what Jesus says and what he does.[5]

"Not on my own authority" and Related Expressions

In 7:17, the "I speak on my own authority"[6] is set over against "the teaching given by God." In the following verse it is said, speaking not merely of Jesus but in general: "Anyone who speaks on his own authority is seeking his own glory. But anyone who seeks the glory of the one who sent him is trustworthy." "Not on one's own authority" then signifies utter obedience to the one who sends, even the Sender. "Not coming of my own accord" (vs. 28) also stands in parallel here with "not speaking on my own authority" (vs. 17). This latter is again connected with "doing nothing on my own authority"; 8:28-29 offers a good example of this. There it is said by Jesus that the Jews will see later "that I am he, and that I do nothing on my own authority, but I speak just as the Father has taught me. He who sent me is with me. He has not forsaken me, because I always do what he wills."[7]

Jesus as the true sent one is conscious of being one with his Sender; he is guided by what the Sender, his Father, has taught him as Son, and he continues to live in and by the power of the Father's nearness. There is a unity of willing, speaking, and acting between Son and Father.

144

Comparable passages are 12:49, 14:10[8] and, above all, even earlier in the gospel, the fundamental exposition in 5:19-30, a direct working-out of Jesus' word in vs. 17, "So long as my Father works, I too am working," that prompts the Jewish adversaries to strive to put Jesus to death because he makes himself equal with God. I shall return to this shortly, but here I wish to point further to Jesus' utterance in 10:17 and 18, which forms a striking but sensible contrast with what has been related just previously. "The Father loves me, because I give my life, in order to take it again. No one takes it from me, but I lay it down of my own accord. I have power to lay it down and to take it up again. This is the charge that I have received from my Father." Precisely he who comes from the Father and acts in keeping with the Father's will has the authority to do something of his own accord--not under compulsion from others.[9]

From Above--From Heaven--From God

We turn now to a complex of expressions which with some variation (and the variation is even greater in the Greek than it is in English: ἄνωθεν, ἐκ τῶν ἄνω, οὐκ ἐντεῦθεν, ἐκ/ἀπὸ οὐρανοῦ, ἀπὸ/ἐκ/παρὰ τοῦ θεοῦ[10]) actually indicate the same thing, "from above"--"from heaven"--"from (or, out of) God." They serve to indicate the contrast between Jesus and his adversaries. In 8:23 Jesus says to the Jews, "You are from below, I am from above." In this respect the believers stand on Jesus' side: "if the world hates you, remember that they have already hated me. If you were of the world, the world would love its own; but because you are not of the world, but I have chosen you out of the world, therefore the world hates you" (15: 18, 19; cf. 17:6, 14-16, 18). Then parallel expressions also are used for the Son and the children. Thus Jesus says of himself, in 8:23, "I am from above," and in 8:42, "I proceeded and came forth from God," while in 8:47 he refers to the believer as "he who is of God." The point

145

concerning Jesus and the believers is their origin, their
source that determines their entire being, and that marks
not merely their being, but all their speaking and acting.
There is also a difference--we shall speak about that
later--but as over against the outsiders they belong together.

   In the series of expressions that concern us here,
the point is, in the first place, (again) the fact of being sent and authorized by God. John the Baptist, an ex-
tremely important witness to Jesus in this Gospel, is
called "a man sent from God" (1:6). Nicodemus, who does
not grasp the real mystery of Jesus,[11] says to him, "Rabbi,
we are convinced that you have come from God as a teacher."
He is thinking in terms of a prophet or teacher like Moses.
The Pharisees speak in the same terms when they say to the
blind man who had been healed, "This man does not come
from God, for he does not keep the Sabbath" (9:16; cf. vs.
29). The expressions used here are not incorrect, yet
there is a fundamental difference between Jesus' coming
from God and being sent by God, on the one hand, and that
of men like John the Baptist on the other hand. To indicate the unique character of Jesus' coming, the "from God"
must be made more precise as "from heaven," "from above."
This is done, then, in Jesus' answer to Nicodemus in 3:11-
21, and in the parallel detached passage in 3:31-36, where
the relationship between Father and Son is unavoidably
brought into the matter.[12]

   What is involved here is a genuine, reliable revelation of God which in God's name is brought by the Son,
who is one with the Father, into a world that has no ear
for it and hence is unbelieving. See 3:31, 32: "He comes
from heaven and is above all. He who comes from this
earth still belongs to the earth and speaks an earthly
language. But he comes from heaven and is above all. He
testifies to what he has heard and seen, and his testimony
is not accepted." "From above" and "from heaven" are expressions for what is radically different about God; they

also serve to ground the authority of Jesus who is speaking here by indicating his origin. Hence we read in vs.
34, "He whom God has sent utters God's words," and this
then is connected with the fact that God has given the
Spirit fully to this one whom he has sent. Anyone who
thus speaks and acts from God can only be identified with
the name of "Son." In vss. 35-36 then it is also said
that the Father loves the Son and has given all things
into his hands. It is in relation to him that the decision is made for belief or unbelief, life or death.

When the related expression, "I have come forth
from God," is used in 8:42, this again is intended to
underscore the unique authority of Jesus' words. Parallel
to it are the expressions, "I have not come of my own accord" and "He has sent me." Just before that (in vs. 40),
Jesus says, "...you seek to kill me, because I have proclaimed to you the truth that I have heard from God." The
opposition that Jesus experiences ultimately goes back to
the devil, as it is said in what follows (vss. 41-47). In
contrast to that, it is only "he who is from God," the believer, who can accept Jesus' words as "words that are
from God" (vs. 47). The same thing is said very plainly
in Jesus' last words to his disciples in chapters 13-17,
where the expression, "have come from God" (along with
others), appears several times (13:3, 16:27-30 and 17:8).
Only the believers have the correct insight into Jesus'
origin and therefore they also believe in his words: "Now
they know that all that thou hast given me comes from
thee. I have given them the words that I have heard from
thee, and they have received them and know truly that I
have come from thee. They have believed that thou hast
sent me" (17:7, 8).

The believers know not only whence Jesus has come,
but also whither he is going. Jesus' coming into the
world presupposes a return. "I have come from the Father
into the world. But now I leave the world and return to
the Father" (16:28). [13] What this implies for Jesus and
the believers is to be considered later.

"The Father who has sent me"

As we have already stated several times in the preceding paragraphs, the divine origin and authorization of
Jesus' words and deeds is very often expressed with a form
of the verb "to send." An emissary is not simply someone
who is sent, but also an envoy, a plenipotentiary; he
speaks and acts in the name of the one who has sent him.[14]
The perfect emissary identifies himself entirely with his
sender. The expressions "he who has sent me" or, in the
third person, "he who has sent him," appear in the Gospel
no fewer than eighteen times,[15] and along with these we
find, in addition, the fuller reference to "the Father who
has sent me (him)" six times.[16] No other single Christological expression appears so often in the Fourth Gospel,
and it is worthy of note that this actually is a theological term. Equally noteworthy is the fact that an active
participle (from the Greek verb πέμπω) is used. Nowhere
is the passive participle "sent" connected with Jesus.[17]
When the author wants to say something about Jesus, he
uses the expression "...whom God (or, he) has sent."[18]
Thus once again an active form of the verb is used, this
time of the Greek verb ἀποστέλλω. The same verb appears
even more often with God as the subject and Jesus as the
object. Thus here also the emphasis is placed upon the
sending activity of God, in which the unity of speaking,
willing, and acting between God and Jesus, Father and Son,
is grounded.[19]

The exposition of the Johannine ἔργον-concept in
Chapter V (see particularly pp. 132-36) is also directly
relevant here, especially what is said there about continuous cooperation. Jesus did not merely receive his commission and instruction, once and for all; he continues to
work in constant dependence upon the Father, καθὼς ἀκούω
κρίνω (5:30; see also vss. 17, 19 and 20, and cf. 11:41-42).
This is the Johannine variation of the OT and Jewish idea
that God is with the one whom he has sent; see, for example, Jer 1:4-10, 19, and the utterance of Nicodemus in

3:3! [20] Jesus also uses the term μετ' ἐμοῦ for his relationship with the Father (8:29; cf. vs. 16 and 16:32).
One notes again and again that the writer of the Fourth
Gospel exhibits a close affinity with all sorts of Jewish
conceptions and theories about prophets, angels, and especially Moses, [21] but that still at the critical moment more
is said than can be expressed in categories of sending.
That the Son is the perfect and, as such, unique emissary
simply can no longer be expressed with the word "prophet,"
and the term "sent one" is just as far from being adequate. [22] To be sure, according to Jewish perspective also,
the son of the sender can function as the most fully qualified envoy, but what is said, with the help of many other
expressions, about the Johannine Son, even goes beyond this
category. See, for example, 5:17-30!

"...making himself equal to God" (5:18)

In 5:17-30 it also becomes evident that, in the
opinion of the evangelist, according to Jewish views, anyone who calls God his Father makes himself equal to God.
In 5:18 we read how the Jews determined all the more to
kill Jesus "because he not only subverted the Sabbath, but
moreover called God his own Father and made himself equal
with God." Their motivation recurs in 10:38 as a direct
accusation: ὅτι σὺ ἄνθρωπος ὢν ποιεῖς σεαυτὸν θεόν (cf.
19:7, ὅτι υἱὸν θεοῦ ἑαυτὸν ἐποίησεν).

These objections also are used by the evangelist in
order further to undergird his own Christian viewpoint.
In 5:17-30 (and in 10:22-38), he undoubtedly is attempting
to provide the members of the Johannine communities with
arguments with which they can defend themselves in the debate with the synagogue and to enable them within their
own circles to think through the implications of the position they have adopted. [23] In his article, "The Divine
Agent and his Counterfeit in Philo and the Fourth Gospel,"
Meeks has shown that here the Jews reproach Jesus with the
same charge that Philo makes against Caligula. He, a man,

is making himself God. What the Christian community says
in defense against that charge is directly linked to what
Philo and others remark about the relationship of Moses
and the prophets to God. About chapter 5, Meeks says:
"The dependence of the messenger on the sender is a leading motif in the Jewish conception of the apostolic prophet....Further the notion that some messengers of God
could be commissioned to perform tasks that are ordinarily
God's works (raising the dead; executing judgment, vss.
21-22) appears in a number of aggadic traditions and is at
least implicit in Philo's account of Moses' miracles."[24]
He points further to the midrash-like argumentation in 10:
34-36. However, he correctly concludes that even here the
Jewish traditions are used in such a way that the Jews
themselves must, according to the experience and the perspective of the Johannine communities, reject this usage
as absurd and blasphemous. He says, "From the Jewish side,
the Christian development of the 'envoy of God' notion has
reached the point of blasphemy, and anyone who makes that
kind of claim about Jesus has to be expelled."[25]

        The Fourth Gospel identifies Jesus as God, and in-
deed at very significant points--at the outset, in 1:1 and
1:18, and at the end in 20:28.[26] The entire intervening
testimony attempts to make clear that here we are not
dealing with a man who has elevated himself to God, but
with the Son, who at a crucial point in world history was
sent by God, and who so fulfilled his mission that he became totally "transparent" to the Father, who spoke and
worked in him (12:45, 14:7-11).

Some Supplementary Observations

        Having arrived at this point, we shall do well to
offer some further elucidation of the relationship of
Father and Son by referring briefly to two points.
        a. In speaking about "from above," "from heaven,"
there is presupposed a picture of the world in which God's
heaven is exalted high above the world of men. Thus one

150

can say that here the author is speaking "mythologically"
and can inquire what is the meaning of this mythic way of
speaking.[27] In doing this, it will be wise to note that
neither the descent of the Son nor his return to the Father
is described anywhere in the Gospel or the Epistles. The
expressions which we are discussing appear only in the
discourses of Jesus and not in the narrative portions of
the Gospel. The "how" is not at all important, but the
"that," expressed in *these* words, is essential. Evidently
the Fourth Gospel cannot in any other way express how
unique is the bond between Jesus and God and how alien is
the world to God and to Jesus. How remarkable it is that
the Son, however, speaking and acting on God's initiative,
has revealed God in the world; and how remarkable it is
that men, in exceptional cases, have accepted this revelation, to live by it.

　　　b. In recent years there has been frequent discussion of a "Christology of function" as contrasted with a
"Christology of natures."[28] The objection then is raised
against the early Christian dogma that, as it is said,
places too much emphasis on the nature of God and the nature of Christ--one may think of such terms as "trinity"
and "the two natures." What is important is not the "nature" but the "action" and "speaking" of God and of Jesus.
The issue here is not whether the early Christian dogma is
thus rightly interpreted; I must say that in the case of
the Fourth Gospel we must be careful with the distinction
that is being made here. Of course with John also, as was
made clear above, all the emphasis is placed on the Son's
acting and speaking in the name of the Father. But it was
also made clear that in order to say something about what
is distinctive in this acting and speaking, John had to go
back to the origin of the one who here spoke and acted; it
does not make sense to play acting and being, function and
nature, off against each other. In its "mythical" discourse the Fourth Gospel is also dealing with the nature
of the Son, in his relationship with the Father.

The Children of God

The Son of God enters the world as an alien, and is neither comprehended nor accepted by the world. Those who do accept him are also themselves aliens in a hostile world. In the history of the Son the children of God recognize their own history. The communities in which the Fourth Gospel and the Epistles arose and were read were conscious of being threatened by a hostile outpost. To quote W. A. Meeks again: "The story describes the progressive alienation of Jesus from the Jews. But something else is happening, for there are some few who do respond to Jesus' signs and words, and these, while they also frequently 'misunderstand,' are progressively enlightened and drawn into intense intimacy with Jesus, until they, like him, are not 'of this world.' Now their becoming detached from the world is, in the Gospel, identical with their being detached from Judaism."[29]

Let us first work out, in somewhat more detail, three aspects of being a child of God: the origin of the believers, their relationship to Jesus, and their relationship to the world.

The Origin of the Believers

In the prologue, the children of God are called "begotten of God" (1:12, 13); here, "of God" is set in contrast to "of blood," "of the will of the flesh," and "of the will of man." That which is divinely new stands over against that which is typically finite and human. In 3:3-8, new expressions are added--"to be born/begotten anew" (in the Johannine perspective that is "to be begotten from above"), "of water and Spirit" (a reference to baptism), and "of the Spirit" (that is, not "of flesh"). Believers are begotten from above; God takes the initiative through the Spirit (of whom man does not know "whence he comes and whither he goes," no more than in the case of Jesus himself).

Hence 8:47 calls the believer "he who is from God"; in the First Epistle also, in 3:9-10, we find the expressions "begotten of God," "children of God," and "from God" parallel to each other. The First Epistle, which speaks often of being "begotten of God" (2:29; 3:9; 4:7; 5:1, 4, 18), in one passage (5:18) also connects this expression with Jesus, "We know that everyone who is begotten of God does not sin (this refers to the believer), because he who was begotten of God (that is, the Son) keeps him."[30] Here the participle used for the Son is different from the one used for the believer; with all the similarity, there is a distinction. This is evident also in the use of the words "children" and "Son." The believers are always called "children" (1:12; 11:52; 1 John 3:1, 2, 10; 5:2), never "sons" (a word that one does find in this connection in Paul; see Rom 8:14, 19; II Cor 6:8; Gal 4:6, 7); they are distinguished from the Son *par excellence*. Yet they are related to him, for they are the ones who have said "yes" to the Son when God sent him into the hostile world. They too may call God "Father," although a distinction still remains; "I go to my Father, who is also your Father, to my God, who is also your God," is the message of the risen Jesus who is about to return to his Father, a message which Mary Magdalene must take to his "brethren" (20:17). Only thanks to the Son the children belong to the great family of God.

The Believers and Jesus

Thus one does not become a child of God apart from the Son.[31] Sometimes the dependence is clearly expressed, as in the texts about the sending of the believers by the Son, who himself is sent. Here we can refer to 4:38, 17:18, and especially 20:21, where after the resurrection Jesus says to the assembled disciples, "As the Father has sent me, so also I send you forth." Here the crucial word is "as." It not only indicates a similarity, but also a difference; the "as" is at the same time also "because."

When Jesus says in 17:18, "As thou hast sent me into the world, so also I send them into the world," reference is made to the similarity between Jesus and those who are his, but it is also indicated that *their* being sent is based on *his* being sent. In the last analysis, each and everyone is dependent upon "the Father who has sent *him*." One may also think of the many other utterances where the little word "as" is used. As an example, I mention 6:57, "As the living Father has sent me and I live through him, so also shall the one who eats me live through me." The terminology is borrowed from the Supper; it is clearly stated how the believer is dependent upon Jesus, and how Jesus is dependent upon the Father.[32]

In 1:12, 13, the "begotten of God" is connected with "receive him" (that is, in this context, the Word), and "believe in his name," in such a way that the human decision is mentioned first, and then God's initiative. Yet faith is a response to, and not a pre-condition of, that initiative. This is evident in the Nicodemus story in chapter 3, where it is said that one must first be begotten/born from above/anew before one can enter the Kingdom of God, and where Nicodemus does not comprehend this and thus also is unable to understand Jesus at the deepest level.

We find something of the same sort in 7:17--only one who wills to do what God wills recognizes what Jesus teaches as something that comes from God. Only those who are "of the truth" listen to Jesus when he comes into the world as a witness to the truth (18:37). But how can you know what is God's will and what is truth without first knowing and accepting Jesus? John does not solve this problem; he does underscore the point that only within the relationship of trust among Father, Son, and children is justice actually done to God's intention. We would like to know what is first and what comes later, and we like to think in terms of cause and effect, but the Fourth Gospel and the First Epistle also simply put things side-by-side,

154

and they attribute all that is good, and all that is
willed and given by God, to his initiative. Thus, very
fittingly, in 3:21, where the author speaks of the divine
light that is kindled in the darkness in Jesus, "He who
does the truth seeks out the light, for there it is evident that it is God who is at work in all his deeds."

The Believers and the World

It is just the children of God who recognize and
confess the Son of God, and therefore they stand together
with the Son over against a hostile world. This is made
clear particularly in the farewell discourses. Reference
is first made in 15:18ff., in the passage that begins with
"If the world hates you, remember that it has already
hated me," and that then, toward the end, especially in
16:1-4, speaks very specifically of "putting you out of
the synagogue" and "killing you." In chapter 17 also we
read that the believers, as aliens in the world and as
disciples of the Stranger from Heaven, remain behind in
the world with their commission (vss. 14-18). There yawns
a great gulf of misunderstanding, unbelief, and enmity between "the world," often represented by "the Jews," on one
side and Jesus with his disciples on the other side. The
prayer in chapter 17 ends with the words: "Righteous Father, the world does not know you, but I know you, and
those whom you have entrusted to me know that you have
sent me. I have taught them who you are, and I continue
to do this, for the love with which you have loved me must
dwell in them, and I myself also must dwell in them" (vss.
25-26).

God, the Son, and the World

It is not improbable that in this strong emphasis
upon the distinction of believers and world, and in the
concentration on the believers, as it is found among other
places in 17:25, 26, the concrete circumstances of the Johannine communities are reflected; these people were

exposed to suspicion and persecution, from the side of
those whom they identified as "the Jews,"[33] and likewise
from all sorts of other forces and groups in the world.

But the question must be posed whether in this concentration on the children of God one has not lost sight
of the world. Why is it said, in this Gospel also, and
precisely here, that God so loves *the world* that he sent
his Son? Is God concerned with the world, or with the
group of the believers?

To the World, Into the World

The one who is sent by God and comes from God
comes into the world. Whenever, in the use of verbs of
"sending" or "coming," the attention is not directed
simply to the "whence," or whenever we do not have simply
a statement of the fact of the sending or coming, "the
world" is given as the destination of that sending or coming.

After the feeding of the five thousand, the men in
Galilee accept Jesus as "the prophet who should come into
the world" (6:14). Martha reaches a profounder level when
she confesses Jesus as "the Christ, the Son of God, who
should come into the world" (11:27).[34] Various times we
hear that God has sent his Son into the world (3:17, along
with "he gave" in vs. 16; 10:36; 1 John 4:9). Then it is
said of him that he speaks to the world what he has heard
from his Father (8:26). He has come into the world for
judgment (9:39)--"I was born and came into the world to be
a witness to the truth," Jesus says to Pilate (18:37), and
just before that he says to the high priest that he has
always spoken "to the world" openly and without hiding
anything (18:20).

Jesus has come into the world as a light (12:46;
cf. 1:9, 3:19). He then also calls himself the light of
the world (8:12, 9:5), just as in 4:42 and 1 John 4:14 he
is called the savior of the world and in 1:29 "the lamb
that takes away the sin of the world" (cf. 1 John 2:2).

He who comes into the world from God is also sent to the
world. God is not interested in the condemnation but in
the saving of the world (3:17, 12:47). In the discourse
about the bread from heaven, it is plainly said that this
bread of life is intended for the world (6:33, 51).

The world can gain insight. Jesus is going to the
Father, via the cross, because "the world must know that
I love the Father and do all that he has commanded me"
(14:31). Obviously then the world also *can* know this and
thus has no excuse, as is clearly said in 15:22-24 (cf.
10:37, 38): "If I had not come and spoken to them..." and
"If I had not done in their presence what no one else ever
had done, then there would be nothing to reproach them
for. But now they have seen that, and yet they will to
know nothing of me and of my Father." In 8:28 Jesus says
to the Jews about the time after the crucifixion, "When
you have lifted up the Son of Man, then you will see that
I am he, and that I do nothing of myself, but proclaim
what my Father has taught me."

Here the reference is to the time when the disciples will act as representatives of the Son. They too are
sent into the world (17:18) and live there without actually belonging to this world (17:11)! If they proclaim the
word, then others will come to believe in Jesus through
that word (17:20). These believers must all be one because of the unity between Father and Son and the "reciprocal indwelling" of Father and Son in the believers.
"Then the world will know," Jesus says to the Father,
"that you have sent me and have loved them just as you
have loved me" (17:23; cf. vs. 21).

Thus the world can gain insight and come to repen-
tance; that is also God's intention in the sending of the
Son. And yet what is said in the Johannine writings about
the world is primarily negative.

The Reaction of the World

In a recent study of the use of the word κόσμος in the Gospel and the Epistles of John, N. H. Cassem comes to a number of interesting conclusions.[35] When we distinguish the positive and negative use of the term, the division is 18 to 9 in the first twelve chapters of the Gospel, and 7 to 30 in chapters 13 through 18. For the First Epistle, the ratio is 3 to 19. The second part of the Gospel and the First Epistle are concerned with the situation of the community in the world after Jesus' departure. All the emphasis clearly falls upon the actual response of the world to the message of Jesus and of his disciples after him; this response is negative, and equally negative is the judgment upon this response. In the first half of the Gospel more emphasis is placed upon God's attitude toward the world; this is quite clearly positive.

A second conclusion is that there is a clear distinction made in the import of "world" dependent on the various prepositions used in connection with the word. As was said above, "to/into the world" appears particularly in connection with words of "sending" and "coming." Thus it stands in the context of God's orientation to the world. Of the fifteen times that the expression "out of the world" appears, it occurs ten times in connection with "being of the world," and that is clearly a negatively regarded state. "Being in the world" is a negatively or neutrally regarded condition.

We can say that God is concerned with the world; this is why Jesus came and why the disciples also are sent forth into the world. But in the concrete confrontation with Jesus it becomes evident that he brings about a division. People say No; those who say Yes are the rare exception--that quite clearly in 3:19-21, which declares that the coming of the light signifies a separation, because men love darkness rather than light. This is the way they are, this is the way the world is, and the outcome is obvious--everyone who does evil things has an

aversion to the light, because he is afraid that his deeds
will be brought to light. God's Son comes to save, not to
condemn, but the judgment brings irrevocable separation
(3:16-18). In the story of the healing of the young blind
man in chapter 9, it is made clear that men *may* see because their eyes are opened. It appears also that men who
think that they see in essence are stone blind. "I have
come into this world," says Jesus, "to bring the decision
(the judgment): the blind begin to see and those who see
become blind" (9:39).

The rejection by the world is declared, not explained. It is just as great a mystery as the faith of
the believers. In some texts, however, the devil is
brought into the picture. Just as faith and good deeds
are ultimately traced to their divine origin, unbelief and
evil works are traced to their devilish origin. When in
chapter 8 (vss. 39-47) the debate between Jesus and his
Jewish adversaries becomes intense, and the Jews appeal to
their having descended from Abraham, Jesus makes it clear
that Abraham is on his side and not on theirs. In their
hatred against Jesus and their efforts to kill him, they
are behaving just like their father, the devil: "You are
of the devil; he is your father, and his desires are your
intention also. He is a murderer from the very beginning"
(vs. 44). Jesus' adversaries simply do not have the right
to say, "God is our Father, God alone" (vs. 41).

This idea is further worked out in 1 John 3:4-12,
where the children of the devil stand over against the
children of God and where Cain is branded as "of the evil
one" because he killed his brother. Evil works and evil
men are literally of the evil one.[36] A couple of times
something is said also about the "prince of this world."
In Jesus' elevation/glorification, it becomes evident that
the reign of that prince is coming to an end (12:31, 16:
11). He has no power over Jesus (14:30). Therefore the
disciples, who now suffer oppression in the world, may be
of good courage: "I have overcome the world" (16:33; cf.

1 John 5:4, 5); or, as it is said in different words in
1 John 2:13, 14, but likewise for encouragement, "You have
overcome the devil."

Whence the "prince of the world" comes and where
he gets his power is not clear. Moreover, it is nowhere
said that man can shift the responsibility off on him. He
is there, and he is at work, as is evident even within the
circle of the disciples in the case of Judas (13:2, 27; 6:
70). The Johannine theology is strongly dualistic, and
that dualism comes to a focus in speaking and acting; but
at the same time the question of origin is constantly being posed, and then everything that is not of God is ultimately of the evil one. But the existence of evil and
of the evil one is not explained, and in the last analysis
the Word, which is related to God in a unique way, is the
power that has created even the world (1:3, 9).

The Father has given all power into the hands of
the Son (3:34, 5:20, 10:17, 13:3, 17:2), and Jesus gains a
victory over the hostile powers in the world, but only
those who accept him have received what God intended to
give them. In the beginning of the prayer in chapter 17
we read, "You have made him lord and master over all men
and have given him power to bestow eternal life upon every
one whom you have entrusted to him." Hence the farewell
discourses begin in 13:1 with the remark that Jesus has
remained faithful to the end to those who belong to him in
the world. And hence the evangelist says in 11:52 that
Jesus died "to gather together again God's children who
are scattered abroad over the whole world."[37] This concerns not only the children of God in Israel, but also
those among the Gentiles (cf. 10:16; 12:19, 20, and especially 12:32).[38] God's intention for the world is realized in the church as the community of those who have accepted and kept the word of Jesus.

The World as a Temporary Dwellingplace

The story of the children of God in a hostile world
is not yet finished. The Son does not remain in the world
but has returned to the Father; those who belong to him
will follow him at the time that is destined for them.
Now a few remarks about this, which must be brief because
Jesus' return to the Father is only one facet of what John
calls Jesus' exaltation or glorification--a typical Johannine complex of ideas that in grand fashion takes Good
Friday, Easter, Ascension, and Pentecost together and interprets them together.[39] We can concern ourselves only
with the four or five Greek words used to indicate Jesus'
return to the Father[40] and ask what this departure signifies for the community that is left behind.

Here also the outsiders comprehend nothing. When
Jesus during the disputes in Jerusalem related in John 7
says, "I shall not be with you long, for I am returning to
him who has sent me" (vs. 33), his adversaries think that
he will go to the Jews in the Dispersion (vss. 35, 36).[41]
In vs. 34 and in a later stage of the discussion (in 8:21,
22), it is underscored that the Jews will not be able to
come where Jesus is going, because "You are from here below, I am from above; you belong to this world, I do not
belong to this world" (vs. 23).

In the farewell discourses of Jesus, the disciples
are prepared for this departure.[42] In the utterances
about this we can distinguish various trains of thought.
In 13:31-38 we hear first that the same thing holds true
for the disciples as for the outsiders: "Dear children, I
shall not be with you much longer. Now I say to you the
same thing I said to the Jews: You shall seek me, but
where I am going you cannot come." But that is not the
final word. To his question, "Lord, where then are you
going?" Peter receives the answer, "Where I am going you
cannot follow me now, but later you will follow me." Here
(see also vss. 37-38) and elsewhere (12:25, 26; 21:19, 20),
"follow" clearly also has the overtone of "follow in the

footsteps, imitate" with all the consequences implied.[43]
In vss. 34-35, the commandment is given for the interim
that people must love each other.

In 17:24, almost at the end of the prayer that concludes the farewell discourses, Jesus asks of God, "Father,
this I desire, that all those whom you have entrusted to
me shall be where I am, and that they shall see the glory
that you have given to me, for you loved me before the
foundations of the world were laid." The Son in his journey travels from the Father to the world, and back to the
Father, from glory to glory. Ultimately, it is said here,
all those whom God has entrusted to Jesus, liberated from
their troubled existence in this world, shall see that
glory and share in it.

In 14:1-3, the idea of Jesus' going away is connected with "preparing a place" and returning to fetch the
believers, "for," Jesus says, "you shall be where I am."
In 14:4-6 the announcement of the departure evokes the
question as to the way. This question is answered with
the well-known words: "I am the way, the truth, and the
life. No one comes to the Father except through me."

Much more might be said here; anyone who studies
the farewell discourses carefully will note how Jesus
therein offers encouragement and admonition to the believers for the time between his departure and their departure. For John also the community lives in an interim
period.

There is however still another word that indicates
the return to the Father and hence demands our attention--
"ascend," which appears three times (3:13, 6:62, 20:17;
cf. 13:1) and which corresponds to "descend," used in 3:13
and particularly in chapter 6 in the discourse about the
bread from heaven, with which Jesus identifies himself
(vss. 33, 38, 41, 42, 50, 51, 58). Still more clearly
than the other terms discussed in this closing section,
these words indicate that in connection with going to the
Father people thought in spatial categories, and that they

actually could not help speaking "mythically." But just
as in the use of "descend" in chapter 6, it is evident
that the point is not at all the spatial idea itself but
rather doing the will of the Father (vss. 38, 44-46) and
the bestowal of life that by virtue of its source conquers
all death, so also in the case of the contrasting "ascend"
the point is not a relocation. In 6:62 and 20:17 it indicates the conclusion of the period of the descent. In his
return the one who descended shows that he truly came from
God; the one who was sent returns to the one who sent him;
he has completed his work.[44] At the same time the ascension, as an element in Jesus' exaltation, introduces a new
phase in the process of revelation (20:19-23).

NOTES

CHAPTER VI

[1]See above, p. 69.

[2]See above, pp. 41-42.

[3]See P. Borgen, *Bread from Heaven. An Exegetical
Study of the Concept of Manna in the Gospel of John and
the Writings of Philo*, NovTSup 10 (Leiden: Brill, 1965),
pp. 158-64; his "God's Agent in the Fourth Gospel," in
*Religions in Antiquity. Essays in Memory of E. R. Good-
enough*, ed. J. Neusner (Leiden: Brill, 1968), pp. 137-48;
and his "Some Jewish exegetical traditions as background
for Son of Man sayings in John's Gospel (John 3:13-14 and
context)," in *L'Evangile de Jean, Sources, rédaction, théologie*, ed. M. de Jonge et al., pp. 243-58; see below,
Chapter VIII, p. 194. Important also are W. A. Meeks's
publications. Besides his *The Prophet-King. Moses Traditions and the Johannine Christology*, NovTSup 14 (Leiden:
Brill, 1967), pp. 301-6, and his "Moses as God and King,"
in *Religions in Antiquity*, pp. 354-71, we should mention
here his important paper, "The Man from Heaven in Johannine Sectarianism," *JBL* 91 (1972), pp. 44-72, in which he
also points to the parallelism between Jesus the Revealer
and the recipients of the revelation. A more recent contribution to the subject is his "The Divine Agent and his
Counterfeit in Philo and the Fourth Gospel," in E. S.
Fiorenza, *Aspects of Religious Propaganda in Judaism and
Early Christianity*, Studies in Judaism and Christianity in
Antiquity 2 (Notre Dame: University of Notre Dame Press,
1976), pp. 43-67. J. P. Miranda's dissertation, *Der Vater
der mich gesandt hat. Religionsgeschichtliche Untersuchung-
en zu den johanneischen Sendungsformeln; zugleich ein Beitrag zur johanneischen Christologie und Ekklesiologie*,
Europäische Hochschulschriften 23, 7 (Bern: Lang, 1972),
gives interesting material, but is not very clear in its
conclusions. His last chapter deals with the concept of
the Prophet. See also the studies by J. A. Bühner,
"Prophet und Engel. Abstieg und Aufstieg Jesu nach dem
vierten Evangelium im Licht der jüdischen Religionsgeschichte," and *Der Gesandte und sein Weg im vierten Evangelium* (Tübingen: Mohr, 1977), which is important particularly for the author's patient search for, and interesting
analysis of, further Jewish parallels to the Johannine
ideas of agency. Interesting also is K. Berger's treatment of the Amen-sayings in the Fourth Gospel, on pp. 96-
117 of his *Die Amen-Worte Jesu. Eine Untersuchung zum
Problem der Legitimation in apokalyptischer Rede*, BZNW 39
(Berlin: de Gruyter, 1970). His conclusion is: "Because

Amen-sayings are only testimonies to what Jesus has heard from the Father, they are set entirely in the context of Jesus' having been sent by God and similarly in the context of the disciples' being sent by Jesus. If one assumes a prophetic figure derivable from Deutero-Isaiah, Jesus appears here as a prophet" (p. 116). See also Berger's "Zum traditionsgeschichtlichen Hintergrund christologischer Hoheitstitel," NTS 17 (1970-71), pp. 391-425, and "Die königlichen Messiastraditionen des Neuen Testaments," NTS 20 (1973-74), pp. 1-44.

[4]On this see M. de Jonge, "Onbegrip in Jeruzalem. Jezus en de Joden in Johannes 7," in Rondom het Woord 15 (1973), pp. 61-80. On 7:14-24, see also Chapter III, above, "Jesus as Prophet and King in the Fourth Gospel."

[5]One may defend the thesis that the evangelist hints at a deeper meaning in all other instances where πόθεν is used (1:48, 2:9, 3:8, 4:11, 6:5). See, e.g., B. Olsson, Structure and Meaning in the Fourth Gospel, ConB, NT Series 6 (Lund: Gleerup, 1974), p. 59.

[6]On the "prophetic" background of this term, see R. Bultmann, The Gospel of John (Philadelphia: Westminster, 1971), pp. 249-50. To the OT parallels mentioned by him, one may add also Jub. 6:35.

[7]See also 8:40, 42-43.

[8]In 5:43 Jesus says that he comes in the name of the Father (cf. 10:25); he contrasts himself with those who appear in their own name--a clearly related expression. Caiaphas (11:51) and the Spirit of Truth (16:13-15) also speak "not of themselves." Cf. also the use of this expression in 15:4 and 18:34.

[9]See J. Blank, Krisis. Untersuchungen zur johanneischen Christologie und Eschatologie (Freiburg: Lambertus, 1964), p. 113: "Because Jesus' activity issues entirely from God and is grounded in God, he has full authority for and freedom in action. Thereby the being and action, οὐκ ἀφ' ἑαυτοῦ, confirms the fact that Jesus is the Son, the eschatological emissary of God, who fulfills the divine will in all that he does." An interesting parallel to 10:17-18 is found in Herm. Man. 11:5.

[10]On the use of παρά, ἀπό, and ἐκ in these contexts, see C. H. Dodd, The Interpretation of the Fourth Gospel (Cambridge: Cambridge University Press, 1953), p. 259, and T. E. Pollard, "The Father-Son and God-Believer Relationships according to St. John: a Brief Study of John's Use of Prepositions," in M. de Jonge et al., L'Evangile de Jean, pp. 363-69. One should not stress the differences (between the prepositions, and in the use of these prepositions in connection with different persons), but rather note the combinations of expressions using different prepositions.

[11]On this, see Chapter II.

[12]See Chapter II, pp. 37-41.

[13]See also 13:3.

[14]See, e.g., K. H. Rengstorf, art. ἀποστέλλω, in *TDNT* 1, pp. 398-406, and the literature mentioned in note 3, above.

[15]4:34; 5:24, 30; 6:38, 39; 7:16, 28, 33; 8:16(?), 26, 29; 9:4; 12:44, 45; 13:20; 15:21; 16:5. Cf. 7:18 and 13:16.

[16]5:23, 37; 6:44; 8:16(?), 18; 12:49; 14:24.

[17]Ἀπεσταλμένος occurs twice in connection with John the Baptist (1:6, 3:28) and once with people sent by the Pharisees (1:24). In addition, it is used once as the translation of the name Siloam in 9:7, clearly referring to Jesus' mission in the world. See also Miranda, *Der Vater der mich gesandt hat*, p. 9. Ἀπόστολος occurs only once in a general statement in 13:16, where ἀπόστολος versus ὁ πέμψας αὐτόν stands parallel to δοῦλος versus κύριος.

[18]3:34, 5:38, 6:29, 10:36, 17:3.

[19]Miranda, *Der Vater der mich gesandt hat*, p. 29, rightly says concerning the use of the two verbs for sending: "In the Johannine usage...a certain consistency can be discerned, which however does not suffice for a conceptual differentiation." This contra Rengstorf, art. ἀποστέλλω, p. 404; Blank, *Krisis*, p. 70, n. 61; and many others, among them J. Seynaeve, "Les verbes ἀποστέλλω et πέμπω dans le vocabulaire théologique de Saint Jean," in de Jonge et al., *L'Evangile de Jean*, pp. 385-89.

[20]For further parallels, see R. Schnackenburg, *The Gospel according to St John* I, Herder's Theological Commentary on the New Testament (New York: Herder and Herder; London: Burns & Oates, 1968), p. 366, n. 61.

[21]See particularly J. A. Bühner's studies on the points raised in this section.

[22]Here one should, of course, also take into account the use of the terms Son of God, the Son, etc., in other early Christian writings, in their relationships to conceptions of prophecy and agency; see the articles by K. Berger mentioned in n. 3, above, and M. Hengel, *Son of God* (Philadelphia: Fortress, 1976). An interesting case, where prophethood and sonship are distinguished and connected, is found in Mark 12:1-8, coming after 11:27-33. See M. de Jonge, "The Use of χριστός in the Passion Narratives," in J. Dupont et al., *Jésus aux origines de la*

Christologie, BETL 40 (Leuven: Leuven University Press; Gembloux: Duculot, 1975), pp. 169-92, esp. p. 180.

[23]Cf. Chapter IV, section IV, in discussion with others. See esp. J. L. Martyn, *History and Theology in the Fourth Gospel* (New York-Evanston: Harper & Row, 1968); "Source Criticism and Religionsgeschichte in the Fourth Gospel," in *Jesus and Man's Hope* 1, ed. D. G. Buttrick (Pittsburgh: Pittsburgh Theological Seminary, 1970), pp. 247-73; and "Glimpses into the History of the Johannine Community," in de Jonge et al., *L'Evangile de Jean*, pp. 149-75.

[24]Meeks, "The Divine Agent," p. 55.

[25]Ibid., p. 59.

[26]See now B. A. Mastin, "A Neglected Feature of the Christology of the Fourth Gospel," *NTS* 22 (1975-76), pp. 32-51.

[27]On this point, see Meeks, "The Man from Heaven."

[28]See, for example, O. Cullmann, *The Christology of the New Testament* (Philadelphia: Westminster, 1959), esp. chapter 9, section 3 (pp. 258-69), and pp. 297-303. See p. 300: "A oneness of essence exists because there is a complete oneness of will." Blank, *Krisis*, pp. 112-13, tells us of a unity that is "not only with respect to mind and will, but ontological and essential." R. E. Brown, *The Gospel according to John (i-xii)*, The Anchor Bible 29 (Garden City, NY: Doubleday, 1966), p. 408 (on 10:37): "...although the Johannine description and acceptance of the divinity of Jesus has ontological implications (as Nicea recognized in confessing that Jesus Christ, the Son of God, is himself true God), in itself this description remains primarily functional and not too far removed from the Pauline formulation that 'God was in Christ reconciling the world to Himself' (II Cor v 19)." See now also Pollard, "The Father-Son and God-Believer Relationships," in which he returns to some earlier statements on moral and ontological aspects of the sonship of Jesus in his *Johannine Christology and the Early Church*, SNTSMS 13 (Cambridge: Cambridge University Press, 1975).

[29]Meeks, "The Man from Heaven," p. 69.

[30]See M. de Jonge, *De Brieven van Johannes* (Nijkerk: Callenbach, 1968, [2]1973), pp. 228-30; cf. C. Haas, M. de Jonge, and J. L. Swellengrebel, *A Translator's Handbook on the Letters of John* (London: U.B.S., 1972), p. 128.

[31]Meeks, "The Man from Heaven," p. 68, rightly points out that "...the Fourth Gospel never provides us with the myth which explains how some men could be from below and others from above." The status of those who are *ek tou theou* "is a *conferred* one, not an ontological one."

[32]See, e.g., 6:57; 10:15; 13:15, 34; 15:9, 10, 12; 17:11, 14, 16, 21, 22, 23.

[33]On the use of "the Jews" in this gospel, see the recent studies of T. L. Schram, *The Use of IOUDAIOS in the Fourth Gospel. An Application of Some Linguistic Insights to a New Testament Problem* (Dissertation, Utrecht, 1974), and R. Leistner, *Antijudaismus im Johannesevangelium? Darstellung des Problems in der neueren Auslegungsgeschichte und Untersuchung der Leidensgeschichte*, Theologie und Wirklichkeit 3 (Bern: H. Lang; Frankfurt: P. Lang, 1974). Also important is W. A. Meeks, "Am I a Jew? Johannine Christianity and Judaism," in *Christianity, Judaism, and Other Greco-Roman Cults* 1, ed. J. Neusner (Leiden: Brill, 1975), pp. 163-86.

[34]On the coming of the Messiah/Christ without any more explicit reference to place, see 4:25; 7:27, 31; cf. 12:13, 15. See also 1:15, 27, 30 (par. to John the Baptist 1:31); 10:10 (as over against those who came before Jesus). In 1 John it is emphatically stated that the coming of Jesus Christ occurred "in the flesh" (4:2, 5:7, and 2 John 7). The same epistle also speaks of the coming of the Antichrist (2:18) and of his spirit (4:3); it is revealed in the emergence of false prophets in the world (4:1). See also Chapter VIII, pp. 200-206.

[35]N. H. Cassem, "A Grammatical and Contextual Inventory of the Use of κόσμος in the Johannine Corpus with some Implications for a Johannine Cosmic Theology," *NTS* 19 (1972-73), pp. 81-91.

[36]In 17:15 and 1 John 5:19 also, one should translate "the Evil One" and not "evil."

[37]Jesus had the charge not to allow to be lost any of those whom the Father had given him (6:39; 10:28, 29; 17:12; 18:9). Judas is the great exception (17:12; cf. 6:64, 70).

[38]See, particularly, Olsson, *Structure and Meaning in the Fourth Gospel*, Excursus III, "Mission in John," pp. 241-48.

[39]See W. Thüsing, *Die Erhöhung und Verherrlichung Jesu im Johannesevangelium*, NTAbh 11, 1/2 (Münster: Aschendorff, [2]1970).

[40]πορεύομαι, ὑπάγω, ἔρχομαι, προσέρχομαι, ἀπέρχομαι, ἀναβαίνω.

[41]A typical bit of Johannine irony, incidentally; see de Jonge, "Onbegrip in Jeruzalem. Jezus en de Joden in Johannes 7," pp. 68-69.

168

^{42}On John 13-17, see also Chapter VII.   Cf. Meeks, "The Man from Heaven," pp. 61-66.

^{43}See also 1 John 2:6, 29; 3:16; 4:17 for expressions about the *imitatio Christi*.

^{44}On this, see also Borgen, "God's Agent in the Fourth Gospel," pp. 137-48, and Bühner, "Prophet und Engel."   Much has been written lately on 3:13; see Borgen, "Some Jewish Exegetical Traditions," and Bühner's studies. The most likely interpretation, in my opinion, is still the one that sees here a denial that anyone (Moses, prophets, apocalypticists) ever ascended to heaven to receive revelation and to see God; the One who descended from heaven gives revelation and life.

CHAPTER VII

ESCHATOLOGY AND ETHICS IN THE FOURTH GOSPEL

Some remarks on the relationship of parenesis, faith, and
expectation in the Gospel and the First Epistle of John

I.   Introduction

Nowhere else in the NT is so much written about
love, and so penetratingly, as in the Gospel and the First
Epistle of John.[1]   Nowhere else is the decisive character
of faith so strongly accentuated, but, as it appears, nowhere else is so little said about the Christian hope as
here (the concordance directs us only to 1 John 3:3).   Yet
in the books about John the word "eschatology" occurs
again and again!   C. H. Dodd speaks about John's "reinterpretation, or transmutation of popular eschatology": "He
has chosen to treat the death and resurrection as eschatological events.   Christ's death on the cross *is* His ascent to the right hand of the Father; and His return to
His disciples after death, which is closely associated, if
not identified, with the coming of the Holy Spirit, *is* His
second advent."[2]   Elsewhere he must, with some regret,
concede that "the author of the First Epistle knows nothing of the reinterpretation of the Advent hope."[3]   Another
influential interpreter of John, R. Bultmann, concludes
his exposition of the theology of John in his *Theology of
the New Testament* in §50 with the expressive title, "Faith
as Eschatological Existence."   For the evangelist, Easter,
Pentecost, and parousia coincide,[4] because in a radically
"demythologizing" way he relates everything to the response that is to be given now: "The judgment, then, is no
dramatic cosmic event, but takes place in the response of
men to the word of Jesus."[5]   Bultmann has less difficulty
than Dodd with the First Epistle because there, precisely
as in the Fourth Gospel, he attributes the futurist utterances to an ecclesiastical redactor.[6]

Dodd and Bultmann, because they have given a
splendid interpretation to certain facets of the Johannine theology, have exerted great influence on the subsequent study; but we cannot and need not here document this
fact.[7] What has just been cited from their work shows us
that we shall do well, before speaking about the relationship of faith and love, first to explore in what respect
faith according to the Johannine view (still) includes
expectation. In the second place we are reminded here
that people have often attempted to solve the problem of
shifts in accent and (apparent) contradictions in the Johannine utterances by speaking of different authors (of
the Gospel and the Epistle), of author and redactor in the
Gospel and in the Epistle, or of various stages of redaction (in the Gospel).[8]

Of course there is no suggestion that the problem
with which we are concerned can be given a detailed treatment here. I shall attempt to indicate a few main points
which in due course should be worked out in more detail.
I begin with the question as to the relationship of faith
and expectation in the First Epistle, in John 13-17, and
in the rest of the Gospel, in order then to go into more
detail on the relationship of love and keeping the commandments, on the one hand, and faith and expectation on
the other hand. With respect to the former question, our
point of beginning shall be the First Epistle of John. It
is advantageous when one can start out from a relatively
simple situation to interpret a highly complicated one (in
particular that in John 13-17). In the epistles we have
to do with a later stage in the history of the Johannine
communities and in the development of the Johannine theology, but one can "reason back" (in doing so one cannot
rule out the possibility that traces of this later development are to be found in the Gospel also).[9]

II. The Community in the Interim

1. 1 John

According to the First Epistle,[10] the community finds itself between two appearances of Jesus. People look back to the first one in faith, bound together with those who can testify to this appearance (1:1-4), and they look forward to the second full of confidence (2:28, 4:17). The first ἐφανερώθη continues to determine the existence of the believers; it makes them justified persons, children of God who cannot sin (3:4-10). Alongside this absolutely formulated "already" stands an equally plain "not yet" (2:28-3:3). Believers are called children of God, and such they are, but it is not yet revealed what they shall be: οἴδαμεν ὅτι ἐὰν φανερωθῇ ὅμοιοι αὐτῷ ἐσόμεθα ὅτι ὀψόμεθα αὐτὸν καθώς ἐστιν (3:2b). It is not certain whether this means being like Christ or being like God[11]--in any case the Christian, however much he may live in communion with God and out of the strength bestowed by God, has not yet reached the goal. He lives in anticipation and sanctifies, purifies, himself, even as Christ *is* pure (present tense--precisely as in 2:2, 29, and 4:17). The Christian may live for the parousia, the day of judgment, with a confidence that is the fruit of the love at work in him (4:17).

In the debate with the false teachers in 2:3-11,[12] the newness of the commandment of love is argued with the testimony that ἡ σκοτία παράγεται καὶ τὸ φῶς τὸ ἀληθινὸν ἤδη φαίνει (vs. 8). The victorious light determines the life of the believers in fellowship with Christ, in whom the new life has begun; there is no doubt about the ultimate victory--the darkness is passing away, irrevocably; similarly, in 2:17 it can be said that the world, with the lust that typifies it, is passing away.

Throughout the Epistle it becomes evident how strongly the author emphasizes the "already" (in addition to 3:4-10; 2:12-14, 20-21, 27, and 3:14, for example); that obviously is not the point of difference with the

false teachers. It is true that emphasis must be placed
upon the point that the first appearance was an appearance
in the flesh (4:2, 5:6) of a concrete living, suffering,
human Son on earth,[13] and furthermore that therewith a
process of living-in-love is set in motion in the circle
of the community, a process that reaches its climax only
in the parousia and the last judgment.[14] In 2:18 the author uses a newly formed term to speak of ἐσχάτη ὥρα, the
final crucial stage in the eschatological process, in
which the false teachers play the role of the adversaries
of Christ who will have no part in the "moment supreme"
because they already stand outside (2:19, 22-25; 3:9-10;
4:1-6).

The "already" does not nullify the "not yet." The
community lives on the strength of the "already," and this
is why the author is so much concerned with a correct view
of Jesus Christ's person and work. But the cosmos still
exists, as a reality which though passing away still is
dangerous,[15] and the imperative that issues from the indicative ought to be taken seriously. Thus the community
develops toward the end that for her obviously does not
signify a caesura but a consummation; nothing more is
said about the ultimate fate of the cosmos.

2. John 13-17

Likewise in the farewell discourses in 13:31-16:33,
with the following prayer in chapter 17, the theme is the
life of the community in the interim. This becomes evident when we compare the introduction to the discourses in
13:31-38 with the conclusion of the prayer in 17:20-26 and
consider the likelihood that in the beginning and the conclusion the intention of the intervening part is summar-
ized.

In this connection, it is of course important to
note that here we have to do with a departure-situation.
Jesus is going to the Father, but his disciples are *not
yet* going (13:33, with reference to 7:33-36; 8:21-22).

Anyone who wishes to follow him will follow later (13:36-
38, 12:25-26), and his way undoubtedly leads through suffering to glory, precisely as does the Son's way (12:25;
cf. 21:18-19). The community finds itself still in the
midst of the world (17:11, 15, 18), only later to be
"where I am" (17:24), beholding the glory which the Son
shares with the Father. That is her privilege, which the
world does not share, for only the community has perceived
that Jesus is the one who is sent by the Father (17:25).
We find the expression "where I am" used in 12:26 also to
indicate the ultimate goal of the true servant of Christ,[16]
and in 14:1-3, where in vs. 3 it is connected with the expression πάλιν ἔρχομαι καὶ παραλήμψομαι. It is only
natural here to think of the stage of the consummation,
which is the point of reference also in 1 John 3:2, 4:17.
This stage is characterized by the state of being "where I
am," i.e., with the Father. Before this stage there lies,
in 17:20-23, the stage of being "in the Father and in the
Son," which is pointed to in 14:18-24 with the words, "in
that day you shall see that I am in my Father and you in
me and I in you"--connected with a coming of Jesus (vs.
18), and of Jesus and the Father (vs. 23). We also find a
"reciprocal indwelling" in 15:1-17 and in 1 John 2:3-6,
24; 3:24; 4:13 (in addition there are many texts with
kindred expressions[17]). The glorified Son lives in and
with those who belong to him, just as the Spirit, who is
sent after him and is closely bound to him, works in and
with him (1 John 3:24, 4:13; John 14:15-17 and 25-26 [thus
just preceding and just following 14:18-24!]; 15:26-27;
16:7-15). Connected with this is a life lived out of love
for love, or, said in another way, a keeping of the commandments, which culminate in the one commandment of love,
that is the other side of the word in which the Son promises God's love (see below, "Ethics in the Interim").

It seems clear to me that the ἔρχομαι of 14:18 (cf.
vs. 23) is related to, but does not coincide with, the
ἔρχομαι καὶ παραλήμψομαι of 14:3.[18] What the Son and the

Spirit "already" are effecting in and with the community
reaches its consummation in what will be actualized "later."
Following 17:24-25, the so-called high-priestly prayer concludes in vs. 26 with the words, "I have made known to them
your name (on earth) and I shall make it known (in the period between departure and consummation), so that the love
with which you have loved me may be in them and I in them."
The emphasis undoubtedly is placed on the special nearness
of the glorified Son with and in the community,[19] but the
climax of everything still remains the crowning of this
association when the community is where he is.

The πρὸς ἐμαυτόν of 14:3 is also used in 12:32,
"And when I am lifted up from the earth, I shall draw all
men to me." "To me" corresponds to "from the earth."
"Lifting up" here implies crucifixion, as vs. 33 says explicitly, and in the context there certainly is a connection with the coming of the Greeks to Jesus in 12:20ff.
On the one hand, in vss. 20-33, what is being discussed is
the ultimate destiny of Jesus' disciples, which is directly connected with the "lifting up-glorification" of the
Son; vs. 32 is clearly connected with 25-26, and 25-26
follow directly after 23-24. In vs. 32 it is made clear
that what is meant is a bringing-together in the Father's
house (14:1-3) of all God's children who are scattered
over the whole world (11:49-51, 10:16). On the other
hand it is clear from the coming of the Greeks (cf. also
12:19 and the allusion in 7:35) that for "John" the coming
together of Greeks and Jews from Palestine and the Diaspora
into the community is already the beginning of realization
of the promised eschatological unity of the people of God.[20]

In chapters 13-17, Easter and Pentecost coincide.
There can be no doubt of that--20:19-23 confirms it. One
cannot speak of a parousia in the sense of an appearing of
Christ upon earth in a way recognizable to all, but of a
consummation. All attention is concentrated on the fate
of the community in the midst of a world that is hostile
but is already in principle conquered; the world has no

future, in contrast to the community which lives for the
final and definitive "being with the Lord."[21]

3. John 1-12

    In the first part of the Gospel it is repeatedly
emphasized that the decision about life and death is made
in the concrete encounter with the Son. Well-known texts
here are 3:16-21, 36; 5:19-27, 30, and of course 1:9-13 in
the prologue. The Son gives life and judges (or condemns)
in the name of the Father; hence "Truly, truly I say to
you that everyone who hears my word and believes in him
who sent me has eternal life and does not come into the
judgment, but has passed from death to life" (5:24). The
text that follows this, introduced with the words "The
hour is coming and now is," indicates that a certain "prolepsis" is meant here, an authentic "already."[22] The same
appears in the important text 11:23-26, in the middle of
the account of the raising of Lazarus. For the last time
in the "book of signs" the life-giving power of the Son is
manifested,[23] and what is said in 5:25 is fulfilled.
Martha utters a fully justified "Johannine" confession of
faith (vs. 27). Just before this, her belief in the
resurrection is corrected in the Johannine sense. After
she has related Jesus' word, "Your brother will arise," to
the "resurrection at the last day," the crucial motif is,
so to speak, Christologically brought out: "I am the
resurrection and the life." This is followed then by a
double saying from which it appears that one who thus believes in Jesus has definitively crossed over the boundary
between life and death. Jesus *is* the resurrection and the
life because the life-giving power of the Father is at
work in the Son. The resurrection is proleptically a
reality; life is a present and thus a *futurum continuum*--
"forever."

    Does this mean that eternity has entered into time
and that life is repeatedly bestowed upon the believers in
the encounter with Jesus? G. Klein says it in good

176

Bultmannian fashion as follows: "Structurally different
from all the hours that are added together to form the
time-continuum, this 'hour' means the eschatological event
of revelation that breaks that continuum, and that lets
past, present, and future be combined."[24]   I doubt whether
this is what is meant here.   In the gospel there are also
(much disputed) futurist utterances, sometimes connected
with utterances in the present tense; 5:28 (alongside 5:
25); 6:39, 40, 44, 54; and 12:48 are repeatedly cited
(only then often to be eliminated as the product of interpolation).[25]   But either for the original author(s) or for
a later redactor or redactors, the combination of present
and future tense must have made sense--for example, in
6:40, where we read: ἵνα πᾶς ὁ θεωρῶν τὸν υἱὸν καὶ πιστεύων εἰς αὐτὸν ἔχῃ ζωὴν αἰώνιον καὶ ἀναστήσω αὐτὸν ἐγὼ
ἐν τῇ ἐσχάτῃ ἡμέρᾳ.   In chapter 11 also ἀνάστασις is allowed to stand beside ζωή and ἀνάστασις is the symbol par
excellence for the life-giving power of the Son.   Nowhere
is a distinction made between soul and body, nowhere is
anything explicitly said of the resurrection of the body
(let alone of "the flesh").[26]   In this not entirely clear
use of the terms "resurrection" and "life" is there not
something of the idea that the life that is given to the
individual and the community in and through the Son still
is moving toward a consummation that lies in the future?
12:26 is parallel to 12:25; perhaps the content of the
later verse does not entirely coincide with that of the
earlier--what 12:26 says corresponds to the stage of the
consummation in the farewell discourses!   In any case, a
"transchronological" interpretation of "the hour" is incorrect.   One could better speak of prolepsis (on the one
hand) and (on the other hand) a *futurum continuum*.

        The difference between chapters 1-12 and 13-17 and/
or 1 John is not in the conception of time or of the es-
chaton, but in the orientation to the revelation in the
world and to the revelation to the community.   In chapters
1-12 Jesus' departure is spoken of only as a departure

that for outsiders means a final farewell (7:33-36, 8:21-22). The light is shining in the world, but at a certain moment it will definitively cease to shine before the world; in 12:35-36 Jesus very clearly says this to the outsiders.[27] Jesus' work is continued by those who hear and keep his word. For these the disciples serve as models (from 2:11 to 20:30-31), in spite of their lack of insight and their misunderstanding that requires further instruction for them--which then is underscored in those passages where the difference in their situation before and after Jesus' departure is in view (2:22, contrasted with 2:11; 12:16; 20:9 and even 14:7-9 and 16:25).[28] For the community there is a future, not for the world--hence the world appears only on the periphery of the ongoing history of the community, as it is announced in John 13-17 and in 1 John and is "corrected" with promises and exhortations.

III. Ethics in the Interim

1. John 13-17

In 13:31-38, in the introduction to the farewell discourses (and to the great prayer), we find, between Jesus' utterance about his departure (vs. 33) and his announcement of Peter's following after him later (vss. 36-38), the new commandment "that you love each other; as I have loved you, that you love each other also. By this everyone will know that you are my disciples, if you have love for one another" (vss. 34-35). Brotherly love is the identifying mark of the community in the interim, and this brotherly love is rooted in Jesus' love for those who are his own.[29] Herewith reference is made back to 13:1b, which is illustrated in the foot-washing and is followed in vss. 12-17 with an exhortation to imitation. The disciples must "wash each other's feet" in imitation of what their Master and Lord has done for them. "I have given you an example," ἵνα καθὼς ἐγὼ ἐποίησα ὑμῖν καὶ ὑμεῖς ποιῆτε (vs. 15). Here the relationship of slave and master, of envoy and sender, is utilized.

Therewith the imperative is grounded in the indicative, and at the same time it is indicated that the imperative is an essential element in the life of the community in the interim. In a life that issues from the "already," the imperative keeps alive the awareness that one is still growing toward the consummation. Neither the community nor the believers have yet arrived, though in a crucial sense they have set out on the right way.[30]

The following chapters exhibit this in various ways. "To love as I have loved you" there appears to be one facet of being incorporated into the activity of the Son, which in fact is the work of the Father. Following 14:10-11, which speaks of "I in the Father" and "The Father in me," and from this draws the conclusion of the unity of Father and Son in word and deed, vs. 12 gives the assurance that "whoever believes in me, the works that I do he shall do also, and greater works than these shall he do." Why? Because Jesus is going to the Father and will do whatever the believers shall ask "in his name." In this way the Father will be glorified in the Son, just as during Jesus' earthly activity (cf. 13:31, 15:8).

What these works are is not defined more precisely here--but what is meant obviously is all that the Son, in the name of the Father, has brought to the world: salvation, light, truth, life, etc. This work is continued in and through the community. In vss. 13-14, heavy emphasis is placed upon "praying in my name" as an aspect of the association with the Son and with the Father (cf. 15:7, 16; 16:23, 24, 26). Verse 15 speaks of "loving me,"--that is, "keeping my commandments"--just as the Son loves the Father and (consequently) acts as the Father has commanded him (14:31).[31] The same expressions appear together in vss. 18-24,[32] where they are connected with the assurance that the Son and the Father will love the believers and will dwell with them.[33] In this connection, vs. 20 speaks

of "I in the Father and you in me, I in you." The (reciprocal) indwelling of the Son and the Father, as a sign of
unity and love, is expanded to include the (reciprocal)
indwelling of (Father and) Son and community, likewise as
a sign of unity and love.[34] Love for Christ leads to
"keeping his commandments," and his "new commandment," the
commandment par excellence, is brotherly love (13:34). In
chapter 14 strong emphasis is placed on the indicative,
but in the expression "keep the commandments" it is made
clear how the imperative grows out of the indicative.

John 15 uses the figure of the vine and the branches
to point to the relationship of (Father,) Son and community. The correct interpretation of the significance of
"bearing fruit" is disputed.[35] Undoubtedly it refers
(again) primarily to the continuation of Jesus' work in
the work of the believers. If the vine bears fruit, it
does so through the branches, and if the branches bear
fruit, they do so thanks to their connection with the vine
(cf. also 12:23-24 and 25-26). The figure of the vine very
clearly is connected with that of the reciprocal indwelling
(vss. 3, 5), and the reality of the hearing of prayer is
underscored (vss. 7, 16). Alongside the possibility of
life and thus of bearing fruit there is also that of death
(vss. 2, 6). Hence the imperative also emerges in the
μείνατε ἐν ἐμοί (vs. 3), parallel to μείνατε ἐν τῇ ἀγάπῃ
τῇ ἐμῇ (vs. 9; cf. vs. 17). The possibility of unfaith-
fulness and apostasy is considered seriously here, just as
in the second part of the chapter (vss. 18-25) reference
is made with strong emphasis to the hostile attitude of
the world toward the community (a consequence of her attitude toward Jesus) (cf. 16:1-4).

In vss. 9-17, in the working-out of "abide in my
love," once again the emphasis is placed upon "keeping my
commandments." Again the fact that the Son keeps the commandments of the Father and abides in his love remains the
basis and guide for the actions of the believers (vs. 10).
The commandment par excellence is again "love each other

as I have loved you" (vs. 12; cf. vs. 17). This love is concretized in the declaration that the greatest love is ἵνα τις τὴν ψυχὴν αὐτοῦ θῇ ὑπὲρ τῶν φιλῶν αὐτοῦ (vs. 13). Here also, what the Son does is the source and guide for the believers, his friends, who do whatever he commands (vs. 14).[36]

The most important contribution offered by chapters 13-17 with reference to our subject thus is set forth. It remains only to point out that in 17:11, 20-23, 24-26, love and indwelling are connected with unity; the unity among the believers is grounded in the unity of Father and Son. That also is a way of saying what is meant in the preceding chapters--the believers are allowed to share in the work of the Father through the Son; hence it can be said that they share in the glory that the Father has given to the Son, and the petition can be made that they may be fully unified, "so that the world may recognize that you have sent me, and that you love them as you have loved me" (17:23; cf. 13:35 and 14:31).

The "already" is dominant; that is obvious. To love is to be incorporated into a great movement of love that embraces Father, Son, and believers. The imperative grows up out of the indicative--it is not (yet) superfluous. The consummation is not yet reached, the world is still present, and it takes a hostile stance toward the community. It can see what is happening in the community in imitation of her Lord; it can even recognize that God is at work here (13:35; 14:31; 17:21, 23),[37] but the reality is that it still hates the disciples just as it hated their Lord when the latter was working in God's name as a man among men. And there always remains the possibility of apostasy even for those who are within the community-- if they are unfaithful to their commitment that they have once made and mistakenly think that they can live only in fellowship with the Lord.

2. 1 John

Just as, with respect to eschatology, no essential
difference can be discerned between the First Epistle and
the Gospel, the view of the First Epistle of the relationship between imperative and indicative is not essentially
different from that of the Gospel. But the Epistle obviously is written in a crisis situation in which people
have dissociated themselves from the community (2:19) and
are propagating a doctrine (with a practice of life issu-
ing from it) that can only be characterized as false prophecy (4:1), heresy (2:2, 4:6), propaganda of the antichrist (2:18, 22; 4:3). Here branches are detached which
appeared to belong to the vine; the writer comes to the
conclusion that these people have never belonged to the
community (2:19). What is posed in principle, but not
very concretely, in John 15 now has become an actuality.
This calls for a more precise statement of the relationship between indicative and imperative, and leads to a
greater emphasis on the imperative because the community
needs to be on the alert against these false teachers and
their practices and against the "world" in general. Thus
emphasis on the imperative goes together with an evident
realization that the community has not yet reached its
goal.

Reading the Epistle against this background, we
note that the author clearly says that anyone who does not
draw the ethical conclusions is wrongly claiming to have a
knowledge of God and to be living in communion with God.
This is said very clearly in 2:3-6 and 7-11, where, as has
already been remarked above (p. 171), a position is taken
in opposition to a number of utterances of the false teachers. Here it is striking that the author can refer back to
the new commandment of John 13:34 as something that the
community has known all along.[38] Moreover, brotherly love
is clearly utilized as the criterion for authentic communion with God--3:10, 17 and 4:8, 20 here speak a clear language.[39] In a situation of conflict in which all are

claiming a knowledge of God, the author wants to teach the community how to distinguish—one knows the tree by its fruits. All are also appealing to the Spirit, and thus the confession is utilized as the criterion for genuine inspiration (2:22-24, 3:24, 4:13, and especially 4:1-6 and 5:6-8). For the author this is the confession that Jesus Christ has come in the flesh (4:2) and has actually suffered (5:6); this confession also has ethical implications. The rule of John 15:13 recurs in 3:16 and 4:10-11 (cf. 2: 6), and seen against the background of the conflict it acquires an especially concrete content.[40] The rejection of the false teachers, who do not belong (2:19) and who, inspired by the antichrist, obviously are ἐκ τοῦ κόσμου (4: 3-6), also leads to a special emphasis on the distance from the world that must be kept by the community. In faith she has overcome the world (2:12-14; 5:4-5, 19-20), but the imperative still is μὴ ἀγαπᾶτε τὸν κοσμὸν μηδὲ τὰ ἐν τῷ κόσμῳ (2:15; see also 16-17; 5:21).[41] We are aware that the "love each other" is limited to the circle of the (pure) believers—it is not different in principle in the Gospel, but there we also find such expressions as 13:35 and 17:24. In the Epistle the horizon is broadened only in 2:2—and there the subject is not what the community does, but what Jesus Christ signifies.[42]

The emphasis on the imperative leads to an extra accentuating of the indicative. For example, in 4:7-21 it is very clearly said that in the Son God first loved us. It is very strongly set forth that the believers are children of God, that is, that they are begotten by God (2:29; 3:2, 7, 9; 4:7). This expression, used also in the Gospel (1:12-13, 3:3-8), is directly connected here with the emphasis on righteousness, love, and indeed with not being able to sin—by virtue of the fellowship of God's children with the Son of God who has shattered the works of the devil (3:8). The "already"-aspect even in the life of the individual believer cannot be more strongly accentuated. This is done in a strictly dualistic framework: "By this

the children of God and the children of the devil are
recognizable: anyone who does not practice righteousness
is not of God, nor anyone who does not love his brother"
(3:10). And yet even the child of God must keep in mind
that he is not automatically sinless, but attention is
drawn to the forgiveness bestowed upon him and the inter-
cession on his behalf (1:8-2:2).[43] "Already" and "not
yet" continue side-by-side; precisely in temptation both
must be emphasized--the community of the righteous must
keep God's commandments.[44]

    The future brings the end of the situation of ten-
sion; for those who persevere in love and in the keeping
of the commandments it signifies consummation and crowning.
The exhortations to "pray in my name" and the promise that
prayers will be heard recur in the Epistle, and there they
are connected with the concept of παρρησία. The believer
now has boldness in relation to God (3:20-22, coupled with
the keeping of the commandments; and 5:14-15), and by and
by will have it at the parousia and the last judgment (2:
28 and 4:17-18), then in full. This is clear in 2:28-3:3
and likewise in the use of the expressions τετελείωται ἡ
ἀγάπη μεθ᾽ ἡμῶν (4:17) and οὐ τετελείωται ἐν τῇ ἀγάπῃ
(4:18). Being "full-grown"[45] is a fruit of "abiding"
(4:16). "Love" here is a richly variegated concept, as is
the expression ἀγάπη τοῦ θεοῦ which is used several times
in this epistle--sometimes the genitive is a *genitivus
objectivus*, or *subjectivus*, or *qualitatis*, or *auctoris*;
frequently it is impossible and even undesirable to make a
distinction, because of the reciprocity in the formulas of
immanence and the close connection between love for God
and love for one's neighbor.[46] "Perfect love casts out
fear," says 4:18. "We shall not be put to shame before
God's judgment-seat," says 2:28. But just as the παρρησία
then is in fact not different from the παρρησία now, it
can also be said that not only in the future but even in
the present "God's love is made perfect in us" (2:5, 4:12).
Of course, that is no occasion for boasting on man's part,

but a consequence of his remaining united with Father and Son.

When C. H. Dodd remarks, "...the thought of coming judgment, here as elsewhere in the New Testament, sharpens the sense of moral responsibility,"[47] he overestimates the significance of the expectation of the future for the ethics of the First Epistle. At the end will be made manifest what is now already a reality. In 2:28-3:3 the author obviously is thinking of the final (definitive) transformation; in 4:16-18 the element of "crowning" certainly is present, but here a comparison with 2:5 and 4:12 makes it clear that it is sometimes difficult to put into words the difference between the "already" and the "then in full."

4. Concluding Remarks

The results of our studies are modest. No essential shifts appear to have taken place in the expectation of the future and in the ethics of the Johannine communities between the writing of the Gospel and the writing of the First Epistle. It appears unnecessary to distinguish a number of redactional layers within chapters 13-17 of the Gospel on grounds of differences in eschatological view or differences of perspective in the relationship of promise and parenesis.[48]

The differences that can be affirmed between Gospel and Epistle are connected, on the one hand, with the fact that in John 1-12 and 13-17 God's revelation in Jesus Christ is illumined both by the aspect of the "coming" and by the aspect of the "going away," and the element of the consummation receives relatively little attention. On the other hand, the eschatology and the ethics of the Epistle are simpler and more direct, because they pertain to a crisis situation in which old certainties must be concretized anew in word and deed. In the situation of the First Epistle, the faith-perspective of "John" was given the opportunity to demonstrate what was of value to it.[49]

NOTES

CHAPTER VII

[1]See "To Love as God Loves," in M. de Jonge, *Jesus: Inspiring and Disturbing Presence* (Nashville: Abingdon Press, 1974), pp. 110-27.

[2]C. H. Dodd, *The Interpretation of the Fourth Gospel* (Cambridge: Cambridge University Press, 1953), p. 395.

[3]Idem, *The Johannine Epistles* (London: Hodder & Stoughton, [3]1953), p. XXXV.

[4]R. Bultmann, *Theology of the New Testament* II (New York: Scribner, 1953), p. 75.

[5]Ibid., p. 38.

[6]R. Bultmann, *The Johannine Epistles* (Philadelphia: Fortress, 1975), p. 44, n. 4 (and the reference given there).

[7]With respect to the eschatology, one will find a good survey of perspectives and literature in R. Schnackenburg, *Das Johannesevangelium* II, Herders Theologischer Kommentar zum Neuen Testament (Freiburg-Basel-Wien: Herder, 1971), pp. 530-44, Exkurs 14, "Das eschatologische Denken im Johannesevangelium." Of somewhat earlier date are L. van Hartingsveld, *Die Eschatologie des Johannesevangelium. Eine Auseinandersetzung mit Rudolf Bultmann* (Assen: van Gorcum, 1962), which also gives information about the views of other interpreters, and the book by Josef Blank, which concerns itself primarily with John 1-12, *Krisis. Untersuchungen zur johanneischen Christologie und Eschatologie* (Freiburg: Lambertus, 1964).

[8]Orientation to Bultmann's theories about the gospel is provided by D. M. Smith, *The Composition and Order of the Fourth Gospel* (New Haven and London: Yale University Press, 1965). A survey of all the hypotheses is given by H. M. Teeple, *The Literary Origin of the Gospel of John* (Evanston: Religion and Ethics Institute, 1974). For the epistles we may refer to E. Haenchen, "Neuere Literatur zu den Johannesbriefen," *TRu* 26 (1960), pp. 1-43 and 267-91, esp. pp. 8-12 and 15-20. See also Chapter VIII, below.

[9]See Chapter VIII and M. de Jonge, *De Brieven van Johannes* (Nijkerk: Callenbach, 1968, [2]1973), pp. 25-29. The mistake of many investigators is that they attempt to discover what is typically Johannine first of all in the Gospel by asserting that "John" utilized all sorts of materials in his own fashion and by employing the hypothesis

that a number of other expressions are less appealing and thus are from a later hand; thus they approach the matter in a more or less "ideal-typical" way. Then they analyze the Epistles, which similarly fail to correspond to the ideal (in the last analysis the ideal of the investigator). Especially in the school of Bultmann, where his analysis of the Epistles is brought under discussion but not his thesis of the ecclesiastical redactor in the Gospel, and where by preference his existentialist conceptual material (including the concept of time) is employed and further enlarged, it appears that in this way, using keen and profound reasoning, people create at least as many problems as they solve. See, among others, J. Heise, *Bleiben. Menein in den johanneischen Schriften* (Tübingen: Mohr, 1969), and (particularly) G. Klein, "'Das wahre Licht scheint schon.' Beobachtungen zur Zeit- und Geschichtserfahrung einer urchristlichen Schule," *ZThK* 68 (1971), pp. 262-326. There we find, for example, the following sentence, which has reference to the expression ἐσχάτη ὥρα in 1 John 2:18: "Thus the development appears to move in the sense of a progressive linguistic apocalypticizing from the absolute use of the non-apocalyptic substantive by way of the secondary appropriation of the apocalyptic toward the acceptance of the apocalyptic substantive" (p. 303). For a thoroughgoing expansion of Bultmann's arsenal of redaction and interpolation theories, see J. Becker, "Aufbau, Schichtung und theologiegeschichtliche Stellung des Gebetes in Johannes 17," *ZNW* 60 (1969), pp. 56-83, and "Die Abschiedsreden Jesu im Johannesevangelium," *ZNW* 61 (1970), pp. 215-46. For the sake of convenience, this author (like G. Richter, outside the school of Bultmann, in a number of publications) starts out from the position that authors always write logically consistent pieces, but that redactors have no need for this consistency. Literary-critical operations starting from these premises will always be highly arbitrary, certainly in writings that have a preference for irony and misunderstanding (consciously used as a literary device), as well as for paradoxes and dialectical tensions. Anyone who wishes to prove developments in theology and consequent differences between Gospel and Epistle, as well as "strata" in the Gospel, will have to dig much deeper and show genuine difference in perspective and shifts in the center of gravity of the argument-- without cherishing the illusion that this can be traced out verse by verse. This is also the merit of G. Klein in his article, in which, alas, he omits from the discussion Bultmann's view of the concept of time in the Gospel.

[10]For detailed comments on the passages cited, I refer to my commentary, *De Brieven van Johannes*, hereafter referred to as *Comm.*, and C. Haas, M. de Jonge, and J. L. Swellengrebel, *A Translator's Handbook on the Letters of John* (London: U.B.S., 1972), hereafter referred to as *Handbook*.

[11]After some hesitation the *Handbook* chooses the former; the *Comm.*, with equal hesitation, opts for the latter.

[12]For the theory that in 2:3-11 and in 1:6-10 a number of utterances of the false teachers are being refuted, see *Comm.*, pp. 13-14.

[13]See *Comm.*, pp. 117-24, and below, Chapter VIII, pp. 200-206.

[14]On the connection between Christology and ethics, see de Jonge, "To Love as God Loves," pp. 113-26.

[15]See 2:12-17; 3:13; 4:3-5; 5:4-5, 19-21.

[16]The pericope 12:20-36 serves on the one hand as introduction to chapters 13-17--it speaks of Jesus' exaltation/glorification and the consequences of it (vss. 20-33). On the other hand, the conversation with the crowd in vss. 34-36, focused on the ἔτι μικρὸν χρόνον τὸ φῶς ἐν ὑμῖν ἐστιν, prepares for the end of Jesus' public appearances (see also vs. 36b!). 12:37-43 then concludes the "book of signs" with a negative judgment on the world's response. By way of transition, the pericope vss. 44-50 then points again to the possibility of faith; see vs. 46: ἐγὼ φῶς εἰς τὸν κόσμον ἐλήλυθα, ἵνα πᾶς ὁ πιστεύων εἰς ἐμὲ ἐν τῇ σκοτίᾳ μὴ μείνῃ.

[17]See *Comm.*, pp. 79-81.

[18]It probably is not accidental that chapter 20 does speak of the coming of Jesus (vss. 19, 24, 26; cf. 21:1, ἐφανέρωσεν ἑαυτὸν πάλιν), but not of his subsequent disappearance. At Jesus' first "coming," the Spirit is given once-for-all (vss. 19-23) with the commission καθὼς ἀπέσταλκέν με ὁ πατὴρ κἀγὼ πέμπω ὑμᾶς. According to 20:17 this takes place at the moment Jesus returns to the Father--see the exegesis of these verses in Chapter I, pp. 3-6.

[19]See also 14:22.

[20]On this, see especially B. Olsson, *Structure and Meaning in the Fourth Gospel*, ConB, NT Series 6 (Lund: Gleerup, 1974), pp. 241-48. The subject here is not the Jews of the Diaspora alone. For a comparable conclusion, see E. Käsemann, *The Testament of Jesus* (Philadelphia: Fortress, 1968), pp. 70-72.

[21]Here we must touch (too) briefly on some difficulties that in part are connected with the fact that in chapters 13-17 we have before us a mixture of discourses which perhaps was later touched up but has not been re-edited (see, e.g., R. E. Brown, *The Gospel according to*

John (xiii-xxi), The Anchor Bible 29A [Garden City, NY: Doubleday, 1970], pp. 581-603). These difficulties in part issue from the fact that the Gospel sums up, under the aspect of "glorification," a number of elements of the preaching concerning the Son that, when they are described separately, necessarily come one after another in time (see also n. 18 and the reference there to Chapter I). Thus after the ἀπ᾽ ἄρτι γινώσκετε αὐτὸν καὶ ἑωράκετε is given in 14:7 in response to Thomas's lack of understanding (and Philip's as well), there comes, in 16:25, a similar promise for the future. And when the disciples think that this promise now has come to fulfillment (vs. 29), they are referred to their future scattering and desertion which has already begun (vs. 32); a question mark is placed after the ἄρτι πιστεύετε in vs. 31. This is undoubtedly connected with the fact that in 16:16-33 the period between death and resurrection is viewed separately (vss. 16-20; cf. the motif of "weeping" and "joy" in 20:11, 13, 14, and 20). The hatred of the world and oppression in the world also are subsequently spoken of, in 16:33 and in 15:18-16:4 as well. The community has the Spirit on her side (15:26-27 and 16:5-14) and may know that Jesus has overcome the world (16:33)--in spite of the perfect tense νενίκηκα, an encouragement in a *transitional* situation (cf. 1 John, for example, 2:12-17 and 5:18-21).

Further, there is the problem of whether the reaching of the goal (identified as "being where I am") by the individual believer in 12:26 coincides with the time referred to in 17:24. In 14:3 many interpreters see reference to something that happens after the believer's death, but it seems to me impossible that this text could be speaking of a continual coming of Jesus and that thus in 17:24 the end result of these "moves" is envisioned. It seems to me more probable that here we are dealing with diverse conceptions side by side (thus Brown, *The Gospel according to John (xiii-xxi)*, pp. 799-800, who also refers to Phil 1:23 and 2 Cor 5:8 along with 1 Thess 4:13-17; 1 Cor 15:51-57), wherein the essential thing is the contrast between now and later and the certainty that both believer and community will reach their final destiny. This problem deserves more detailed study.

[22]Cf. 4:23 (following 4:21), where there is anticipation of the time when the gift of the Spirit will make possible a worship in Spirit and in truth, and 16:32, where the disciples' situation after Jesus' death is regarded as proleptically present at the time of the farewell discourse (see also n. 21).

[23]See Chapter V, pp. 124-26.

[24]Klein, "Das wahre Licht," p. 295.

[25]See, e.g., the (highly cautious) argument of Schnackenburg, *Das Johannesevangelium* II, pp. 144-47.

[26]Not even in the passage 6:51b-58, where eternal life and resurrection are connected with partaking of Jesus' flesh and blood; by way of contrast, see Ign. *Smyrn.* 1-7!

[27]See what is said above in note 16. One should also compare 9:4-5 and 11:9-10, and of course 8:12. The ἔτι μικρόν is definitive for the world, but not for the community (see also 14:19). Klein, "Das wahre Licht," pp. 269-91, sees it (here also) altogether differently: "In summary it may be said that for the author of the Gospel of John, light and darkness are forces at work in a similarly undifferentiated fashion in past, present, and future of the world-epoch" (p. 275). The Gospel and the Epistle are supposed to be employing a totally different concept of time here also. Incorrect in principle and confusing with respect to the conclusions reached is Klein's (like Bultmann's) constantly speaking of "man" and forgetting to differentiate between "community" and "world."

[28]See Chapter I, pp. 7-12.

[29]R. Bultmann, *The Gospel of John* (Philadelphia: Westminster, 1971), p. 525, correctly says on this passage: "For καθώς expresses the integral connexion between the ἀλλήλους ἀγαπᾶν and Jesus' love which they have experienced; it does not describe the degree of intensity of the ἀγαπᾶν (Loisy), nor does it depict the way that Jesus took as the way of service; rather it describes the basis of the ἀγαπᾶν. And that is why the ἵνα-clause is repeated with the stressed καὶ ὑμεῖς; it thereby becomes clear that precisely this ἀλλήλ. ἀγ. is the fulfillment of the purpose of Jesus' love." See also p. 384, n. 3.

[30]G. Richter, in his *Die Fusswaschung im Johannesevangelium*, Biblische Untersuchungen 1 (Regensburg: Pustet, 1967), especially on pp. 285-320, incorrectly sees the parenetic section 13:12-17 as a secondary insertion. Equally one-sided is J. Becker when, in his article "Die Abschiedsreden Jesu im Johannesevangelium," he concludes, from his theory of a fully realized eschatology, that the ethical passages 13:34-35, 14:15, and 15:1-6 presuppose a different and later situation than the rest of the Gospel (he rightly points to the many parallels with the First Epistle). He fails to recognize the internal connection of indicative and imperative because he fails to recognize that the community finds itself in tension between a new beginning and consummation. See further Heise, *Bleiben*, and cf. O. Prunet, *La morale chrétienne d'après les écrits johanniques* (Paris: Presses Universitaires de France, 1957), and N. Lazure, *Les valeurs morales de la théologie johannique* (Paris: Librairie Lecoffre, 1965).

[31]Cf. 10:18, 12:49-50 (with ἡ ἐντολὴ αὐτοῦ ζωὴ αἰώνιός ἐστιν also), 15:10.

[32]See vss. 15, 21, 23 (τὸν λόγον μου), 24 (τοὺς λόγους μου and ὁ λόγος), and cf. 15:10, 12 (ἐντολή as in 13:34), 14, and 17 (ἐντέλλομαι).

[33]See vss. 21, 23, and cf. 16:27, where it is clearly said, moreover, that love for Jesus is equivalent to believing that he has come from God. The Father's love for the Son is spoken of in 3:35, 5:20, 10:17, 15:9, and 17:23-24. According to 15:9, Christ's love for those who are his is grounded in the Father's love for him (καθώς is used again).

[34]With respect to the relationship of Father and Son, cf. 10:30 and 10:38, and (with the community also in view) 17:11, 21-23, 24-26 (see below also). About the connection within variety of the diverse formulations employed here, see R. Borig, *Der wahre Weinstock. Untersuchungen zur Joh. 15,1-10*, SANT 16 (München: Kösel, 1967), pp. 199-236.

[35]Ibid., pp. 237-46.

[36]Cf. 10:11, 17-18, and 13:37-38.

[37]God's revelation is indeed also addressed to the world, and the world (theoretically) can also come to faith; see also 3:16-17; 6:33, 51; 8:28; and 15:22-24. The *de facto* response, however, is indicated in 1:9-11. Faith and acknowledgment are the exception, and they are ultimately based upon divine intervention (1:12-13). See Chapter VI, p. 156.

[38]See *Comm.* on this passage and the excursus on "From the Beginning" on pp. 32-34.

[39]See also 5:1-2, the meaning of which is disputed; cf., e.g., *Comm.* and *Handbook* on this passage.

[40]On this, see de Jonge, "To Love as God Loves," p. 119. The author knows how to make this rule concrete for everyday life also in 3:17.

[41]On this pericope and especially on the use of the word "world," see my *Comm.*

[42]See de Jonge, "To Love as God Loves," pp. 123-26.

[43]For the relationship between 1:5-10 and 3:4-10 and the connection with the combination of the "already" and the "not yet," see *Comm.*, pp. 155-59; cf. also the notes on ἀνομία in 3:4 (pp. 141-43) and on "mortal sin" in 5:16-17 (pp. 226-28).

[44]See 2:3-4, 7-8; 3:22-24; 4:21-5:3; the plural alternates with the singular, and in 2:5 with "the word"-- de Jonge, "To Love as God Loves," pp. 117-20. Important also is I. de la Potterie's exegesis of 2:12-14 in "La connaissance de Dieu dans le dualisme eschatologique d'après I Jn. II, 12-14," in *Au service de la parole de Dieu. Mélanges offerts à Mgr A. M. Charue* (Gembloux: Duculot, 1969). De la Potterie sees in the background the idea of the new covenant. Cf. also *Comm.*, pp. 73-77, and the literature cited there.

[45]See *Comm.*, pp. 78-79.

[46]See de Jonge, "To Love as God Loves," pp. 120-23, and *Comm.*, pp. 78-79.

[47]Dodd, *The Johannine Epistles*, p. XXXV.

[48]On the whole question of different redactions, see Chapter VIII, below.

[49]In the above, 2 John has been left out of consideration because the data in this brief epistle add nothing new to the picture that we can sketch on the basis of 1 John. On the theory (in my opinion an incorrect one) that 2 John is secondary in relation to 1 John and represents a still further "ecclesiasticized" stage of the Johannine theology, see *Comm.*, p. 236, and the note on that page in the supplements to the second printing.

CHAPTER VIII

VARIETY AND DEVELOPMENT IN JOHANNINE CHRISTOLOGY

Introduction

Many studies have been devoted lately to the various aspects of the problem of development in Johannine thought. Literary critics concentrate on the problems connected with the delineation of possible sources and of the redactional activity which shaped the Gospel. Often a second redaction is assumed which reflects the use and adaptation of the Johannine Gospel material in the communities for which the Johannine Epistles were written. The main question is to what extent we can speak of differences in outlook between the various authors or redactors or, alternatively, of changes in the theology of Johannine Christianity brought about by the changes in circumstances in which it lived and to which it had to respond. For that reason scholars dealing with sources, redaction(s) and theology(-ies) in the Fourth Gospel tend to give much attention to investigation of the historical situation(s) reflected in the Gospel and the Epistles, especially in the various sources and/or the stages of redaction detected in the Gospel. Many elements essential for the analysis of the developments of Johannine theology remain, of necessity, hypothetical and therefore, we are still far from a general consensus on the matter. Every scholar assumes that traditional material was used in the composition of the Fourth Gospel, but there is difference of opinion as to its nature. Everybody agrees that we may speak of a typical Johannine vocabulary, style, and theology; but there are many sudden transitions in language and content and (seeming) inconsistencies. How does one explain them? Do they, in one case, point to earlier (written) source-material with its own bias, and do we have to assume different stages of redaction in another?

A good survey of recent opinion can be found in
L'Evangile de Jean, Sources, rédaction, théologie, a report of the Colloquium Biblicum Lovaniense 1975, with an
introduction by the present author, published in 1977 as
Vol. 44 in the Bibliotheca Ephemeridum Theologicarum Lo-
vaniensium. The contributions of authors of different
backgrounds collected there are representative of the various methods employed in Johannine studies today. Typical
of much recent German and American literature on John is
James M. Robinson's article, "The Johannine Trajectory,"
in J. M. Robinson-H. Koester, *Trajectories through Early
Christianity*.[1] A very full and balanced picture of Johannine Christianity is given in D. Moody Smith, "Johannine
Christianity: Some Reflections on its Character and Delineation."[2] It should be compared with O. Cullmann's
recent *The Johannine Circle*.[3]

The most important and most widely accepted theory
in the field of Johannine source-criticism is that of a
Signs source. The origin and growth of the hypothesis of
the Signs source has lately been described in great detail
by Gilbert van Belle.[4] What the theory of a Signs Source
(or in his case, a Signs Gospel incorporating Passion
material as well) may mean in terms of the study of the
development of Johannine Christology is shown by one of
the influential modern protagonists of the theory, R. T.
Fortna, in his "Christology in the Fourth Gospel: Redaction-critical Perspectives."[5] U. B. Müller, in his *Die
Geschichte der Christologie in der johanneischen Gemeinde*,[6]
tries to prove that John 1:14, 16 also belong to an early
stage of christological thinking in the Johannine communities, closely connected with that represented by the Signs
Source. His work connects with that of J. Becker;[7] like
this scholar, he also devotes much attention to the later
"ecclesiastical" developments of the Johannine theology
which we find in the First and Second Epistles and in a
number of passages in the Gospel, particularly in the
farewell discourses.[8] Interesting, because of their

concentration on the stages in the history of the Johannine communities supposedly reflected in the Gospel and
the Epistles, are the studies of J. Louis Martyn.[9]

In this introductory survey, we must also mention
R. Schnackenburg's brief "Rückblick auf die Entstehungsge-
schichte des vierten Evangeliums" at the end of the third
volume of his commentary.[10] It is "a survey in retrospect"
in which the author briefly indicates the development of
his own ideas during the many years he worked on his commentary. His views are representative of much cautious
"middle of the road" scholarship (Roman Catholic as well
as non-Roman Catholic) of the present day. Schnackenburg's
survey shows that the problem of the variety within the
unity found in the Johannine writings has presented itself
with increasing force during the past decades and will have
to be resolved by every scholar who occupies himself with
the Fourth Gospel and the Johannine Epistles.

(1)   For Schnackenburg, the Fourth Gospel is the work of
an evangelist, a great theologian who was responsible for
the very special historical picture and theology of the
Gospel, reflecting the theological problems and debates at
the time of writing. The evangelist used sources. Already in the introduction to his first volume (pp. 64-67),
Schnackenburg supposed the existence of a Signs Source.
During his work on Volume II, dealing with chapters 5-12,
the theory of the Signs Source became increasingly important for him, and during the writing of Volume III he also
felt compelled to assume the existence of a pre-Johannine
Passion-source behind John 20. He emphasizes, however,
that he wants to proceed with caution because, after all,
we cannot know precisely what these sources actually con-
tained. Our main purpose should be to explain the text of
the Gospel before us; sources are only important insofar
as they help to explain the meaning of the author who can
be shown to have used them.

Gradually, the theory of a final redaction of the (3)
(probably not yet completed) Gospel by later members of

the Johannine community became more and more important
for Schnackenburg. The work of the redactor(s) is visible
in chapter 21, in 13:12-27 and 13:34f., and in chapters
15-16 and 17. Schnackenburg underlines that this redaction did not alter the theological perspective of the Gospel but adapted it to the needs of the Johannine community.
The natural place for the additions were the farewell
discourses.

This section may be concluded with a reference to
(the first installments of) a comprehensive assessment of
recent Johannine scholarship, H. Thyen's "Aus der Literatur zum Johannesevangelium" in *Theologische Rundschau*.[11]
Of importance for our present purpose are his part 3,
"Aufweis der Forschungstrends an neueren Interpretations-
versuchen des Johannesprologs" (pp. 53-69, 222-52) and
some sections of part 4.1, "Die johanneische Redaktion"
(pp. 289-330). On pp. 328-30, the author gives an outline
of the subjects he intends to treat in the next installments of his article.[12] He announces that he will not pay
much attention to the problem of Johannine sources
("Semeia-, Rede-, Passionsquelle") although much important
work has been done in this field lately. He professes to
be rather skeptical with regard to the various source-
theories and of their presuppositions concerning the
treatment of traditional material by later authors/redac-
tors; he prefers a consistently redaction-critical approach. Thyen avoids the term "evangelist" because he
does not believe in the existence of one figure adopting
and adapting material from written documents before him.
He also criticizes recent scholars who regard the work of
the "evangelist" as an original work of genius and the
activity of (a) later redactor(s) as ecclesiastical alter-
ation. Throughout we find redaction, and redaction is always the result of rethinking, reinterpretation, and
bringing up-to-date of earlier tradition. It is also the
work of a living community rather than of an individual.
Thyen, therefore, refuses to distinguish between "the

Gospel" and the (ecclesiastical) redaction, but prefers
the terms "Grundschrift" and "(johanneische) Redaktion."
This Johannine redaction went much further than the activity commonly ascribed to the ecclesiastical redactor.
The Johannine redaction made the Gospel what it is now and
before the last stage we can only speak of a "Grundschrift."

This becomes clear in his treatment of the various
approaches to the Prologue in part 3, particularly in his
discussion with G. Richter[13] (pp. 222-41). With Richter
and others, Thyen assigns 1:14-18 to the final redaction
of the Gospel. For Richter, this is a second redaction of
a Gospel that was written with the intention to prove that
the man Jesus is the Messiah, the Son of God (20:31). The
evangelist himself did not emphasize Jesus' manhood; he
had, in fact, to defend his message against people for
whom that manhood was so obvious that they could not believe in Jesus' claim to be the Son of God. Only a few
redactional passages in the Gospel, like 1:14-18, are
definitely anti-docetic, just as 1 and 2 John. For Thyen
not only 1:14-18, and the other texts mentioned by Richter,
are anti-docetic, but also 20:30f. and in fact the whole
Gospel which is for him the result of an anti-docetic reinterpretation of the "Grundschrift" against another party
in Johannine Christianity which interpreted this (at the
most gnosticizing) document in a docetic and gnostic way.[14]

Some Remarks on Method

The many questions raised in the literature briefly
referred to in the introduction--which is only a small part
of what could have been mentioned--cannot be dealt with
here. Thyen's consistently redaction-critical approach is
in many ways similar to the method employed in the preceding chapters of this volume, and there is basic agreement
on the thesis that the present Gospel as a literary product with a consistent theology of its own should be the
starting-point of all analysis. Thyen, however, still
assumes source-material, even a "Grundschrift," and a

thoroughgoing redaction, and he looks for ways and means
to distinguish between the two. In the present approach
both supposedly redactional and supposedly traditional
elements are treated as integral parts of a new literary
entity, which has to be studied on its own, because it
functioned as a whole among people who did *not* take its
prehistory into account.

This approach goes together with a certain scepti-
cism concerning the possibility to distinguish between redaction and source(s).[15] Certain elements are so essential in their present (narrower and wider) context that
they must be regarded as integral parts of the document in
question. It is often impossible, however, to be sure
that what remains after these elements are removed as
"redactional" really represents the text of the source;
the author[16] may have introduced subtle changes in what he
had before him, or he may be quoting from memory or just
re-telling a story. Everything which does not obviously
bear the stamp of the author's mind may, nevertheless, go
back to the author, including certain tensions or (seeming) inconsistencies.

It is not surprising, therefore, that so far little
has been said in this volume about the possibility of development in Johannine christology. The introduction to
Chapter V made clear that the passages on "the signs" were
to be treated as parts of the present Gospel and elements
in the argumentation of the Gospel. In Chapter VII we
noticed a number of differences in emphasis in matters of
ethics and eschatology between the Gospel and the First
Epistle but we could not distinguish between different
redactional stages in chapters 13-17. Admittedly the composition of these chapters is not very clear to us; we are
inclined to consider them as a rather loose combination of
a number of similar but not entirely congruent passages.
In Chapter VII, however, we did not distinguish between
"earlier" and "later" passages, let alone an "original"
and an "ecclesiastical" level of redaction. The rather

loose composition of the farewell discourses may be the
natural outcome of an attempt of the "author(s)" of the
Gospel to bring together as much material as possible
dealing with the situation of the community after Jesus'
departure to the Father.[17]   In this connection we should
also point back to the last section of Chapter IV (pp. 97-
102), where a plea was made for caution in attempts to reconstruct the historical circumstances in which the Fourth
Gospel originated and to which it responded. This caution
is all the more necessary when we deal with reconstructed
sources and earlier stages of redaction. In fact no author escapes reasoning in a circle. One notes difficulties in the Fourth Gospel and differences between the Gospel and the Epistles and traces them back to stages in the
development of theological thinking in communities which
had to give answers to concrete challenges from without or
within. We get different pictures of (a) living Johannine
community(-ies) creating living theology-in-response, and
the ideas about what must have happened again influence
theories of redaction. In his conclusion, U. B. Müller
speaks of "differenzierungsscheue Exegese" which will reject much of what he and others have been doing as purely
hypothetical. This cannot be denied, he says; yet a hypothesis proves its value if it helps to clarify problems
and contributes to their solution.[18]

The approach advocated in this volume certainly
tends to play down the differences and inconsistencies in
a certain writing, for the very reason that it consistently views them as differences and inconsistencies within
the framework of that writing. It also tends to be unhis-
torical, but not because it denies the "Sitz im Leben" and
the "communication-in-situation"-aspect of the literary
document, but because it realizes that some writings, particularly a Gospel, may be used only with great circum-
spection as historical sources.

Does this mean that, given the limitations of the
chosen method, we are not in a position to discuss any

developments in Johannine Christology at all? This does
not necessarily follow. For one thing, comparison between
the views concerning Jesus Christ in the Gospel and those
in 1 and 2 John is possible and may lead to certain conclusions with regard to the developments in Johannine
Christology. Next, we may ask to what extent this comparison with the Epistles helps us to detect elements in the
Christology of the Gospel which we have overlooked so far.
In this connection it will prove necessary to say something about the relationship between 20:30-31, "the so-
called first ending," and chapter 21. This, in turn, will
lead to some observations concerning other passages dealing with the beloved disciple.

*Some Important Features of the Christology of the First
Epistle*[19]

        In the Nestle-Aland text of the Johannine Epistles
the word χριστός occurs 11 times. Although for obvious
reasons the manuscripts differ in a number of these instances, all modern editors[20] are in agreement with Nestle
at this point. Only Westcott and Hort add a twelfth instance between square brackets, reading ὃς ἐὰν ὁμολογήσῃ
ὅτι 'Ιησοῦς [Χριστός] ἐστιν ὁ υἱὸς τοῦ θεοῦ with B in 1 John
4:15.

        In four cases we find 'Ιησοῦς Χριστός directly
linked with ὁ υἱὸς αὐτοῦ. In each instance this combination is so placed within the sentence as to put all emphasis on the christological statement. In 1 John 1:3b a
long and involved argument ends with the joyful asservera-
tion καὶ ἡ κοινωνία δὲ ἡ ἡμετέρα μετὰ τοῦ πατρὸς καὶ μετὰ
τοῦ υἱοῦ αὐτοῦ 'Ιησοῦ Χριστοῦ. With this statement at the
beginning of 1 John may be connected a similar one at the
end of this letter, καὶ ἐσμὲν ἐν τῷ ἀληθινῷ, ἐν τῷ υἱῷ
αὐτοῦ 'Ιησοῦ Χριστῷ (5:20).[21] In both cases the unity between God and Jesus Christ, Father and Son, which receives
so much attention in the Gospel and in the Epistles of
John is presupposed and stressed. The same applies to the

formula ἵνα πιστεύσωμεν τῷ ὀνόματι τοῦ υἱοῦ αὐτοῦ Ἰησοῦ
Χριστοῦ in 1 John 3:23 and to the introductory greeting in
2 John 3, ἔσται μεθ᾽ ἡμῶν χάρις ἔλεος εἰρήνη παρὰ θεοῦ
πατρός, καὶ παρὰ Ἰησοῦ Χριστοῦ τοῦ υἱοῦ τοῦ πατρός, ἐν
ἀληθείᾳ καὶ ἀγάπῃ.[22]

In 1 John 2:1 Jesus Christ is said to act as
παράκλητος, one who pleads our cause *with the Father*.
Jesus Christ is not called the Son here, but again his intimate relationship with God is emphasized. In this text
he receives the epithet δίκαιος, a "messianic" designation
in Acts 3:14, 7:52, 22:14 as in 1 Enoch 38:2 and 53:6. It
is, however, far from certain that a messianic meaning or
overtone is intended here. In 1:9 God himself is called
πιστὸς καὶ δίκαιος in connection with his forgiveness for
those who confess their sins. In 2:29 and 3:7 the righteousness of Jesus is mentioned as an example for his followers who as true children of God should be like the One
who is Son of God par excellence (see 3:7-10). Jesus
Christ, who is righteous, lives in communion with God and
is therefore able to intercede for the sins of those who
believe in Him. Πολὺ ἰσχύει δέησις δικαίου ἐνεργουμένη
(Jas 5:16; cf. 17-18 and Prov 15:29)!

Another emphatic statement is οὗτός ἐστιν ὁ ἐλθὼν
δι᾽ ὕδατος καὶ αἵματος, Ἰησοῦς Χριστός (1 John 5:6) which
follows on a passage which begins with the formula πᾶς ὁ
πιστεύων ὅτι Ἰησοῦς ἐστιν ὁ χριστός in 5:1 and ends with
a similar statement ὁ πιστεύων ὅτι Ἰησοῦς ἐστιν ὁ υἱὸς
τοῦ θεοῦ in 5:5. Does this imply that the designation
χριστός and the expression ὁ υἱὸς τοῦ θεοῦ are not only
closely linked, but also interchangeable? The answer to
this question should, I think, be in the affirmative. The
whole argument in 5:1-5 revolves round the question, who
are truly born from God, and the answer is clearly, those
who believe in the Son of God and love the children of
God. It would have fitted the author's argumentation if
he had begun with the expression ὁ υἱὸς τοῦ θεοῦ or with
ὁ γεννηθεὶς ἐκ τοῦ θεοῦ as in 5:18.[23] Nevertheless, the

belief in Jesus as the Son of God is mentioned only at the
end, and the section opens with a reference to the belief
in Jesus as ὁ χριστός. The author must have found no
difficulty here because for him and his readers the two
terms were virtually synonymous.[24]

This is also clear in 1 John 2:22f. and 2 John 9.
The denial ὅτι 'Ιησοῦς (οὐκ) ἔστιν ὁ χριστός, which characterizes the Antichrist, is a denial of both Father and
Son, and a sure sign that one is not in communion with Son
and Father. To the author and his readers the χριστός is
clearly the υἱός; the denial that Jesus is the χριστός
reveals that one lives far from the Father who sent Jesus
as his Son on earth. He who is so "progressive" that he
does not abide ἐν τῇ διδαχῇ τοῦ χριστοῦ,[25] does not have
God, but he who abides in that doctrine has both the Father and the Son.

In 1 John 4:2f. and 2 John 7, we find a further
specification which is essential to the author's argumentation and deserves, therefore, our special attention. Here
the formula 'Ιησοῦν Χριστὸν ἐν σαρκὶ ἐληλυθότα (2 John 7,
ἐρχόμενον ἐν σαρκί) is used to denote the content of the
correct Christian ὁμολογία. In 1 John 4:2 the grammatical
construction is not very clear and therefore translations
and interpretations differ. Moffatt's translation, "Jesus
as the Christ incarnate," would imply that the author intended to give a further explication of the formula used
in 1 John 2:22 and 5:1. Still, in that case he would have
used the definite article before χριστόν, and/or before ἐν
σαρκὶ ἐληλυθότα. In the case of the use of ἐν σαρκὶ ἐληλυθότα as an attribute to 'Ιησοῦν Χριστόν, we should also
expect the article after Χριστόν.[26] Considering the fact
that in vs. 3 the simple τὸν 'Ιησοῦν is used as equivalent[27] of the full formula in vs. 2, we should take 'Ιησοῦν
Χριστὸν ἐν σαρκὶ ἐληλυθότα as whole, and translate, "to
confess Jesus Christ as having come in the flesh."[28] The
emphasis falls not so much on Jesus Christ's coming in the
flesh as on his humanity (see also the use of the perfect

participle!). To the author, the confession "Jesus is the Christ" can only mean that Jesus Christ is regarded as a real human being. It is evident that the author's opponents were docetists,[29] and that 1 John considers it necessary to state quite clearly that Jesus Christ was a real man (1:1-4), who died a real death (1:7, 4:10, 5:6). The point at stake is the correct *interpretation* of the formulae Ἰησοῦς ἐστιν ὁ χριστός and Ἰησοῦς ἐστιν ὁ υἱὸς τοῦ θεοῦ and this interpretation is given in 1 John 4:2.

2 John 7 takes up this interpretation but expresses it in a slightly different form; the present participle ἐρχόμενον is used instead of the perfect participle ἐληλυθότα. It is generally taken to refer to the coming of Jesus Christ into the world, regardless of the time-aspect. The Gospel speaks of one "who comes from above" (John 3:31), the Second Epistle speaks of one "who comes in the flesh" (cf. also John 6:14, ὁ προφήτης ὁ ἐρχόμενος εἰς τὸν κόσμον; 11:27, ὁ χριστὸς ὁ υἱὸς τοῦ θεοῦ ὁ εἰς τὸν κόσμον ἐρχόμενος).[30]

Two further points should be noted:

1. Though ὁ χριστός and ὁ υἱὸς τοῦ θεοῦ are used synonymously, the author seems to favor the latter expression. "Son of God" (or "His Son," "The Son," etc.) is used 22 times in the First Epistle, and also twice in the second one. Especially striking is the fact that after 1 John 5:6, only υἱός is used (no less than 8 times in 15 verses). χριστός occurs again together with τῷ υἱῷ αὐτοῦ in 1 John 5:20b where the author, as was noted above, returns to the terminology used in 1 John 1:3.

2. Besides χριστός, the Epistles also use the words χρῖσμα (3 times, in 1 John 2:20 and 27) and ἀντίχριστος (4 times, in 1 John 2:18, 22; 4:3 and 2 John 7), neither of which occurs elsewhere in the NT. From the context in 1 John 2:18-27, it is clear that the use of these terms is intentional, and serves the author's argumentation. The "liar" who denies that Jesus is the Christ is the antichrist (vs. 22) who has come into the world

(vs. 18) in the persons of many antichrists, many de-
ceivers (vs. 26), who propagate a false doctrine and
clearly do not belong to the church. The author assures
his readers (vss. 20, 27): They are the *antichrists*, but
you have received the *chrisma*. You know the truth, they
belong to the world of falsehood.

This is not the place to go into the complicated
problems of the meaning and the background of the words
χρῖσμα and ἀντίχριστος.[31] The principal difficulty is
presented by the fact that the links in terminology are
clearer than the underlying chain of thought. It is evident that the author's refutation of his opponents and
exhortation of his children remain within the circle of
Christian faith and practice. The terms ἀντίχριστος and
χρῖσμα (like χριστός itself) needed no explanation in the
communities to which the Epistles were addressed, notwithstanding the fact that we do not find these terms in any
of the other writings of the NT, including the Gospel of
John. There is no indication that the controversy within
the "Johannine" Christian communities was influenced by
Christian-Jewish controversies concerning the messiahship
of Jesus. The term "antichrist" is neither a Jewish term
nor a clear equivalent of a Jewish expression. The use of
χριστός or χρῖσμα does not reveal any allusion to the Jewish background of the "anointing" of Jesus, and *a fortiori*
no connection is made between the "anointing" of the
Christians and the messiahship of Jesus.[32]

From this rather rapid survey of the use of the
word χριστός in the Johannine Epistles one thing emerges
clearly: This word is used as a *Christian* term, which has
lived its own life in the Christian church, and especially
in the Christian communities to which the Epistles were
addressed. Χριστός is synonymous with "Son of God" and
the central problem is the connection between the unity of
Father and Son and Jesus' concrete manhood--for the author
an essential element in the relationship between the Son
of God and the children of God. In the author's christology

χριστός is one, traditional, term among others, and certainly not the most important one. His christology centers around the statements ὁ ὁμολογῶν τὸν υἱὸν καὶ τὸν πατέρα ἔχει (1 John 2:23) and (ὁμολογεῖν) Ἰησοῦν Χριστὸν ἐν σαρκὶ ἐληλυθότα (1 John 4:2). For him the opponents who deny the ἐν σαρκί deny the Son and therefore God himself.

This christological emphasis is of great christological importance. That Jesus came "in the flesh" means that he died on the cross. The blood of Jesus (5:6) removes sin (1:7, 9; cf. 3:6, 8). God sent his Son as a ἱλασμός for our sins (4:10; and not only for our sins but also for those of the whole world, 2:2). This emphasis on the humanity and humility of Jesus Christ also has ethical consequences: "By this we know love, that he laid down his life for us; and we ought to lay down our lives for our brethren."[33]

The First Epistle was written in a crisis-situation. People who have left the Johannine communities (2:19) try to lead the Christians astray to whom the author is writing (2:26, 3:7). The Epistle tries to counteract the evil effects of the (in his view Pseudo-) Johannine teaching of the opponents, and its christological argument serves to attack it at its roots. The readers are exhorted to go back to "the beginning"[34] and the author emphasizes that he speaks in the name of a group ("we") which testifies to what it has heard and seen (1:1-4).[35]

Much more can be said concerning the situation behind the First (and Second) Epistle--although we should realize that we see it through the eyes of its author-- than with regard to that presupposed in the Gospel. And because the author as well as his opponents obviously started from a few common basic tenets in the Johannine communities, it is tempting to go back to the point where their roads separated.[36] We may, for instance, suppose that at some stage Johannine theology was characterized by a great emphasis on the glory of Jesus the Son of God; at

the moment this emphasis led to a denial of the humanity
and crucifixion of Jesus, others felt compelled to develop
an explicitly anti-docetic christology.[37] This historical
question cannot be discussed here. It is important, however, to ask whether any of the elements which are characteristic for the christology of 1-2 John are found in the
Gospel and to see in what respect the picture given in the
previous chapter of this volume has to be supplemented.

Anti-Docetic Elements in the Fourth Gospel?

In the preceding chapters, it has become clear that
χριστός is used in the Fourth Gospel in the Jewish (Samaritan) sense of the word or with a Christian meaning presupposing, but correcting, Jewish usage. The term "Son of
God" is used to bring out this Christian meaning, but is
not (yet) identical with χριστός. The double expression
'Ιησοῦς Χριστός occurs twice (in 1:17 and 17:3) in a
context which presupposes the unity of Father and Son; in
this case we may speak of a usage comparable to that of
the Epistles (where this expression is found no less than
eight times).

There is clearly a shift in emphasis here between
the Gospel and the Epistles, but not necessarily a difference in christology. The Epistles are directed toward a
situation of conflict between (true and false) Johannine
Christians; the Gospel presupposes reflection on the issues at stake in the debates between Jews and Christians,
and between Christians of various background.[38]

Of more importance is the emphasis on the ἐν σαρκί
and on the death of Jesus Christ. Jesus' opponents in the
Gospel do not doubt that the person before them is human,
but find it impossible to believe that this human being
has received unique authority from God. 6:42 is significant here: "Is this not Jesus, the son of Joseph, whose
father and mother we know?" and also 5:18 (leading up to
10:33-39 and 19:7) "...This was why the Jews sought all
the more to kill him, because he did not only break the

sabbath, but also called God his father, making himself equal with God."[39] Considering the fact that Jesus is portrayed here in debate with outsiders who could not penetrate into his innermost secret, it is not surprising that the difficulty does not lie in the fact that he is a man.

But are there, perhaps, indications that the Gospel wants to preclude wrong notions about Jesus' manhood among its Christian readers? Thyen maintains that 20:30, 31 have an anti-docetic thrust;[40] he connects these verses with 19:35 and with the preceding Thomas-story which in vss. 25, 27 (cf. vs. 20) presupposes 19:34. Now it is obvious that the stories in vss. 19-23 and 24-29 (like 19:38-42) assume that Jesus died on the cross. It remains to be seen, however, whether they are explicitly anti-docetic; it is not at all clear that they want to combat other views on Jesus' death and resurrection. And if the preceding sections are not anti-docetic, there is no reason to regard 20:30, 31 as such. This is different in the very explicit 19:35, to which we shall return below.

Not wanting to go into all the details concerning the exegesis of 1:14-18 and the place of these verses in the history of Johannine thought, I content myself with the remark that even the use of the word ἐγένετο in the crucial expression ὁ λόγος σὰρξ ἐγένετο in 1:14 cannot prove the anti-docetic thrust of this verse.[41] In a small article written against G. Richter's exegesis of this verse,[42] K. Berger rightly pointed to Justin, *Dial.* 127.4 and 128.1 where πῦρ γέγονε is interpreted as φαινόμενος ἐν πύρος δόξῃ..., (cf. *Apol.* 63.10, 16). Neither the ἐγένετο nor the following ἐσκήνωσεν meditates on the exact nature of the manhood of the Logos; as the following "we saw his glory, etc." shows, the essential point is that the believing community living in communion with the eye-witnesses is able to say that they were allowed to recognize Jesus Christ as the only-begotten Son of the Father (cf. 1:12, 13) and to receive "grace and truth" through him. The emphasis is on the fact that true life springs from the revelation of God through this unique man at a particular point of time. Certainly a "naive docetic" interpretation of 1:14 is not very likely; it is quite another thing, however, to maintain that the verse is explicitly anti-docetic.

Apart from 19:35, there is one other passage which deserves our attention--6:32-59, followed by vss. 60-71. The latter verses were already briefly discussed in Chapter I.[43] The true disciples in vss. 67-71 are able to say ῥήματα ζωῆς αἰωνίου ἔχεις (vs. 68). This is parallel to τὰ ῥήματα ἃ ἐγὼ λελάληκα ὑμῖν πνεῦμά ἐστιν καὶ ζωή ἐστιν in vs. 63b--a sentence preceded by the statement τὸ πνεῦμά ἐστιν τὸ ζωοποιοῦν, ἡ σὰρξ οὐκ ὠφελεῖ οὐδέν.[44] The disciples who refuse to follow Jesus any longer do not accept his words as life-giving, (as source of) Spirit and life. They say: σκληρός ἐστιν ὁ λόγος οὗτος· τίς δύναται αὐτοῦ ἀκούειν (vs. 60). Also later, after the Son of Man has returned to the Father, they will not be able to believe; they do not look beyond "the flesh which is of no avail."

But what exactly shocked them? Their reaction is characterized in vs. 61 as γογγυσμός, just as that of the Jews in 6:41. Is their difficulty the same as that of the Jews? Verse 52 would seem to point in that direction. Verses 53-58 are directed against the Jews who protest against Jesus' word in vs. 51. This final part of Jesus' discourse on the Bread from Heaven emphasizes the unity between the believers and Jesus through the eating of the flesh of the Son of Man and the drinking of his blood. Many people have ascribed this concluding passage to an ecclesiastical redactor, and it is certainly not impossible to assume that the discourse on the Bread from Heaven ever existed in a shorter form.[45] But vs. 58 forms a good "inclusio" with vss. 32-35, and it is quite apposite that the disciples in vs. 60 react to the last part of the discourse which so clearly speaks about the unity between the believers and Jesus in eucharistic terminology.[46] The

209

difficulty of the Jews is the difficulty of the outsiders, the problem of the disciples is typically one of insiders, at least of people who want to be insiders but discover that they can remain disciples no longer. Undoubtedly the present Gospel wants to warn its readers against the reaction of the backsliding disciples portrayed in this chapter. Everyone who fails to acknowledge that unity with Jesus is only possible through his death on the cross must know that he has stepped outside the orbit of divine revelation and true life and no longer belongs to the circle of disciples. And as to the parallelism between Jews and "docetists," we may quote P. Borgen, "...John tries to show that the docetic spiritualists in the Church are like Jewish externalists, because both reject the Incarnate One as the only mediator between God and man."[47]

Chapter 6 constitutes a complicated and closely-knit whole. Only in this chapter do we meet disciples who forsake Jesus, and the reason for their departure is indicated in vs. 60, which is a reaction to the Discourse on the Bread including its last section, vss. 53-58. It is, of course, possible to assume that 51b-58 were added later to an already existing Gospel, but in that case the difference between the reaction of the disciples and that of the Jews is not clear, and one may ask why the disciples were mentioned at all.[48] It would seem that those who regard vss. 51b-58 as an ecclesiastical and/or anti-docetic addition should also leave out vss. 60-66 and 67-71. If this is so, we have to conclude that in this case a very incisive literary-critical operation is necessary to distinguish between the present Gospel and the earlier text which it incorporates.[49]

Our conclusion must, therefore, be that the present Gospel does not only presuppose reflection on the issues at stake in the debates between Jews and Christians and between Christians of various background, but that it also reacts to difficulties within the Johannine communities and between those communities and people who have left

them. What is a major christological issue in the First
and Second Epistles is a minor one in the Gospel, but the
necessity of "anti-docetic emphasis" is (already) there.
To that purpose also, 1:14 and the Thomas-story 20:24-29,
although not anti-docetic in themselves, could be used,
and the formula Ἰησοῦς ἐστιν ὁ χριστὸς ὁ υἱὸς τοῦ θεοῦ
could be used against "Jews" and docetic (ex-)disciples.

Jesus' death on the cross is, in the Fourth Gospel,
primarily a stage in his return to the Father, characterized as δοξασθῆναι and ὑψωθῆναι.[50] The soteriological
effects of Jesus' death as such do not receive much emphasis.[51] Nevertheless, there is no suggestion anywhere that
Jesus did not die a real death. There is only one text,
19:35, which seems to consider it necessary to emphasize
this. After 19:34 has recorded that "blood and water"
flowed from Jesus' side after one of the soldiers had
pierced it with a spear, vs. 35 adds, "He who saw it has
borne witness--his testimony is true, and he knows that he
tells the truth--that you may also believe." The ἵνα καὶ
ὑμεῖς πιστεύητε links this verse with 20:31; the first
part should be connected with 21:24--all the more because
in the present context the eye-witness referred to in 19:
35 can be no other than "the beloved disciple" mentioned
in 19:25-27 and at the end of chapter 21. Verse 34 is a
difficult verse in a very complicated passage (vss. 31-37),
but vs. 35 referring back to vs. 34 certainly has an anti-
docetic thrust (cf. also 1 John 5:6-8).[52]

It is possible to distinguish different lines of
thought in vss. 31-37 (which itself stands rather uncon-
nected beside vss. 38-42)[53] and various theories of redaction have been put forward. Verse 35, as an interpretative comment, plays an important role in the pericope; it
may come from a later redactor but need not necessarily be
secondary. If, in fact, the anti-docetic element forms an
integral part of chapter 6, there is no reason why 19:35
should have been added later.

The Passages on the "Beloved Disciple"

The eye-witness in 19:35 is the "beloved disciple," mentioned in a number of passages in the Gospel and a particularly important figure in chapter 21, generally considered to be an appendix to the Gospel. As we have consistently tried so far to interpret the present Gospel as a whole, and maintain that 6:51b-58 and 19:35 are an integral part of the Gospel, it may be useful to look briefly into the relation of chapter 21 to the rest of the Gospel and to attempt to analyze the function of the "beloved disciple" in the book. This disciple was, on purpose, not discussed in Chapter I and should, therefore, receive attention here. Again, I concentrate on the literary composition and leave the many problems connected with the relation between sources and redaction(s) and historical questions (e.g., that of the identity of the beloved disciple) out of account.[55]

John 21 is an epilogue but, as H. Thyen[56] reminds us, not necessarily an appendix by another author than the one who wrote 20:30-31. The "disciple whom Jesus loved" remains anonymous though his identity is known to the ἀδελφοί in vs. 23 and to the "we" group who wrote vs. 24. Both in vs. 7 and in vss. 20-22 this disciple is connected with Peter. In vs. 7, Simon Peter comes into action after the disciple has told him "It is the Lord!" In vss. 20-22 there is a parallelism between Peter's following (cf. 13: 36) and that of the beloved disciple, though that of the latter does not include a martyr's death. Jesus' word ἐὰν αὐτὸν θέλω μένειν ἕως ἔρχομαι, τί πρὸς σέ; was misunderstood by "the brothers," we are told in vs. 23. People took this literally, and thought that the beloved disciple would not die before the parousia. The beloved disciple did die, however, and the group responsible for vs. 24 and, no doubt, the final redaction of the latter part of the chapter or more, give another interpretation of this saying.[57] This **disciple** remains with the believers, even after his death, **as witness** (ὁ μαρτυρῶν present!) in what

212

he has written (ὁ γράψας ταῦτα). He is an absolutely
reliable witness, we are assured (cf. 19:35; note the
perfect μεμαρτύρηκεν there).

It is clear that for the "we" of 21:24 (cf. 1:14!),
the testimony of "the disciple whom Jesus loved" is essential. The testimony of the "we"-group is founded on his
testimony; here the *pluralis ecclesiasticus* and a *singu-
laris apostolicus*, exemplary of the *pluralis*, come together. This group wants to make clear that this disciple,
after all, "*wrote*" the Gospel.[58] The dependence of the
whole "Church" on the beloved disciple is indicated by the
dependence of Peter on this disciple's insight and witness
in vs. 7.

Not without reason, vs. 20 refers back explicitly
to chapter 13 where the beloved disciple is mentioned for
the first time and is described as ἀνακείμενος....ἐν τῷ
κόλπῳ τοῦ Ἰησοῦ. The parallel with 1:18 has often been
noted. He is the disciple par excellence,[59] his unique
position of trust towards Jesus somehow reflects Jesus'
unique relationship with the Father. In 19:25-27 the beloved disciple succeeds Jesus as son in that he becomes
and acts as a son for Jesus' mother.[60] Peter is, again,
dependent on this disciple and asks him for an explanation
of Jesus' word on the traitor (vs. 21). The disciple
hears what Jesus says to Judas, he knows what it means
that Judas goes away and what will happen, but, strangely
enough, does not tell Peter or any of the other disciples
(vs. 28!); he keeps his information to himself. The same
is true in 20:2-10.[61] The beloved disciple believes after
he has seen the empty grave and all that is in it, but he
does not share his insight with Peter or anyone else; the
story goes on as if he had not been there and had not
understood anything (vss. 17-18, 19-23, 24-29).

This aspect of the role of the beloved disciple
may well be intentional. He is in a unique position within the inner circle of the disciples; all others, symbol-
ized by Peter, are dependent on his insight. In fact

for the Johannine community, in which he is the central
figure, his witness to, and interpretation of, events is
fundamental for the Gospel it sends out into the world.
Yet the difference between chapters 13 and 20, on the one
hand, and 21:24 on the other, wanted to make clear that
his inside knowledge became decisive after Jesus' return
to the Father. ()This disciple knew who, in the inner
circle, was going to betray Jesus (note the repeated mention of treason in 13:2, 11, 18-19, 21-30).[62] He stood at
the foot of the cross (19:25-27 in contrast to 16:32!)²and
knew that Jesus had really died (19:34). He understood
that Jesus had risen bodily from the dead (20:8) and he
was the first to recognize the risen Lord on the border of
the lake of Tiberias (21:7). He is the one who guarantees
the reality of Jesus' death and resurrection and shows
what it means to have life in communion with this Jesus,
the Christ and the Son of God. 19:35 is by no means an
isolated saying in the Gospel.

NOTES

CHAPTER VIII

[1]J. M. Robinson and Helmut Koester, *Trajectories through Early Christianity* (Philadelphia: Fortress, 1971). The article is chapter 7 and can be found on pp. 232-68.

[2]D. Moody Smith, "Johannine Christianity: Some Reflections on its Character and Delineation," *NTS* 21 (1974-75), pp. 222-48.

[3]O. Cullmann, *The Johannine Circle* (Philadelphia: Westminster, 1976).

[4]G. van Belle, *De Semeia-bron in het vierde evangelie. Ontstaan en groei van een hypothese* (Leuven: Universitaire Pers, 1975). The book is written in Dutch, but all essential quotations are given in the original languages.

[5]R. T. Fortna, "Christology in the Fourth Gospel: Redaction-critical Perspectives," *NTS* 21 (1974-75), pp. 489-504.

[6]U. B. Müller, *Die Geschichte der Christologie in der johanneischen Gemeinde*, SBS 77 (Stuttgart: Katholisches Bibelwerk, 1975).

[7]J. Becker, "Wunder und Christologie," *NTS* 16 (1969-70), pp. 130-48.

[8]Müller, *Die Geschichte der Christologie*, pp. 53-68; cf. J. Becker's articles mentioned in Chapter VII, n. 9, and his "Beobachtungen zum Dualismus im Johannesevangelium," *ZNW* 65 (1974), pp. 71-87, and "J 3, 1-21 als Reflex johanneischer Schuldiskussion," in *Das Wort und die Wörter* (Festschrift Gerhard Friedrich), ed. H. Balz and S. Schulz (Stuttgart: Kohlhammer, 1973).

[9]See J. L. Martyn, "History and Theology in the Fourth Gospel," *Jesus and Man's Hope* 1, ed. D. G. Buttrick (Pittsburgh: Pittsburgh Theological Seminary, 1970), pp. 247-73, and his contribution, "Glimpses into the History of the Johannine Community," in *L'Evangile de Jean. Sources, rédaction, théologie*, ed. M. de Jonge et al. (soon to be published), pp. 149-75.

[10]R. Schnackenburg, *Das Johannesevangelium* III, Herders Theologischer Kommentar zum Neuen Testament (Freiburg-Basel-Wien: Herder, 1975), pp. 463-64, the last section of Exkurs 18, "Der Jünger, den Jesus liebte."

216

[11]At the time of the writing of this chapter, three installments had appeared of H. Thyen's "Aus der Literatur zum Johannesevangelium," in *TRu* 39 (1974), pp. 1-69, 222-52, and 289-330. This author also had access to H. Thyen's "Entwicklungen innerhalb der johanneischen Theologie und Kirche im Spiegel von Joh. 21 und der Lieblingsjünger exte des Evangeliums," in *L'Evangile de Jean*, pp. 259-99.

[12]Thyen, "Aus der Literatur zum Johannesevangelium"; I quote from p. 329: "4.12. Joh. 21 und der Lieblingsjünger; 4.13. Joh. 6 und die Sakramente; 4.14. Redaktionelle Reapokalyptisierung der johanneischen Eschatologie?; 4.15. Joh. 13, die Abschiedsreden und die Verheissung des Parakleten; 4.16. 'Scheu und Glaube,' die johanneischen Ostererzählungen und die beide Kanawunder; 4.17. Joh. 3 und das Täuferbild." On 4.12, cf. now Thyen, "Entwicklungen innerhalb der johanneischen Theologie," and on 4.15, cf. "Johannes 13 und die 'kirchliche Redaktion' des vierten Evangeliums" in *Tradition und Glaube. Das fruhe Christentum in seiner Umwelt* (Festgabe für K. G. Kuhn), ed. G. Jeremias, H. W. Kuhn, and H. Hegermann (Göttingen: Vandenhoeck & Ruprecht, 1971), pp. 343-56.

[13]G. Richter, "Die Fleischwerdung des Logos im Johannesevangelium," *NovT* 13 (1971), pp. 81-126, and 14 (1972), pp. 157-76. See also Müller, *Die Geschichte der Christologie*, "Nachtrag," pp. 74-76.

[14]Here Thyen uses a number of ideas from L. Schottroff's *Der Glaubende und die feindliche Welt. Beobachtungen zum gnostischen Dualismus und seiner Bedeutung für Paulus und das Johannesevangelium*, WMANT 37 (Neukirchen: Neukirchener Verlag, 1970).

[15]See also the introduction to Chapter V. We should note that Thyen does not doubt the possibility of reconstructing at least some parts of the "Grundschrift," however skeptical he may be with regard to the delineation of sources.

[16]I use the word "author" here because I want to avoid the word "redactor." It is clear that a document like the Fourth Gospel may have been a product not of a single author, but of a believing community. At this point Thyen and I do not differ.

[17]In any case, we cannot assume that our standards of consistency were applied at any hypothetical earlier stage of redaction of these discourses; see Chapter VII, n. 9.

[18]Müller, *Die Geschichte der Christologie*, p. 69.

[19]In this section, I take up the first part (pp. 66-71) of my contribution, "The Use of the Word ΧΡΙΣΤΟΣ in the Johannine Epistles," to *Studies in John* presented to Prof. Dr. J. N. Sevenster, NovTSup 24 (Leiden: Brill, 1970), pp. 66-74. It was written before the work on the Gospel, resulting in the other studies in this volume, had started. The second part of the article, giving a comparison with the use of χριστός in the Gospel, was taken up and expounded in Chapter IV.

I assume the literary unity of 1 John (against Bultmann and others; see my *De Brieven van Johannes* [Nijkerk: Callenbach, 1968, [2]1973], pp. 11-14), and reject R. Bergmeier's theory ("Zum Verfasserproblem des II. und III. Johannesbriefes," *ZNW* 57 [1966], pp. 93-100, followed by R. Bultmann in *The Johannine Epistles*, Hermeneia [Philadelphia: Fortress Press, 1973], p. 107, n. 2) that 2 John is a later ecclesiastical falsification based on 1 John, as unnecessary and not capable of proof (for further details, see *De Brieven van Johannes*, pp. 235-37, and the note on p. 236 in the second edition).

[20]I consulted Tischendorf, Westcott and Hort, Weiss, von Soden, Vogels, Merk, B. F. B. S. text (second edition), B. F. B. S. Greek-English Diglot, and *The Greek New Testament*.

[21]G. D. Kilpatrick, in the B. F. B. S. Greek-English Diglot, omits the second ἐν τῷ as a possible dittography and reads τὸν ἀληθινὸν θεόν in the immediately preceding clause. For further details and argumentation, see G. D. Kilpatrick, "Some Notes on Johannine Usage," in *The Bible Translator* 11 (1960), pp. 173-77, and "Two Johannine Idioms in the Johannine Epistles," *JTS* N.S. 12 (1961), pp. 272-73. Kilpatrick tries to show that in the Gospel and Epistles of John ἀληθής is always used predicatively, and ἀληθινός attributively. In all instances where an exception to this rule may be found, the text is uncertain.

[22]Here a number of textual witnesses add κυρίου before Ἰησοῦ; see, e.g., the apparatus in *The Greek New Testament*.

[23]In this verse, this expression is used alongside πᾶς ὁ γεγεννημένος ἐκ τοῦ θεοῦ. This latter phrase denotes the believers; the former most likely refers to Jesus Christ; cf. John 6:39; 10:28-29; 17:12 (, 15); and Rev 3:10. For a discussion of the problems connected with this verse, see my *De Brieven van Johannes*, ad loc.

[24]5:5 should be compared with 4:15, ὃς ἐὰν ὁμολογήσῃ ὅτι Ἰησοῦς ἐστιν ὁ υἱὸς τοῦ θεοῦ, again in a context which refers to the communion of the true believers with God. The addition Χριστός after Ἰησοῦς in B is perfectly intelligible (see also 5:6, Ἰησοῦς Χριστός, directly after

5:5), but therefore probably secondary; cf. also the addition of Χριστός by A *Koinē* Vulg and many other witnesses in 1 John 1:7.

[25]Τοῦ χριστοῦ may be *genitivus objectivus* or *genitivus subjectivus*. In view of John 7:16-17; 8:28, 40; 15:15, and 18:19, the latter solution is the more likely one, but the former is by no means impossible. This question, however, is of only secondary importance for the purpose of this article.

[26]If only to avoid confusion; see BDF 270.3, and N. Turner, *A Grammar of NT Greek* (Edinburgh: T. & T. Clark, 1963), pp. 185-86. It should be noted that in 1 John 2:1, δίκαιον follows Ἰησοῦν Χριστόν without an article; cf. John 12:9, ὁ ὄχλος πολύς.

[27]There are, however, a great number of variants at this point. See, e.g., the apparatus in *The Greek New Testament*. After Ἰησοῦν, κύριον is added in ℵ and Χριστόν in the *Koinē*-text and others. ℵ, the *Koinē*-text, and most other MSS also add ἐν σαρκὶ ἐληλυθότα, a reading given in brackets by von Soden (with the non-addition as alternative reading). These additions clearly intend to give a fuller and more precise formulation in accordance with the preceding verse, and are not likely to be original. Therefore, the equivalent of Ἰησοῦν Χριστόν ἐν σαρκὶ ἐληλυθότα in vs. 2 will indeed have been a simple τὸν Ἰησοῦν.
The interesting question whether in vs. 3 ὃ μὴ ὁμολογεῖ or ὃ λύει should be read before τὸν Ἰησοῦν need not detain us here. G. D. Kilpatrick gives ὃ λύει in the B. F. B. S. Greek-English Diglot, but all other modern editors prefer ὃ μὴ ὁμολογεῖ. For further particulars, see *The Greek New Testament*; R. Schnackenburg, *Die Johannesbriefe*, Herders Theologischer Kommentar zum Neuen Testament (Freiburg-Basel-Wien: Herder, [2]1963), p. 222; and de Jonge, *De Brieven van Johannes*, ad loc. In the latter work, an interesting suggestion by Dr. J. Smit Sibinga is recorded to the effect that ΠΝΕΥΜΑΟΛΥΕΙ is a misreading for ΠΝΕΥΜΑΟΜΗΟΜΟΛΟΓΕΙ, Γ not being written in some ancient MSS (see H. St. J. Thackeray, *A Grammar of the Old Testament in Greek* [Cambridge: Cambridge University Press, 1909], pp. 111-13).

[28]Compare, e.g., John 9:22, ἐάν τις αὐτὸν ὁμολογήσῃ Χριστόν, and especially the variant reading, ἐάν τις ὁμολογήσῃ αὐτὸν Χριστόν in P66 φ al.; see BDF 157.2. In 416.3 the theory of an *accusativus cum participio* construction (as with verbs of perception and cognition) is dismissed in favor of the theory of the use of a double accusative.

[29]It is not certain that they used a consistent terminology to express their docetic views; for further details, see de Jonge, *De Brieven van Johannes*, pp. 117-24.

[30]For further comment, see Schnackenburg, *Die Johannesbriefe*, pp. 301-13. Cf. also 1 John 2:18, ὁ ἀντίχριστος ἔρχεται.

[31]See Schnackenburg, *Die Johannesbriefe*, pp. 145-49, and 152-53, and de Jonge, *De Brieven van Johannes*, pp. 101-108 and 109-14. On χρῖσμα, see especially the excellent article by I. de la Potterie, "L'onction du chrétien par la foi," *Bib* 40 (1959), pp. 12-69.

[32]Compare, by way of contrast, the use of χρίειν in the NT. In Luke 4:18 we find a quotation from Isa 61:1, and in Acts 10:38 an allusion to the same text. In Heb 1:9 there is a quotation from Ps 14:8. All these texts refer to the anointing of Jesus, as the expression ἐπὶ τὸν ἅγιον παῖδά σου Ἰησοῦν, ὃν ἔχρισας in Acts 4:27, where Ps 2:1-2 is quoted immediately before. In 2 Cor 1:21, Paul connects the "anointing" of the believers with their being established together, εἰς Χριστόν. In this connection he emphasizes the gift of the Spirit.

[33]See Chapter VII, above, pp. 181-84 (and 171-72); de Jonge, "To Love as God Loves," in *Jesus: Inspiring and Disturbing Presence*, trans. John E. Steely (Nashville-New York: Abingdon Press, 1974), pp. 110-27. U. B. Müller rightly emphasizes the soteriological aspect of this christological emphasis in 1 John (*Die Geschichte der Christologie*, pp. 53-68).

[34]See 2:7, 24; 2 John 5, 6; cf. John 15:27. In 1:1, 2:13, 14, and 3:8, obviously "the beginning of creation" is meant; 3:11 is purposely ambiguous--see de Jonge, *De Brieven van Johannes*, pp. 32-34.

[35]On the close and indispensable connection between *pluralis ecclesiasticus* and *pluralis apostolicus* in the Gospel and here, see also Chapter I, n. 62.

[36]See, e.g., de Jonge, *De Brieven van Johannes*, pp. 14-24.

[37]According to Müller, the opponents radicalized the early Johannine tradition which he finds represented in John 1:14-16 (*Die Geschichte der Christologie*, pp. 65-68); Thyen ("Aus der Literatur zum Johannesevangelium," p. 239) thinks of an explicit gnosticizing of tenets in the "Grundschrift" which itself lies before the docetic-antidocetic controversy. The term "naive docetism" was made popular by E. Käsemann in *The Testament of Jesus* (Philadelphia: Fortress, 1968).

[38]See Chapter IV, section IV.

[39]See also Chapter VI, pp. 148-49.

[40]So most clearly in part I of Thyen, "Entwicklung-
en innerhalb der johanneischen Theologie und Kirche."

[41]So H. Thyen in his "Aus der Literatur zum Johannesevangelium," p. 227, following Richter, "Die Fleischwerdung des Logos," pp. 87-89.

[42]K. Berger, "Zu 'Das Wort ward Fleisch' Joh. I
14a," *NovT* 16 (1974), pp. 161-66. See also Müller, *Die
Geschichte der Christologie*, pp. 74-76.

[43]See Chapter I, above, pp. 14, 16, 18.

[44]The various possibilities of interpretation of
this verse can be found in R. Schnackenburg, *Das Johannes-
evangelium* II, Herders Theologischer Kommentar zum Neuen
Testament (Freiburg-Basel-Wien: Herder, 1971), ad loc.
Verses 60-65 receive much attention in F. Porsch, *Pneuma
und Wort. Ein exegetischer Beitrag zur Pneumatologie des
Johannesevangelium*, Frankfurter Theologische Studien 16
(Frankfurt: Josef Knecht, 1974), pp. 161-210.

[45]See, e.g., Schnackenburg, *Das Johannesevangelium*
II, pp. 85-89, for a survey of authors and arguments.

[46]"The purpose is not to give doctrinal instruction
about the eucharist as such, but rather to use the eucharistic ideas to throw light upon the reality of incarna-
tion"--thus P. Borgen, *Bread from Heaven. An Exegetical
Study of the Concept of Manna in the Gospel of John and
the Writings of Philo*, NovTSup 10 (Leiden: Brill, 1965),
p. 166. Many authors, however, speak about "the eucharistic discourse." In Ign. *Smyrn.* 7:1, we meet docetists
who also have divergent ideas on the eucharist. To what
extent the "false teachers" in 1 John had similar opinions
is not clear; see de Jonge, *De Brieven van Johannes*, pp.
212-17, on 1 John 5:5-8. In any case it seems right to
stress that the essential problem in John 6 and 1 John 5
is in the field of Christology.

[47]Borgen, *Bread from Heaven*, p. 184. Both parties
reject the confession "Ἰησοῦς ἐστιν ὁ χριστός" (cf. 1
John 2:22).

[48]The nearest parallel would be 8:31, where "Jewish
Christians" are exhorted to remain in Jesus' word in order
that they may really be his disciples.

[49]Significantly, Thyen, who assumes a eucharistic
reinterpretation of the Discourse of the Bread in 6:48-58,
supposes that vss. 60-63 originally mentioned "Jews" and
not "disciples"; see his "Entwicklungen innerhalb der johanneischen Theologie und Kirche," p. 17, referring to
section 4.13 of his "Aus der Literatur zum Johannesevangelium."

[50]See, e.g., W. Thüsing, *Die Erhöhung und Verherrlichung Jesu im Johannesevangelium* (Münster: Aschendorff,
1959, ²1970).

[51]Compare 1:29, 6:51, 11:50-51, 17:19, 18:4. The
First Epistle is here far more explicit.

[52]Compare also G. Richter, "Blut und Wasser aus der
durchbohrten Seite Jesu (Joh. 19,34b)," *MTZ* 21 (1970), pp.
1-21.

[53]See Chapter II, p. 33.

[54]See, e.g., the survey in T. Lorenzen, *Der Lieblingsjünger im Johannesevangelium*, SBS 55 (Stuttgart:
Katholisches Bibelwerk, 1971), pp. 53-59.

[55]For literature, see ibid., and, particularly,
Thyen's studies mentioned in notes 11-12 together with
Schnackenburg, *Das Johannesevangelium* III, Exkurs 18, "Der
Jünger, den Jesus liebte." For the relation between the
beloved disciple and the author of the Gospel, see Schnack-
enburg and also Cullmann, *The Johannine Circle*, pp. 71-85.

[56]Thyen, "Die Entwicklungen innerhalb der johanneischen Theologie und Kirche." No manuscript gives us a
text of the Gospel without chapter 21.

[57]See Thyen's criticism of other interpretations in
his discussion of these verses in ibid., and Schnackenburg,
Das Johannesevangelium III.

[58]The participle γράψας is sometimes taken as cau-
sative (cf. 19:22), but in the context it certainly means
more. What the disciple witnesses (all along) stands now
on paper. The authority behind this Gospel is the disciple.

[59]Compare also 13:23 with ἀγαπήσας τοὺς ἰδίους κτλ.
in 13:1.

[60]In a way, 19:25-27 is the most cryptic of the
passages dealing with the beloved disciple. See, again,
Schnackenburg, *Das Johannesevangelium* III, ad loc., with
a survey of ancient and recent interpretations. According
to Thyen, this passage also emphasizes that Jesus had an
earthly mother and was truly human himself (cf. 6:41).
This is certainly not evident. It is difficult to say
with certainty whom Mary (and the other women) represent;
a connection with 2:4 is intended. Mary expects everything from Jesus, and although she was first mistaken
about the ὥρα, she will be led to full understanding after
her Son's death by the beloved disciple (vs. 27: ἀπ'
ἐκείνης τῆς ὥρας).

[61]In his "The 'Other Disciple' in Jn. 18:15-16,"
ETL 51 (1975), pp. 113-41, F. Neirynck has already shown
that the expression πρὸς τὸν ἄλλον μαθητὴν ὃν ἐφίλει ὁ
'Ιησοῦς in 20:2 refers back to the disciple mentioned together with Peter in 18:15, 16, and to 13:23. Also in
chapter 18, Peter is dependent on the other disciple, but
only to get access to the court of the high priest. Notwithstanding Thyen's spirited plea for it I do not think
that we can be sure that the anonymous companion of Andrew
in 1:37-39 is implicitly identified with the beloved disciple.

[62]For Thyen the situation of the Johannine Epistles
is reflected here; see his "Johannes 13 und die 'kirchliche Redaktion' des vierten Evangeliums," esp. pp. 354-
56. He sees a special connection with the conflict with
Diotrephes in 3 John and is inclined to identify the
"beloved disciple" and "the elder" in 2 and 3 John (see
the end of his "Entwicklungen innerhalb der johanneischen
Theologie und Kirche").

INDEX

226

230